STRENGTHENING
THE UNITED NATIONS

STRENGTHENING
THE
UNITED NATIONS

Commission to Study the Organization of Peace

Arthur N. Holcombe
CHAIRMAN

HARPER & BROTHERS PUBLISHERS
New York

CONTENTS

v

vi   Contents

COMMISSION TO STUDY THE ORGANIZATION OF PEACE

Research Affiliate of the
AMERICAN ASSOCIATION FOR THE UNITED NATIONS

Honorary Chairman

JAMES T. SHOTWELL

Chairman

ARTHUR N. HOLCOMBE

Drafting Committee for the Tenth Report

QUINCY WRIGHT, *Chairman*
INIS L. CLAUDE, JR., *Rapporteur*
CLYDE EAGLETON
CLARK M. EICHELBERGER
STEPHEN M. SCHWEBEL

Policy Committee for the Tenth Report

(In addition to Officers and Drafting Committee)

DANA CONVERSE BACKUS
HARDING F. BANCROFT
CLARENCE A. BERDAHL
DONALD C. BLAISDELL
ROY BLOUGH
WALDO CHAMBERLIN
DANIEL S. CHEEVER

BENJAMIN V. COHEN
NORMAN COUSINS
OSCAR A. DE LIMA
LAWRENCE S. FINKELSTEIN
RICHARD N. GARDNER
ARTHUR J. GOLDSMITH
LELAND M. GOODRICH

vii

FRANK P. GRAHAM

DONALD HARRINGTON

H. FIELD HAVILAND, JR.

WILLARD N. HOGAN

ELMORE JACKSON

PHILIP E. JACOB

PHILIP C. JESSUP

HANS KOHN

GERARD J. MANGONE

SAMUEL J. NOUMOFF

MRS. FRANKLIN D. ROOSEVELT

PAUL E. SMITH

LOUIS B. SOHN

C. M. STANLEY

RICHARD W. VAN WAGENEN

JAMES P. WARBURG

HARRIS WOFFORD, JR.

RICHARD R. WOOD

Chairmen of the Study Committees

(Responsible for Chapters 1–12 of Part 2)

ROY BLOUGH

DANIEL S. CHEEVER

NORMAN COUSINS

CLYDE EAGLETON

LAWRENCE S. FINKELSTEIN

H. FIELD HAVILAND, JR.

WILLIARD N. HOGAN

GERARD J. MANGONE

LOUIS B. SOHN

RICHARD W. VAN WAGENEN

RICHARD R. WOOD

QUINCY WRIGHT

FOREWORD

The United Nations was designed for an age that is rapidly passing away. What gunpowder and printing did to the Middle Ages, atomic bombs and electronic communications are doing to what we used to call Modern Times. The new super-powers are widening the gap between themselves and the lesser powers, while the latter make an agonizing reappraisal of the alternatives to a precarious independence. The old colonial empires are in process of liquidation, and yet the new national states cannot assure the defense of their peoples. The endless adventure that is the government of mankind enters a new phase, in which the nations must look more to reason than to tradition for their guide.

The Organization, established under the United Nations Charter, has met the challenge of this new age with imagination and vigor. The new states have eagerly sought membership, manifestly believing that with their limited access to the new weapons there is a better prospect of security within than outside the fold. The super-powers, possessing greater strength than they dare to use, manifestly believe that they too are more secure within a new order sustained by the organized opinion of mankind. The faith seems to grow stronger with survival beyond each new crisis that the United Nations can be a major factor in holding a fast-changing world together. It is a tribute to the adaptability of the young Organization that its Members continue to cling to their determination to make it the instrument for saving succeeding generations from the scourge of war.

When Franklin D. Roosevelt and his associates were planning a new general international organization to preserve his fourth freedom, the freedom from fear of war, they could not know that the bold experiment which he had authorized in response to Albert Einstein's grim warning would turn out in such a way as to make war "unthinkable." Now a dozen years have passed since the terrible bomb fell on Hiroshima and President Eisenhower is evidently not the only world statesman who regards war as unthinkable. The unthinkability of war has become a challenge to a fresh look at the problem of international organization. The action of the tenth United Nations General Assembly in authorizing a Charter Review Conference, to be held at a date to be fixed by a later General Assembly, attested the disposition of the most responsible world statesmen to accept this challenge. It is now clear to all who can bear to gaze on the contemporary international scene with open eyes that the great and unavoidable task of world statesmanship is to hasten the process of adapting the United Nations to the growing demands of this exigent new age.

The Charter of the United Nations is a document not to be meddled with lightly. It contains the plan of an Organization which has shown itself to be both rigid enough to withstand the shocks of unexpected crises and flexible enough to accommodate itself to changing circumstances. This adaptable Organization could perhaps, by the prudent exercise of its existing powers, grow bigger and stronger without formal amendments to the Charter, and with good fortune survive into the unpredictable period ahead when far greater demands than heretofore are likely to be made upon it. But weaknesses in its structure and processes have been apparent from the beginning, and no convenient opportunity to correct them should be neglected. The proposed Charter Review Conference may supply such an opportunity.

People who look forward to a more law-abiding, orderly, and peaceful world find themselves in a real dilemma. The United Nations is weak, because the world's statesmen will not trust it with greater power. They will not trust it with greater power, because it is weak. We seek ways to break this vicious circle. We do not wish to lower public confidence in an Organization which is our best protection against the tragedy of another world war, but we cannot admit that intelligent statesmen, by taking thought, are unable to speed up the process of adjusting our system of international organization to the insistent requirements of the coming age of atomic power and worldwide electronic communications.

We do not regard a Charter Review Conference, if one should be held in the near future, as a means of supplying the world with a definitive constitution. More time will be needed for such a development. We do contend that it is possible to take some firm forward steps now. We think that a Charter Review Conference might be helpful, though much can be done to strengthen the United Nations by the General Assembly without such a Conference. Even more could be done by the governments of the leading Member States, if they could be persuaded to work more resolutely through the United Nations. We insist that it is important to make the necessary effort without further delay. There is no way in which sovereign states of the traditional kind can be made strong enough to protect their peoples by the force of their own arms alone. There is no rational alternative to strengthening the United Nations.

Our program consists of proposals of three kinds. We recommend a few changes in the United Nations Charter; we recommend a greater number of changes in the policies and practices of the Organization; and we recommend some changes in the policies and practices of our own government, encouraged in this part of our program by our hope that other governments will follow a good example when set by the Government of the United States. To those whose confidence in the adaptability of the United Nations inspires a determination to transform it without delay into a much more vigorous and effective organization, our proposals may seem excessively modest. To those who have little or no confidence in the United Nations, the same proposals will seem untimely, audacious, and even rash. We can only reply that our program calls for moving forward in what we believe to be the right direction at as fast a pace as fits the spirit of the times and the temper of the nations. We have emphasized those changes which seem to be most feasible in the immediate future and most capable of guiding the further development of the Organization in the way it should go. We are confident that their adoption would clear the road for more far-reaching improvements which might be expected to follow without undue delay.

This Tenth Report of the Commission to Study the Organization of Peace is the product of a genuinely collective effort. The conclusions reached by the Commission are based upon the findings of twelve special study committees which have surveyed the record of the United Nations up to now and have appraised the proposals from various quarters for strengthening the Organization. We have also used materials published in earlier Commission Reports, particularly our Ninth Report, which dealt with the problems of a Charter Review Conference. Responsibility for the contents of the reports of the Study Committees rests exclusively with their respective members, who have signed their names thereto. The Commission Report was prepared by a special Drafting Committee, assisted by a Policy Committee, whose members have already been listed by name, but is published by direction of the Commission as a whole and upon the particular responsibility of those members whose names are attached thereto. Signers of the Commission Report or of any of the Committee Reports whose approval is conditional or limited in any important way have indicated their reservations at appropriate places. They alone are responsible for their opinions, but the Commission has authorized their publication in the interest of freedom of thought and expression for all its members. Sixty-five members of the Commission have taken an active part in the preparation of this Report. Many of them have given much time and effort to the work. Eighty-seven members listed on pages 54-55 have signed it.

For generous aid in the preparation and publication of this Report we are indebted to the General Service Foundation of St. Paul, Minnesota. We are grateful for the confidence of its Trustees. They of course are not responsible for our treatment of our subject or for our Recommendations.

ARTHUR N. HOLCOMBE, *Chairman*
Commission to Study the Organization of Peace

part 1

TENTH REPORT OF THE COMMISSION

part I.

FINAL REPORT OF THE
COMMISSION

I.   Summary of Recommendations
II.   Text of the Report

I

Summary of Recommendations

In formulating its recommendations for strengthening the United Nations the Commission to Study the Organization of Peace has not confined itself to proposals for amending the United Nations Charter. Important gains in strength are possible by action of United Nations organs and Members under the Charter as it stands. However, a few recommendations will require amendments, notably those dealing with membership (1), the composition and voting procedure of the Security Council (4, 5), and institutional sanctions (14). The recommendations concerning the World Court (11), the Economic and Social Council (17), human rights (20), international law and conventions (21) and public information programs (22) are addressed primarily to the Government of the United States. The remainder of the recommendations are addressed to the General Assembly or other organs of the United Nations.

1) *Membership.* The Commission adheres to the fundamental proposition that the United Nations should be a universal organization. To this end, we believe that all states able to discharge the obligations of membership should be admitted if they apply. Whether the applicant satisfies this condition should be decided by a procedural vote of the Security Council and by a two-thirds vote of the General Assembly. (See pages 31, 241)

2) *Representation of Member States.* We urge general acceptance of the principle that decisions concerning the right of a government to represent a Member State in the United Nations, reached by a two-thirds majority vote in the General Assembly, should be followed by

3

all organs of the United Nations and by the specialized agencies. (See page 31)

3) *The Secretary-General.* The Commission suggests that the General Assembly pass a resolution declaring itself competent to appoint an Acting Secretary-General, if the office should become vacant and the prompt election of a new Secretary-General as provided in the Charter (Article 97) should not prove feasible. The Acting Secretary-General should be fully empowered to exercise the functions of the office until such time as he might be replaced by a Secretary-General chosen in the normal manner. (See pages 31-32, 241)

4) *The Security Council.* We look, as an ultimate goal, to a Security Council continuously adaptable, in composition, to the dynamics of a world in which the roster of the most important and powerful states is subject to change.

Advantage should be taken of the growing demand for enlargement of the Security Council to improve its representative character. A moderate expansion of the Council should include provision to ensure implementation of the first criterion for elective members, that is, contribution "to the maintenance of international peace and security," as well as of the second, "equitable geographical distribution." (See pages 32-33, 239-249)

5) *The Veto Power.* The practicable aim in regard to the veto is that which was stated in the Vandenberg Resolution of June 11, 1948: the removal of the veto on the admission of new Members and on the functioning of the Security Council in the field of pacific settlement (Chapter VI). The gradual restriction of the veto power should next extend into the area of peace preservation (Chapter VII), enabling the Council to make recommendations to the Members concerning the existence of threats to or breaches of the peace or of acts of aggression, concerning provisional measures in such cases, and concerning sanctioning measures if such provisional measures are not observed. (See pages 33, 79-80, 241, 247-249)

6) *Domestic Jurisdiction.* We deplore the practice of raising the issue of domestic jurisdiction (Article 2, paragraph 7) upon inscription of a problem upon the agenda of United Nations organs, since debate in itself cannot properly be considered intervention in the domestic jurisdiction of a state. However, the organs of the United

Nations should give more serious attention to claims that specific resolutions are beyond their competence and should more frequently request the advisory opinion of the World Court on such claims. (See pages 34-35, 128-130)

7) *Representation and Voting in the General Assembly.* We urge the United Nations to continue its examination of possible changes designed to produce a more equitable system of representation and voting in the General Assembly. (See pages 35, 128-130)

8) *Investigatory Authority.* We believe that the General Assembly should declare the scope of the investigatory authority of the United Nations, and recommend appropriate measures to ensure that Members will receive and cooperate with investigatory missions. The authority of the Security Council by a procedural vote (Article 29), or of the General Assembly by a two-thirds vote (Article 22) to initiate such investigations, and the obligation of the affected Member States to accept them (Articles 104 and 105), should be recognized. Moreover, we urge the General Assembly to confirm the right of the Secretary-General, in person or through deputies, to visit and negotiate with the governments of Member States (Articles 97, 99, 104 and 105). (See pages 36, 79-81)

9) *Permanent United Nations Force.* A permanent United Nations Force should be made to emerge from the experience of the United Nations in Palestine, Korea, and Egypt. We recommend a force composed of at least 2,000 individual volunteers on active duty, plus a larger number of men in trained contingents, including air force units, committed specifically to the Organization by Member States. This Force should be held in genuine readiness for use under the authority of either the General Assembly or the Security Council. A permanent United Nations Commander, assisted by an advisory committe of Member States and working in close cooperation with the Secretary-General, should provide the essential professional direction of the Force. (See pages 36-38, 65-68, 86-88)

10) *Use of Rapporteurs.* We suggest that the United Nations develop the practice of dealing with a dispute or situation, either before or after preliminary debate, by referring it to private negotiation under the auspices of a *rapporteur* to be appointed by the Secretary-General in consultation with the President either of the General Assembly or

of the Security Council. If the process of quiet consultation does not produce agreement, we recommend that a resolution proposed by the *rapporteur* should be given priority over any other draft resolution in the public debating and voting process. (See page 39)

11) *The World Court.* We urge the United States to take the lead in promoting resort to the World Court in contentious cases of appropriate nature. To this end it should modify the reservation attached to its ratification of the optional clause. We also urge the United States to take the leadership in persuading the organs of the United Nations to make more use of the Court for advisory opinions. (See page 39)

12) *Non-Self-Governing Territories.* The Commission believes that the provisions of the Charter relating to the government and development of non-self-governing territories (Article 73) constitute international obligations for Members of the United Nations and that the General Assembly is competent to inquire into the observance of those obligations. On this basis, we believe that Member States administering such territories should accept the obligation of reporting to the United Nations on political progress as well as on economic, social, and educational developments.

We support the claim of the General Assembly that it has competence to decide what territories are non-self-governing and when they cease to be so because of changes in their constitutional status.

The Committee on Information from Non-Self-Governing Territories which, like the Trusteeship Council, has a balanced membership between administering and non-administering states, should be made permanent. The General Assembly should enlarge its functions so that it can make recommendations to Member States. (See pages 40, 138-146)

13) *Acquisition and Administration of Territory.* We believe that the United Nations is capable not only of administering territory, but of acquiring title under international law through cession by the state with title or through prior claim to territory or space to which no state has title.

We believe that the United Nations should undertake the responsibility of administering certain contested areas of international importance for water or air transport, and certain uninhabited areas like

Antarctica, at the request or with the consent of states having claim to such territories. With respect to the bed of the high seas beyond the continental shelf and to outer space, which are outside the jurisdiction of any state, we urge the General Assembly to declare the title of the international community and to establish appropriate administrative arrangements. (See pages 40-41, 208-223)

14) *Sanctions Against Illegal Behavior.* We recommend that urgent attention be given to the development of United Nations sanctions against internationally illegal behavior likely to disturb international peace and security, but not involving actual hostilities. The first requirement of such a program is confirmation of the allegation of illegal action. If such a charge is not referred by the parties to the World Court as a contentious case for its decision, the General Assembly or Security Council should investigate the facts of the situation and secure the advisory opinion of the World Court before making a formal finding against the offending state. However in cases carrying an imminent threat to the peace or involving clear-cut refusal to comply with a mandatory decision of an international agency, a more summary procedure would be necessary. Next, the resources of peaceful adjustment and moral pressure should be fully explored. If finally necessary, the United Nations should bring into play the power of the General Assembly to recommend or of the Security Council to order, and of either organ to coordinate the application of, all possible sanctions short of the use of armed force. These would include economic sanctions and what might be called "institutional sanctions"— deprivation of the privileges and benefits which derive from membership in the United Nations system. (See pages 42-43, 78-83)

15) *Breaches of the Peace.* We recommend continuance of the practice of dealing with actual hostilities by provisional orders, calling for cease-fire and withdrawal, and of employing armed force only if hostilities are continued. While there is need for flexibility to meet the circumstances of each case, the Commission recommends that, apart from necessities for self-defense against armed attack, situations involving aggression should be dealt with by the United Nations, not by nations or collective defense agencies acting independently. The United Nations should call upon and coordinate the action of its Members and of such agencies when forces directly available to it are inadequate. (See pages 43-44, 83-86)

16) *Disarmament Negotiations.* We recommend that negotiations for the regulation of armaments under United Nations auspices be pursued vigorously, though we recognize that agreement for armaments control will probably have to be linked with political accommodation. We believe that some forms of international control are feasible and would foster attitudes conducive to political accommodation. Avenues to be explored include control arrangements in limited geographic areas, inspection to prevent sudden attacks, pilot projects to test the effectiveness of such inspection, limitation or elimination of nuclear explosions dangerous to human life and health, international control of intercontinental ballistic missiles and space satellites, and balanced reduction of military forces and limitation of military production. (See pages 44-45, 59-74, 218-220)

17) *The Economic and Social Council.* We recommend that the Economic and Social Council examine the functional commissions and eliminate those not found to be essential. We suggest that the Council make greater use of experts, appointed in their individual capacities as required for temporary service. We urge states which are elected to the Council to give recognition to the potential importance of that body by delegating persons of high standing and outstanding competence as their spokesmen in the Council. Thus revitalized, the Economic and Social Council should provide dynamic leadership for the United Nations in the development of a genuinely international outlook upon economic problems, and vigorous initiative in the exploration of economic frontiers which give promise of offering new possibilities for raising the level of human welfare. (See pages 45-46, 185-186, 193-197)

18) *United Nations Development Agency.* We cannot urge too strongly the desirability of setting the United Nations to the task of promoting and operating bold programs of technical assistance and capital investment. It is particularly important that special high-priority programs be initiated to further the development of non-self-governing territories and to assist such new states as may require external aid in formulating and carrying out economic development projects.

We recommend the establishment of a United Nations Development Agency as the central authority for coordinating the programs of technical assistance and capital investment carried out by the specialized agencies, and for the operational management of the present and future activities of the United Nations itself in the economic development field. This Development Agency should be clearly recognized as a part of the United Nations, but it should be sufficiently autonomous to make decisions concerning the use of funds by an appropriate form of weighted voting. Such a system should be designed to ensure that the major contributing states will have a degree of influence commensurate with their importance in the support of United Nations economic programs. The Development Agency might be so constituted that the major contributors of funds would always occupy seats and the beneficiary countries would have rotating regional representation. Provision might be made that projects be prepared by regional subsidiaries for presentation to the Development Agency and that all programs be approved by a majority of the major contributors. (See pages 46-48, 200-206, 234-235)

19) *Autonomous Agencies.* We advocate the immediate establishment and the vigorous support of the International Atomic Energy Agency. Inasmuch as the principle of inspection has been incorporated in its Statute, the United States and other major atomic powers should bring their bilateral programs under the Agency.

We emphasize the importance of giving increasingly vigorous support to the specialized agencies and of putting into effective operation the Inter-Governmental Maritime Consultative Organization and the Organization for Trade Cooperation. The United Nations should promote the coordination of the specialized agencies both through improved formal arrangements and through the development of more effective collaboration under the proposed United Nations Development Agency. (See pages 48, 177-178, 183-186, 200-206)

20) *Human Rights.* We believe that the most fruitful approach to the task of developing legally binding standards of human rights would be to attack the problem piecemeal. A series of conventions dealing with single or small groups of issues pertaining to human rights should be negotiated. Persistent effort should be made to promote the moral influence of the Universal Declaration of Human Rights as a factor in shaping legal systems and determining governmental policies. (See pages 49, 105-121)

21) *International Law and Conventions.* We urge the United States to contribute to the development and codification of international

law by encouraging the work of the International Law Commission, and by participating actively in making general treaties on topics suitable for international action. In particular, we urge the United States to ratify the United Nations Convention on Privileges and Immunities. (See pages 49-50, 155-158, 168)

22) *Public Information Programs.* We recommend that the United Nations expand its programs of public information; develop more effective means for evaluating the impact of these programs; seek more adequate dissemination of United Nations news, literature, and broadcasts in the territories of Member States; and strengthen the relations between the Economic and Social Council and non-governmental organizations. We urge the United States to assist in this effort by demonstrating greater respect for freedom of movement by observers and correspondents covering United Nations activities, as well as by United Nations personnel (See pages 50, 99-104, 160-165)

23) *Revenues.* We urge the United Nations to promote continuous and intensive exploration of possible new sources of revenue to supplement governmental contributions and to take timely action to exploit such sources as circumstances permit. (See pages 51, 259-262)

24) *Program budget.* We suggest that the United Nations develop a program budget, combining all programs—such as relief, welfare, and technical assistance activities—falling outside the realm of standard or normal operations, and clearly distinguished from the administrative budget. For the present, the program budget should be supported by the voluntary contributions of Member States and by such other revenues as the Organization may receive, while the administrative budget should continue to be covered by assessments upon Member States. However, we urge that agreement should be reached as soon as possible upon an arrangement whereby the contributions of Members to the program budget will be made on the basis of a special scale of assessment. In order to provide reasonable protection for the wealthier states against inequitable demands upon their treasuries, it is essential that the program budget should be prepared and controlled by a suitable weighted voting process. (See pages 51-52, 258-259, 262)

II

Text of the Report

INTRODUCTION

From Jeremiah's day to our own, men have been saying, "Peace, peace; when there is no peace." Today, there is no peace—no universal peace, no stable and secure peace, no just peace, no peace which permits human beings to concentrate on solving the basic problems and exploiting the magnificent opportunities which confront them in their quest for the good life. The human situation in the mid-twentieth century is tragic, and it could easily become catastrophic. The tragedy lies in the unhappy circumstances—the misery, the oppression, the injustice—within which great masses of human beings live out their lives; it lies in the peril of universal destruction which casts its shadow over the hard-won achievements of the human race; it lies in the conflicts and maladjustments which frustrate the realization of new-found potentialities for raising the life of mankind to unprecedented levels of dignity, fulfilment, and comfort.

In this situation, the United Nations stands as a symbol of humanity's hope for survival and creative achievement. Support for the United Nations is not a matter of crying "Peace, peace; when there is no peace." It does not involve reliance upon magical incantation to banish from consciousness the reality that there is no peace, or to banish from reality the tragic fact that peace has not been achieved. Rather, we believe support for the United Nations expresses the conviction that humanity has adequate resources for transcending its perilous and unsatisfactory situation, and the determination that those resources shall be mobilized with ever-greater intelligence and imagination to the end that peace shall be achieved. We believe in the

11

possibility; we recognize the urgency; we maintain the hope; we accept the challenge.

The Commission rejects complacent satisfaction with the United Nations as it is. The United Nations is neither as effective as it must be nor as effective as it can be. We also reject the impatient assertion that the United Nations, as it is, contributes so little to the ordering of international relations and the improvement of human welfare as to be virtually useless. The fact that the United Nations cannot do everything that needs to be done should not be allowed to obscure the fact that it can do, and is doing, many things that are of vital importance to the peace and welfare of the world.

We do not place our faith in the mechanism of a balance-of-power system, but we insist upon the fundamental significance of power, as we have done consistently from the beginning of our existence as a Commission.[1]

We do not look to institutional formulas alone to solve the world's problems, but we emphasize, as we have done since 1940[2], the necessity of developing global institutions capable of promoting a maximum degree of orderliness in an evolving world society. We undertake to deal resolutely with the problems and possibilities of the present, unencumbered by nostalgia for an idealized past or by wistfulness for an ideal future.

We accept and advocate the concept of international organization. We are cognizant of the considerable progress that has been made in the development of serviceable international institutions. We are aware of the inadequacies of the institutional system associated with the name of the United Nations. We are conscious of the formidable difficulties which impede the improvement of that system. We recognize the imperfection of our knowledge concerning the ultimate shape of the structure which will be required for the effective operation of the global society. We confess the incompleteness of our

---

[1] "Law has always been maintained by force. A nation, today, like individuals in the past, must choose between continuous and probably incompetent self-defense against aggressors, or collective action against them. In the former case, it may claim complete freedom, but will probably not be able to maintain it; in the latter case, it must give up some of its freedom in order to secure collective support for the rights which the community agrees that its members should have. This is the explanation of law and government among human beings; and it is through law and government that order has been maintained among human beings." *Preliminary Report and Monographs,* April 1941, p. 281.

[2] *Ibid.,* pp. 10-11.

understanding of the processes by which such a structure can be made a workable and working reality. But we may not refuse to give such help as we can in the necessary struggle to strengthen the existing international institutions.

In endorsing the concept of international organization, the Commission recognizes that the task of creating a better world order involves something both of cultivation and of construction. It is in some measure an "agricultural" problem and in some measure an "engineering" problem, requiring both the nurturing of favorable social trends and the designing of suitable institutional forms. As we put it in our *Preliminary Report*, "The Commission deeply appreciates that mere form without substance is of little value. No system of laws and organization can be of value without the living faith and spirit behind and in it. No world organization can succeed without mutual confidence on the part of its members."[3]

We recognize the overriding importance of national policies, as distinguished from international mechanisms, in world affairs today. There is a reciprocal interaction between these elements, but in the present stage of history the behavior of states has a greater impact upon international institutions than the decisions of international institutions have upon states. In the long run, we hope and believe that the agencies of the world community will have a decisive effect upon the behavior of individual and collective units within that community. Nevertheless, we decline to place limitless faith in the potentialities of international mechanisms. The Commission can conceive of no future in which the success of efforts to maintain world order and promote universal human welfare will not depend heavily upon the moral decency and political wisdom of human beings, leaders and followers. For as long as we can foresee, these human beings will be organized primarily in national states.

For the present the Commission is concerned to promote the strengthening of the United Nations. We employ the term, "strengthening," in its broadest sense, referring to the objective of *increasing the effectiveness* of the Organization and its affiliates in the performance of functions that are essential to a developing world order. In recent months, the Commission, acting as a unit and as a group of Study Committees, has given sustained attention to questions relating to the desirable and possible course of the future development of the

[3] *Ibid.*, p. 6.

United Nations. Out of this deliberation have come the Committee Reports which are included in this volume, as well as this Report of the Commission, with its recommendations. We have attempted to steer between the actual and the desirable, recognizing that necessity and reason may continually push the actual toward the better, even though not all the way to the ideal. The intertangled crises of our time give urgency to the project of strengthening the United Nations, and our faith in the creative intelligence and moral adaptability of mankind gives us hope that the elaboration of such a project will contribute in some measure to the realization of this high purpose.

The United Nations—Original Plan and Present Reality

Functions

The Preamble of the Charter begins with an expression of determination "to save succeeding generations from the scourge of war"; and Article 1, setting out the purposes of the United Nations, lists first the purpose "to maintain international peace and security." These are not accidents of the drafting process. Motivations were undoubtedly mixed and varied at San Francisco, but it is nonetheless clear that the statesmen who gathered in the momentous Conference of 1945 regarded the new venture in international organization as first and foremost an effort to develop effective means of preventing war. General recognition of the world's need—and the need of each nation—for an agency to maintain peace was the primary factor making possible the creation of the United Nations. In accordance with this overriding objective, the Charter places heavy emphasis upon outlawing the arbitrary use of threat of force, promoting the peaceful settlement of disputes and the peaceful adjustment of war-breeding situations, limiting and regulating armaments, and developing effective international measures against unauthorized use of force.

If the Preamble and Article 1 begin with references to the function of preventing war, they do not end there. They continue with reference to such tasks as promoting respect for human rights and the rights of nations and peoples, developing law-abidingness in international relations, contributing to the realization of justice in the relations among nations, and launching cooperative attacks upon problems of the economic, social, cultural, and moral welfare of mankind. Moreover, the subsequent provisions of the Charter for the creation of an

Economic and Social Council and a Trusteeship Council as "principal organs" of the United Nations, for the development of a system of specialized agencies, and for the assertion of international interests in promoting the well-being of non-self-governing territories provide clear indication that the United Nations was from the beginning expected and intended to function not only in the arena of conflicts, bearing directly upon peace and security, but also in adjacent fields.

The comprehensiveness of the functional roles assigned to agencies of the United Nations system by the Charter reflects more than the belief that the new Organization, while giving priority to the political function of keeping the peace, might without undue strain undertake the performance of additional functions. Basically, it reflects the view that all the problems of social existence are interrelated, and that the conditions of peace can be created only by simultaneous and co-ordinated efforts to solve a variety of problems which are connected with the problem of war, as well as to come to grips directly with that central issue. The priority of peace is supported, not repudiated, by the Charter's establishment of a multifunctional system of international organization.

In the years since the Second World War, nothing has happened to disprove the assumption of the founders of the United Nations that the elimination of war is mankind's number-one problem. On the contrary, the phenomenal development of new and extraordinarily destructive weapons has transformed peace from an ideal devoutly to be hoped for into a fundamental necessity of elementary survival. The ranks of the peace-seekers have been expanded to include not only all men of good will but also all other men of good sense. Moreover, the world has been troubled by conflicts and competitions, frictions and frustrations, ambitions and animosities, more than sufficient to confirm the wisdom of the decision concerning priorities which was made at San Francisco. When war carries with it a threat to the very survival of civilization, the urgency of dealing effectively with all threats to the peace is self-evident.

However, the existence of formal agreement upon the priority of the peace-keeping function has not prevented confusion in the actual development of the activities of the United Nations. Unfortunately, clarity of purpose does not exclude uncertainty and disagreement as to methods of achieving that purpose. The United Nations has discovered that dedication to the maintenance of peace provides no clear answer to questions concerning the means which can and should be adopted in the quest for peace.

No better example of the confusion about method, which has over-shadowed the clear objectives of the United Nations, can be found than the uncertainty which has surrounded the subject of organized resistance to armed aggression. The Charter is ambiguous in this regard. It proclaims in general terms the intent to establish a system of collective security against aggression, but it also includes provisions suggesting that the system was not designed to operate in opposition to the will of any one of the Great Powers.[4]

This original defect of the Charter has been compounded because circumstances have prevented the translation of the security scheme from paper provisions to political reality. Under these circumstances Members of the United Nations have wavered in uncertainty about the feasibility and desirability of assigning significant responsibilities to the Organization for dealing with the problem of aggression. When it became clear that the primary danger of war derived from situations in which the Charter imposed serious restrictions upon the function-ing of its projected collective security system, the initial reaction was to develop an extra-United Nations system of regional alliances to cope with that danger. Two distinct viewpoints supported the propo-sition that the security function of the United Nations might be elimi-nated or drastically reduced. One held that a global organization could not discharge this function and that the United Nations should there-fore make way for more effective regional agencies. The other held that the United Nations should play down its enforcement function in order to maximize its effectiveness as an impartial conciliator. How-ever, response to the hostilities in Korea and the passage by the Gen-eral Assembly of the Uniting for Peace Resolution reflected a revival of the conviction that the United Nations could and should play a significant role in organizing collective resistance to aggression. More-over, this reinstated concept was characterized by a new ambitious-ness. It opened up the possibility of collective action against a Great Power and its satellites—a possibility which the statesmen of San Francisco had been unwilling to contemplate.

There has been no renewed drift toward the overt repudiation of the concept of the United Nations as an enforcer of the peace. This does not mean that the Organization is committed to the launching of

[4] Cf. Articles 1 (1) and 27 (3).

collective military action against any and all acts of unauthorized force. In Korea, where the Soviet Union was only indirectly involved, such action was taken. In the Hungarian crisis of late 1956, however, where the Soviet Union was directly involved, such action was not seriously contemplated. In the Egyptian case, where the General Assembly voted in disapproval of the military action undertaken by Israel, Britain, and France, the decision of those states to halt their action permitted the Assembly to avoid what might otherwise have become an urgent question. Should the United Nations organize collective forces for combat under the complicated political and legal circumstances which characterized the case, or could it, if it tried? The most that can be said at this time is that the Members of the United Nations have refused to accept its exclusion from the role of initiator of collective-security action. They have insisted upon opening up and holding open the possibility that the Organization may be used to organize voluntary military collaboration of Member States as a device for halting aggression, by whomever launched. Beyond this it cannot be said that clear agreement has been achieved within the Organization on the relative merits of, or the interrelationships among, the various methods which are theoretically available to it for the direct promotion of its primary objective, the maintenance of peace.

The clarity of the Organization's formal adherence to the priority of its peace-preserving function is also offset by the fact that it is *not* clear that all its Members genuinely accept that priority. Devotion to peace in the abstract is one thing; the motivations of foreign policy in concrete situations may be something quite different. The United Nations in operation, contrasted with the abstract idea of a general international organization, is a collection of Member States pursuing and attempting to gain the Organization's aid and support in pursuing a multitude of national purposes of varying relevance to and compatibility with the objective of keeping the world at peace. That objective, having been established as ideologically sacrosanct, is not openly challenged, but the record indicates that in fact some Members of the United Nations have given primary consideration to various other purposes. Among these have been speeding the liquidation of colonialism, promoting economic progress in underdeveloped countries, gaining diplomatic triumphs over their rivals, creating blocs, and waging propaganda battles. The nations are less disposed to subordinate their policies to the needs of United Nations peace-keeping operations than to make the United Nations the tool of their own national purposes—purposes which may or may not be conducive to the maintenance of peace.

However difficult it may have proved for the Organization to adhere firmly to the principle that its peace-preserving function has priority, it is evident that the functional development of the United Nations has produced in full measure the proliferation of activities which were provided for in the original scheme of the Charter. The governments of the mid-twentieth century have displayed an extraordinary inclination to expand the list of subjects with which they are prepared to have international agencies deal. As this is an era of big government, so it is an era of big international organization. No better evidence of this trend is needed than citation of the fact that a conservative reaction has set in. This reaction is characterized by claims familiar in domestic controversies about big government—that too much money is being spent, too many functions are being usurped, and too much intrusion into local affairs is taking place. The movement for the Bricker Amendment in the United States and the more broadly-based anxiety for the safeguarding of "domestic jurisdiction" could hardly have arisen if the United Nations had settled down to cultivate a modest little garden instead of taking virtually the whole world of human problems as its area of concern. It should be noted, however, that if states resist the enlargement of the scope of the United Nations system, states also—and oftentimes the *same* states—press new functional responsibilities upon the Organization. The expanding universe of international organization is the product not only of converging calculations of national advantage, but also of a general conviction that global peace and welfare may be served by international action. It must be taken as a fact of life that the United Nations and its affiliated agencies are being called upon, and will be called upon, to concern themselves with problems of ever-increasing variety.

Powers

The founding fathers of the United Nations were building on the ruins of an organization which had proved powerless to prevent the catastrophe of World War II. They were building for a world that had been shattered by the impact of uncontrolled national power. Hence, it is natural that they should have been deeply concerned with the problem of providing adequate power for the Organization to which they were assigning such ambitious and vital responsibilities. The question of what powers should and could be entrusted to the new world Organization was a persistent theme of all the studies, negotiations, and conferences which led to the creation of the United Nations.

Power is always a difficult concept to analyze, and never more so than in connection with international institutions. It may be broken down into such elements as legal authority to make decisions, procedural arrangements facilitating decision-making in actual political circumstances, and realistically usable capacity for securing compliance with such decisions as are reached. For instance, it might be said (1) that the Congress of the United States has legal authority, limited only by the Constitution as interpreted by the Supreme Court, to pass civil rights legislation; (2) that its actual political ability to pass such legislation is limited by the difficulty of overcoming the Senatorial filibuster and, conceivably, the Presidential veto; and (3) that its capacity to secure obedience is to be measured not in terms of American military strength (which is not realistically usable for this purpose) and only partially in terms of available police strength (which has limited utility for this purpose) but primarily in terms of its resources for exerting influence and pressure by non-coercive methods. Thus, the statement that Congress has "power" to uphold the civil rights of Americans is true only if it is not taken as a simple statement. The powers of international organizations are subject to a similar kind of analysis.

Another useful approach to the analysis of power is to concentrate on the third element of the above scheme, "realistically usable capacity for securing compliance," and to emphasize the variety of methods which may be available for achieving the desired result. Thus, the Commission, in its Fourth Report, treated the problem of power in terms of four categories: the power of the sword, the power of the purse, the power of the word, and the power of the law.[5] This scheme has the merit of pointing directly to the crucial fact that the limits of power are not coterminous with the limits of "enforcement" in the literal sense. To rely again upon examples from the American political scene, it is evident that the observer who looks only for nightsticks, guns, and jail keys will fail to discover the most significant elements

---

[5] Commission to Study the Organization of Peace, *Fourth Report*, Part I, "Security and World Organization," November 1943, pp. 33-35.

of the compound which energizes the system. This includes, for instance, the power of Congress to spend money, the power of the President to make speeches, and the power of the Supreme Court to wrap the robe of the law-speaker around its collective body. Again, this sort of analysis is applicable to the powers of international agencies.

The Charter reflects the recognition that the power of the sword is indispensable to the management of international relations. It envisages agreements by Member States to put military contingents at the disposal of the United Nations. It anticipates organizational planning for the utilization of those forces. Likewise it confers upon the Security Council the legal authority to make decisions, both positive and negative, concerning the international use of force. In looking toward the creation of an acceptable system for the limitation of national military establishments, the framers of the Charter showed interest in the question of the relative armed strength of the United Nations and of the states which might require coercive control. In allowing the claim of the Great Powers for a right to veto decisions to invoke sanctions, they acknowledged the modesty of their expectations concerning the military capability of the United Nations against a Great Power and deliberately conceded the impracticability of giving the Organization more than a conditional grip upon the hilt of the law-enforcing sword. The Charter contemplates no global Leviathan, but neither does it imagine that all swords are really plowshares.

The drafters of the San Francisco plan, in seeking power resources for the United Nations, looked well beyond the tip of the sword. Fundamentally, the powers with which they sought to equip the Organization were powers of a non-coercive nature. They included: the power to discuss, criticize, and propose; the power to receive reports and conduct investigations; the power to publicize and condemn; the power to urge, influence, and persuade; and the power to promote adjustment, lend assistance, and confer benefits. From one end of the Charter to the other, the evidence is plain that the United Nations was intended to possess, and expected to use, capacities far wider in scope than the literal capacity to compel.

The decision to endow the Organization with powers of the sort described above did not represent an urge to develop necessarily inferior substitutes for unattainable "real" power. The creation of the Charter reflected the conviction that the power to achieve an orderly world must be a compound of capacities to induce and capacities to compel—that the mobilization of rationality and decency is as vital to the objective as the mobilization of force. This conviction has often been too lightly brushed aside by those who can find realism only at the tip of a sword. Realistically, non-coercive capacity has the merit of being politically *usable* in an era when military capacity has become so dangerous that an international decision to use it is politically improbable. Moreover, this sort of power possesses an important advantage over military force. When it is used, it tends to produce rather than to destroy the conditions which are essential to the realization of the ideal of global order.

As the Charter has been translated into an evolving reality, the pattern of United Nations power has undergone continuous alteration. The truth is that power cannot be *conferred* upon an organization by the makers of its constitution. They may express an intention that it shall have power, but it can actually use only such power as it *develops*. Hence, it is not surprising that the practical situation of the United Nations with respect to power in 1957 should be different from that envisaged by the Charter.

The coercive capacity of the United Nations has fallen far below the expectations of its founders. The military units envisaged in Articles 43 and 45 have not been placed at the disposal of the Security Council. The political impediment to the decision-making power of that organ, the veto, has loomed insurpassably large. There remains the legal power of the Security Council to counter aggression with the force of the community—usable only if the Great Powers agree.

The failure to realize the anticipated coercive capacity of the Security Council has been partially offset by the unanticipated entry of the General Assembly into the field of enforcement action. Under the impetus of the Korean operations, when the Security Council was able to sponsor multilateral military resistance to aggression only because of peculiar circumstances which are not deemed likely to recur, the Assembly asserted a capacity to take similar action in future contingencies. Consequently, it may be said that the United Nations has developed a possibility of acting forcibly which is different from, but in accordance with, the scheme laid down in the Charter, provided it puts its determination of policy in the form of a recommendation to the Member States instead of a decision.

Nevertheless, there remains a large gap between theoretical capacity and usable power. In political terms, the likelihood of the General Assembly's reaching a decision to recommend the use of force is greater than that of the Security Council's attaining the requisite vote for deciding to take armed action. As the membership of the United Nations is progressively expanded by the admission of new African and Asian states, such a recommendation by the General Assembly may become less likely. The coercive power of the United Nations is not, at the present time, the major factor in the security calculations of statesmen. The hard fact is that, so far as enforcement is concerned, there exists an inverse relation between the requirements upon international organization and the resources at its disposal. The same factors that make the task of safeguarding security a bigger and harder job also tend to weaken the capacity of the United Nations to take coercive action.

If the development of the United Nations has produced a less significant capacity for compulsion than was intended, the opposite is true of many of the other powers with which the statesmen of San Francisco undertook to invest the Organization. The non-coercive capacities indicated in the Charter have, by and large, not been permitted to wither into insignificance, but have been subjected to an intensive cultivation which has produced phenomenal growth. These capacities have flourished most prominently in the General Assembly. Note, for instance, the repeated assertions of its capacity to expose to public debate, to subject to international criticism, to proffer international advice, and to claim international interest in areas never before brought under the jurisdiction of international institutions. Far from remaining a dead letter, the authority of the United Nations to concern itself with colonial policy has been exploited and expanded to the point where the General Assembly claims a capacity approaching legislative competence. A similar development has taken place in the field of human rights.

It would appear that measurable progress has been made toward creation of a new category of international law—the United Nations resolution. It is more than a recommendation and less than a full-fledged legal instrument in the old established sense. In short, the power of the word has moved perceptibly toward identification with the power of the law. The exploitation of the possibilities of the power of the international purse may not be far behind. While it is true that the United Nations purse is a slender one, and that its periodic replenishment is a matter of continuous uncertainty, it is also true that United Nations programs of assistance have tended to assume more than marginal significance for numerous governments and peoples, and that the Organization's growing capacity to confer or to withhold material benefits carries with it a potentially increasing power to persuade. Finally, it may be noted that the powers of the Secretary-General have tended to become increasingly important as the United Nations has developed from a Charter blueprint to a working institution, elevating him to the stature of an international statesman and global chief executive.

Clearly, these growing powers of the United Nations are subject to the possibility of misuse. Some observers would insist that the actual and potential abuse of these powers, or some of them, poses such a serious problem that the Organization, in its present form at least, should be debarred from exercising them. Any serious student of the United Nations will find instances in which he doubts that the Organization has used its powers wisely or justly.

Moreover, these are imperfect powers in the sense that they have no guaranteed effectiveness. Enthusiasts have frequently overrated the potency of world opinion mobilized by international agencies. It is the beginning of wisdom to recognize that some nations will never, and no nation will always, submit to the non-coercive pressures which the United Nations has developed. The map of world affairs is dotted with disputes that have not yielded to the processes of peaceful settlement, and with injustices that have not been remedied in response to United Nations appeals. More broadly, the evolving powers of the United Nations have not been effectual in preventing the development, or in bringing about the end, of such fundamental conflicts as the cold war or the strife over colonialism. It must be granted that the United Nations can be defied. But states have manifested great interest in blocking the passage of resolutions which they would feel impelled to defy. Furthermore, states have anxiously resisted the expansion of the Organization's competence to pass resolutions which they are capable of defying. These facts offer evidence that the non-coercive varieties of power have a considerable significance.

Structure

The founders of the United Nations adopted a structural scheme which reflected an urge to divide the functions and separate the powers of the new institutional system. They deviated sharply from the League of Nations model in providing for a Security Council which would assume "primary responsibility for the maintenance of international peace and security,"[6] and for a General Assembly which would exercise broad supervision over all activities other than those especially entrusted to the Security Council. In the negotiating and drafting process at San Francisco, the sharp line of division was considerably blurred; the General Assembly was made competent to consider a matter which.is a primary responsibility of the Security Council but on which that body proves unable to exercise its functions. The Charter, however, retains the basic concept of the differentiation of function. This concept was expressed in the adoption of provisions for a Trusteeship Council, an Economic and Social Council, and a network of specialized agencies, all of them operating within particular sectors of the broad field assigned to the General Assembly. The specialized agencies were envisaged as autonomous international organizations, affiliated with and coordinated by the United Nations but not integral parts of its mechanism. Somewhat similarly, the way was left open for the creation of regional agencies which would be formally outside the United Nations system but subject in considerable measure to the direction and control of the Security Council in so far as they might concern themselves with activities in the area of peace and security. The Security Council was given a Military Staff Committee with specialized advisory functions related to military and disarmament questions. The structural blueprint was completed by provisions for a United Nations Secretariat and an International Court of Justice, but the plan was flexible enough to permit the creation of other organs and agencies of types not explicitly authorized in the Charter.

This design was the product of a number of factors. It reflected the organization-building habits which had been acquired by the international community over a period of roughly a century, and in particular the architectural lessons which had been drawn from the League experiment. It represented a practical adjustment to the fact that certain international bodies, notably regional organizations and specialized agencies, were already going concerns or fully elaborated projects. It expressed a conviction concerning the merits, from the standpoint of efficiency, of a scheme based upon division of labor and decentralization of authority. Finally, it represented a delicate political agreement concerning the distribution of power among the Members of

[6] Charter of the United Nations, Article 24, paragraph 1.

the United Nations. The special position of the Great Powers in the Security Council, the balance between administering authorities and states not administering trust territories in the Trusteeship Council, and the equal vote given to all Members in the General Assembly indicate the general nature of this agreement.

The evolution of the institutional structure of the United Nations has been characterized, in the first place, by a tendency toward proliferation. This is related to the fact that the Organization has moved steadily toward the expansion of its functions and its techniques for influencing state behavior. Given the original bias, implanted in the Charter, toward institutional specialization, it is not surprising—although it has sometimes been alarming to students of administration—to find that the United Nations has spawned a numerous progeny of commissions, committees, and subordinate bodies of various kinds. The organizational chart of the international community has become exceedingly complex and not altogether neat. Experts might disagree as to whether this situation of institutional untidiness is indicative of a healthy growing process or of a constitutional addiction to complexity on the part of those who devote themselves to organizing a world order. In any event, the United Nations has displayed an adequate capacity for creating whatever structural additions it may require, if not for subjecting its pattern of organization to a continuous process of rationalization.

A second major feature of the constitutional history of the United Nations to date has been the lapse into desuetude, or less drastically, the decline in use, or the modification of the originally intended significance, of certain organs. Most notably, the Security Council has played a diminishing role in the system. This has resulted largely but not entirely from the severe impact of Great Power conflict upon its capacity for effective operation. The Military Staff Committee, having been immobilized by disagreement among its members, has become moribund. The Interim Committee of the General Assembly, launched with great fanfare in 1947, has seldom been heard from since. The Economic and Social Council, while maintaining a vigorous schedule of meetings and presiding over an impressive network of subsidiary groups, has not brought the results expected of a principal organ. The International Court of Justice has not been utilized as much either for advisory opinions or judgments as was the Permanent Court of International Justice during the League period. The experience of the United Nations suggests that international organization tends to produce an excessive amount of machinery, much of which is either left to rust in disuse, or is not used with full effectiveness.

This feature of the Organization's structural evolution is intimately related, as both cause and effect, to the third major feature: the steady rise in importance of the General Assembly. This phenomenon is the product of the convergence of a number of political factors. Small states, taking advantage of the conflict among the Great Powers, which has robbed the Security Council of vitality, have pressed for the primacy of the Assembly. The Western powers, frustrated by the Soviet veto in the Security Council, have undertaken a compensatory build-up of the Assembly. The Soviet Union, bent on global competition rather than negotiation with the Western powers, has turned to the Assembly as a suitable arena for the political struggle. Leaders of the anti-colonial movement, checked by the balanced composition of the Trusteeship Council, and underdeveloped countries, discouraged by opposition in the Economic and Social Council to their demands for ambitious economic programs, have sought to exploit the possibility of outvoting conservative forces in the Assembly. States which do not occupy seats in the Councils and other organs of limited membership have insisted upon the transfer of issues to, or the reconsideration of issues in, the one organ in which all members have equal and permanent membership. States which do enjoy membership in the smaller organs have tended to use low-level representatives in those bodies and to insist that the decisions of those bodies be reviewed—and their deliberations repeated—by the higher ranking teams assigned to the annual sessions of the Assembly.

The upshot of all this is that the principle of the differentiation of function, as between the Security Council and the General Assembly, has been cast into the discard. The scheme of division of labor, involving the supervisory Assembly and the specialized Councils, has tended to break down. The concept of decentralization has given way to a situation in which the General Assembly is the dominant organ within the United Nations.

This alteration is in large measure a function of the transformation of the basic nature of the United Nations. If the Organization is to be above all else a forum for global discussion, mobilization of world opinion, and crystallization of the best possible approximation of a global will, then clearly the logical and appropriate focal point for these enterprises is not an organ with restricted membership, but a body as nearly universal in representative scope as the General Assembly. But this monopolization of function by the Assembly carries with it significant disadvantages and dangers. The sheer bulk of the agenda threatens to overcome that body. The monotonous repetition in the Assembly, first in committee and then in plenary session, of debate already conducted in the specialized Councils casts a reflection upon mankind's good sense. More importantly, the tendency of the Assembly to exercise direct dominance over the activity of the United Nations in all sectors of the field occupied by the Organization represents a breach of the political bargains which were struck at San Francisco. Aside from this consideration it simply is not self-evident that such a body as the Assembly—with its greater resemblance to a public forum than to an intimate negotiating conference, and with its formal dedication to the proposition that petty states and superpowers have equal weight—is a suitable and sensible organ for doing the greater part of what needs to be done by international action in our time. Nevertheless, judging from the fact that a similar drift marked the evolution of the League of Nations, we might conclude that the tendency of the Assembly to become the primary organ is typical of the development of international political organizations.

The final feature of the process of structural evolution which deserves particular attention is the high development of the autonomy of the specialized agencies and the relative ineffectiveness of efforts to envelop them as coordinated elements within a general United Nations system. This development, which is intimately related to the general proliferation of international institutions, would seem to constitute a notable exception to the centralizing tendency noted above. The specialized agencies constitute a type of institution that has seemed immune to the absorptive power of the General Assembly. Indeed, it seems likely that the tendency of the Assembly to draw all the strings of the United Nations within its own grasp has, paradoxically, contributed to the laxity of the Organization's hold upon the specialized agencies. By diminishing the stature of the Economic and Social Council, the Assembly has handicapped the organ which was charged with the task of bringing the specialized agencies within a working system of coordination.

This is not to say that no useful operating relationships have been established within the system. Both formal and informal arrangements for collaboration and coordination have been made, in accordance with the special agreements negotiated between the United Nations and each of the specialized agencies. Limited coordination has been promoted by consultation among the administrative leaders of the organizations. The joint enterprise of the Expanded Program of Technical Assistance carries promise of encouraging the most practical and meaningful sort of cooperation among its participants, which include the United Nations and seven of the specialized agencies.

Nevertheless, it is clear that the concept of decentralization has held sway in the relations of the United Nations with its affiliated agencies. The trend has been toward the hardening of autonomous features, not the development of integration within the United Nations system.

MAJOR PROBLEMS OF THE UNITED NATIONS AND RECOMMENDATIONS FOR THEIR SOLUTION

It should be clear to everyone, from the severest critic of the United Nations to its most devoted supporter, that the United Nations, as it has developed up to the present time, falls far short of optimum capacity as an agency for coping with the problems of world affairs. This deficiency relates as significantly to *positive* as to *negative* aspects of the global task. The Organization is seriously inadequate for meeting the challenge either of humanity's great opportunities or of its grave perils.

We do not wish to minimize the historic importance, and the promise for the future, of the creative innovations and institutional developments which the United Nations has to its credit. Nevertheless, attention may well be focused upon the constitutional and political limitations which handicap international organization in the present era. There is the basic problem of inadequate constitutional authority to take measures which may be deemed essential to the realization of established objectives. When legal competence is not lacking, effective action may be prevented by formal barriers to decision-making, such as the veto rule in the Security Council. When the decision-making process is not thus handicapped, essential policies may yet fail to command the support needed to put them into effect, as a result of bias, lack of courage, lack of vision, or whatever other factors may influence the votes of Member States. If all these hurdles are surmounted, decisions may be nullified by the insufficiency of available means for enforcing or otherwise securing compliance or cooperation. Even if adequate means are theoretically available, the willingness and determination of Member States to use them may be lacking. Their reasons may extend from reluctance to risk war to refusal to spend money. Thus, there are many potential frustrations for international organization between the acceptance of vital responsibilities and the performance of necessary and proper functions.

The inadequacies of the United Nations may be analyzed usefully in terms of "gaps," original and acquired, within its system of functions and powers. A strong case can be made for the proposition that the original scheme of the Charter established a large gap between the functions assigned and the powers attributed to the Organization. In any event, such a gap has come to exist. The task has grown steadily larger and more difficult with the spectacular explosion of atomic energy, the crude threat of Communist aggression, and the delicate problems of adjustment between ascendant nationalism and decadent colonialism. Rising expectations, soaring aspirations, and growing opportunities for improvement of human conditions have added further to the functional requirements of the United Nations. Given this increase in functional demand, the power supply provided for in the Charter was clearly inadequate. Unfortunately, the development of the powers of the Organization has followed no such simple course of consistent expansion. Unanticipated power resources have been discovered and tapped, but these have been at best compensatory assets, tending to offset the loss of resources which the Charter promised but could not deliver. The original purposes expressed in the Charter may have been unduly modest; the evolved functions of the United Nations may be unduly ambitious; at any rate, there is no doubt that a serious gap exists between the responsibilities which the Organization has accumulated and the capacities which it has developed.

It may be that mankind's best hope lies in the possibility that this gap will prove to be a *spark gap*—not a broken connection leading to disaster, but a breach which by its very existence will produce a flash of creative power. This conception assumes a capacity of human beings to respond to the challenge of danger and opportunity which we would not discount, but we would point out that there are stringent limitations upon the scope of international reform directly attainable by human ingenuity and resolve. The temptation to dream of "legislating" the problems of the United Nations into oblivion is one that must be resisted. We cannot by taking thought, or drafting blueprints, or proposing amendments to the Charter, banish the reality of national power, or control the manner in which states use their votes in the United Nations, or produce enhanced sensitivity of governments to world opinion, or determine the way peoples interpret their vital interests and feel about the justice of their national demands. At best, we can hope to influence the development of international institutions and to contribute toward coordinating the political forces of our world within a system of order.

The Commission does not profess, in this Report, to offer solutions for all the problems of the United Nations, or even for all the major ones. We have deliberately refrained from attempting to cover all the ground which has been explored by the various Study Committees whose Reports are included in this volume. We have felt no obligation as a Commission either to agree or to disagree with all the recommendations included in these Reports. We have undertaken to concentrate our attention upon a limited number of problems, selected because we deem them both important and susceptible to at least partial solution by the methods which we are agreed in recommending.

Problem-Area I: The Organizational Problems of the United Nations

Whatever else the United Nations may be and should be, it is an agency for attempting to bring order and justice into the political relationships which exist among states and peoples. It is fitting, then, that we should first focus our attention upon its deficiencies of organization in this broad area of its operations.

A problem of major concern is posed by the fate which has overtaken the Security Council. This organ, designed to serve as the primary element in the political concerns of the system, has been reduced to relative inactivity. The Security Council must be ranked as a casualty of the Cold War, of the Soviet disposition to use the veto power to forward its immediate interests, and of the urge of small states for equal representation in international organization.

To a very considerable extent the United Nations has compensated for the ineffectiveness of the Security Council by shifting its functions to the General Assembly. Nevertheless, the possibility that the use of the veto may prevent the Security Council from reaching decisions remains a serious handicap to the United Nations in dealing with certain organizational questions which vitally affect its operation. The ending of the Council's participation, or the restriction of the rule of unanimity in its participation, in decisions on such questions is essential to the development of the United Nations as an effective system.

This observation applies, first, to the issue of the admission of new Members to the Organization. *The Commission adheres to the fundamental proposition that the United Nations should be a universal organization. To this end, we believe that all states able to discharge the obligations of membership should be admitted if they apply. Whether the applicant satisfies this condition should be decided by a procedural vote of the Security Council and by a two-thirds vote of the General Assembly.* The basic question of the representative scope of the United Nations is not one to which the veto power should apply.

A closely related problem is that of reaching decisions concerning the right of a government to represent a Member State in the United Nations. *We urge general acceptance of the principle that decisions on issues of this type, reached by a two-thirds majority vote in the General Assembly, should be followed by all organs of the United Nations and by the specialized agencies.* While we recognize that the latter, under existing constitutional arrangements, cannot be bound by decisions of the General Assembly, we think it highly desirable that the specialized agencies should give serious attention to decisions of the Assembly on questions of representation. We regard it as mandatory for the proper functioning and development of the United Nations that disputes on issues of this sort should be settled by a single decision, uniformly applicable to all parts of the system, and we think it is obvious that the appropriate body for reaching a decision of such constitutional importance is the General Assembly.

In one other respect, there is need for agreement to develop an alternative to a procedure which involves the Security Council. Under Article 97 of the Charter, the election of a Secretary-General is dependent upon a decision of the Security Council to recommend a candidate to the General Assembly; in practice this decision requires the unanimity of the permanent members of the Council. Since the Charter makes no provision for a situation in which the Security Council may find itself unable to produce a recommendation, a stalemate in the Council may prevent the vital post of Secretary-General from being filled in some future contingency. In 1950 the General

Assembly averted such a calamitous development by taking extraordinary action to extend the term of Secretary-General Lie, but this was possible only because the incumbent was willing and able to continue his service. Hence, that precedent provides no assurance against a long-continuing vacancy in the office in the event of the death or disability of the Secretary-General. To meet this problem, *the Commission suggests that the General Assembly pass a resolution declaring itself competent to appoint an Acting Secretary-General, if the office should become vacant and the prompt election of a new Secretary-General as provided in the Charter (Article 97) should not prove feasible. The Acting Secretary-General should be fully empowered to exercise the functions of the office until such time as he might be replaced by a Secretary-General chosen in the normal manner.* In making this recommendation, the Commission does not wish to minimize the importance of the consideration that the Secretary-General should enjoy the confidence of all the Great Powers, if he is to serve with full effectiveness. We do consider it essential, however, to establish procedures minimizing the danger that the Organization might be left for an extended period without a Secretary-General. To that end, we suggest the elimination of the Security Council's capacity to block the filling of the office on a provisional basis.

Beyond this point, the Commission does not advocate reducing the Council's role in the United Nations. On the contrary, we are convinced that there is a fundamental need for revitalizing the Security Council. Ultimately, the task is not to circumvent the stalled Council, leaving it stranded in oblivion, but to make it go. The United Nations needs such an organ as the Security Council was intended to be, and adaptations to its failure to function effectively can never fully compensate for this failure.

We look, as an ultimate goal, to a Security Council continuously adaptable, in composition, to the dynamics of a world in which the roster of the most important and powerful states is subject to change.

Advantage should be taken of the growing demand for enlargement of the Security Council to improve its representative character. A moderate expansion of the Council should include provision to ensure implementation of the first criterion for elective members, that is, contribution "to the maintenance of international peace and security," as well as of the second, "equitable geographical distribution."

This alteration, which should be achieved as soon as possible, would have the fundamental purpose of contributing to the psychological revitalization of the Security Council. The low estate of the Council is not attributable solely to the fact that the veto has paralyzed its operation. A part of the difficulty lies in the fact that too few governments are interested in making the Security Council a significant element in the operating mechanism of the United Nations. It is to be hoped that the proposed change would stimulate a broader concern for making the Council work effectively.

A second necessary element in the project for rehabilitating the Security Council is the reduction of the impact of the veto power upon its capacity for exercising its functions. *The practicable aim in regard to the veto is that which was stated in the Vandenberg Resolution of June 11, 1948: the removal of the veto on the admission of new Members and on the functioning of the Council in the field of pacific settlement (Chapter VI). The gradual restriction of the veto power should next extend into the area of peace preservation (Chapter VII), enabling the Council to make recommendations to the Members concerning the existence of threats to or breaches of the peace or of acts of aggression, concerning provisional measures in such cases, and concerning sanctioning measures if such provisional measures are not observed.*

The Commission believes that this limited reduction of the veto power is an essential objective whose achievement will contribute significantly to the revitalization of the Security Council. No prescriptions are available for producing the progressive relinquishment of the veto power. This result is clearly dependent upon the diminution of the tensions of the Cold War and the basic adjustment of relationships among the Great Powers. Perhaps the most that can be done at the institutional level is to promote the development of a general interest in making the Security Council an effective agency, thereby creating a demand which cannot be ignored by the possessors of the veto power.

It is to be hoped that the alteration of the composition and the voting rules of the Security Council along the lines which we have suggested would enable that body to achieve reinstatement as a genuinely useful organ of the United Nations. Given its psychological and procedural revitalization, the Council could play a role in the management of global political affairs for which no other international agency is suited.

The General Assembly, unlike the Security Council, has not proved deficient in capacity to register its will through the passage of resolutions, and its functional development has been marked by rapid growth rather than by atrophy. The Assembly is unlikely to be displaced—and, indeed, should not be displaced—from its acquired political role. The central problem of the Assembly, relevant also to the Security Council in so far as that body has been able to reach formal decisions, has been that of making its resolutions conduce to meaningful and useful results.

In the broadest terms the political inadequacy of the United Nations, and particularly of the General Assembly, is exemplified by the passage of resolutions which prove to be ineffectual. The United Nations speaks, but its voice is ignored. Its expressed purposes are neglected and frustrated. Its will is defied and thwarted. The popular image of a weak and futile United Nations is compounded of such elements as the long unresolved dispute over Kashmir, the perpetuation of a divided Korea, the settled attitude of intransigence in South Africa, the endemic conflict between Israel and the Arab states, and the contemptuous defiance exhibited by the Soviet Union as it sits astride the mangled body of Hungarian independence. The critical question arises: what can be done to enhance the real significance of the United Nations as a directing and controlling force in international politics?

Attention should be directed first to the perennially contentious issue of the boundary between domestic jurisdiction and international competence. In practice the United Nations has not been debarred by claims of domestic jurisdiction (based upon Article 2, paragraph 7) from dealing with issues which a significant majority of its Member States have wished to subject to international debating and voting processes. The Organization has on occasion overridden claims of this sort with such abandon as to inspire sincere anxiety among some qualified observers and bitter resistance within some governments. The problem is not that of the undue functional confinement of the United Nations; it is the problem of the weakening of the moral and political influence of the United Nations by the majority's disregard for the essential principle of a constitutional system that limitations of competence should be regarded with respect by those who command the votes. This is not to say that we are agreed upon the thesis that the United Nations has in fact expanded its activities beyond the limits that would be permitted by a legitimately and desirably liberal construction of the Charter. It is to say that the Organization has tended to undermine its authority by failing to give assurance to Member States that their claims of domestic jurisdiction will be fairly considered, not arbitrarily brushed aside.

We deplore the practice of raising the issue of domestic jurisdiction (Article 2, paragraph 7) *upon inscription of a problem upon the agenda of United Nations organs, since debate in itself cannot properly be considered intervention in the domestic jurisdiction of a state. However, the organs of the United Nations should give more serious attention to claims that specific resolutions are beyond their competence and should more frequently request the advisory opinion of the World Court on such claims.*

This suggestion does not rest upon the naive belief that political controversy over questions of the Organization's competence can be eliminated, or that the inherently political questions regarding jurisdiction can be transformed into simple legal problems which can be neatly solved by judges. The issue of domestic jurisdiction which arises in the United Nations system can no more be put to final rest than can the issue of states' rights in the American federal system. Nevertheless, we believe that the effectiveness of the United Nations can be improved if Member States will display greater moderation and a stronger sense of responsibility, both in claiming immunity from United Nations action on jurisdictional grounds and in dealing with such claims when raised by other states. Only in such a political atmosphere can the Organization develop its moral authority to the fullest.

We recognize that the problem of securing respect for the resolutions of the General Assembly is intimately related to the problem of establishing a fairer system of representation and voting in that body. The present one-state-one-vote rule is clearly unrealistic, and has become a serious impediment to the development of the Assembly's prestige as the collective spokesman of a global viewpoint. *We urge the United Nations to continue its examination of possible changes designed to produce a more equitable system of representation and voting in the General Assembly.*

Problem Area II: Political and Legal Functions of the United Nations

A primary objective of any campaign to strengthen the United Nations must be to increase the Organization's capability in the realm of pacific settlement of disputes. We have expressed the hope that the

Security Council may ultimately become able to operate in this field without the stultifying influence of the veto,[7] but the immediate problem is to improve the equipment of both major organs, and particularly the General Assembly, for producing peaceful solutions in situations of actual or potential conflict.

The development of the investigatory power of the United Nations beyond the capacity of the Security Council under Article 34 is a vital part of the approach to this problem. International investigation has merits which go far beyond the obvious utility of providing accurate information to serve as the basis of United Nations decisions or recommendations. The presence of a United Nations observation agency in a troubled area may conduce significantly to the relaxation of tensions and the moderation of the policies of disputants.

Because we regard the legal capacity of the United Nations to conduct investigations in the territory of Member States as a vital element in the Organization's equipment for dealing with problems of international peace and security, we believe that the General Assembly should declare the scope of this capacity, and recommend appropriate measures to ensure that Members will receive and cooperate with investigatory missions. The authority of the Security Council by a procedural vote (Article 29) or of the General Assembly by a two-thirds vote (Article 22) to initiate such investigations, and the obligation of the affected Member States to accept them (Articles 104 and 105) should be recognized. Moreover, we urge the General Assembly to confirm the right of the Secretary-General, in person or through deputies, to visit and negotiate with the governments of Member States (Articles 97, 99, 104 and 105).

It is doubtful that there could be a more favorable omen for the future of world peace than a steadily developing capacity of the United Nations both to launch prompt and unimpeded inquiries into situations of friction and conflict and to utilize its Secretary-General as a statesman representing the interests of the international community.

Recurrent crises in international affairs during the last decade, which have required the United Nations to improvise machinery for maintaining the peace of the world, have illustrated the unmistakable need for a limited reservoir of military manpower to be placed constantly at the disposal of the Organization. A *permanent United*

[7] See p. 33, above.

Nations Force should be made to emerge from the experience of the United Nations in Palestine, Korea, and Egypt. We recommend a force composed of at least 2,000 individual volunteers on active duty, plus a larger number of men in trained contingents, including air force units, committed specifically to the Organization by Member States. This Force should be held in genuine readiness for use under the authority of either the General Assembly or the Security Council. A permanent United Nations Commander, assisted by an advisory committee of Member States and working in close cooperation with the Secretary-General, should provide the essential professional direction of the Force.

The point should be made unmistakably clear that we propose a *policing force*, not an army—an instrument for the promotion of peaceful settlements, not an agency for waging an international war against an aggressor state. The possibility cannot be excluded that this force might become involved in full-scale military conflict, but the purpose should be to establish a corps of United Nations servants, not a legion of martyrs to the cause of international organization. Such a force might be of inestimable value in observing troubled areas, in providing temporary occupation of areas where conflict is imminent, in supervising the stabilization of situations in which cease-fire and withdrawal orders have been issued, in patrolling armistice lines, in maintaining order in disputed territories while settlements are being arranged, in supervising plebiscites, and the like. Supplementary functions of a United Nations Force might include, or ultimately come to include, the guarding of internationally owned facilities such as the installations which may be acquired by the projected International Atomic Energy Agency, participation in the control mechanism of an international system for the regulation of armaments, and provision of police services in areas which may be placed under the long-term or permanent administration of the United Nations. There can be little doubt that the United Nations could usefully employ such a force as we recommend, and, in the long run, a substantially larger force.

The usefulness of a United Nations Force must depend upon the willingness of United Nations organs to put it to use, which in turn will depend upon the willingness of the states involved in disputes to permit it to be used. We think it is evident that no peaceful settlement procedure can be imposed upon a resistant state without defeating its fundamental purpose. Hence, we do not propose departure from the established principle that the application of the techniques of institutionalized pacific settlement is subject to the consent of the state or states most directly affected. The essential consent to the functioning of a United Nations Force must be produced by the moral pressure of the Organization and the growing prestige of a United Nations system which proves itself worthy of the confidence and serviceable to the real interests of the nations.

Investigation and policing are of no ultimate value unless the political process of promoting settlement—the process which they are intended to facilitate—is carried forward with skill and, more fundamentally, with wisdom. There is no sense in recommending that people be skillful or wise, although there may be a great deal of sense in suggesting that people avoid the hopeless search for a system which will work wonders for the world even without the assets of human skill and wisdom. Nevertheless, we believe that the world can do better than merely to sit back and hope that the United Nations will develop and utilize the requisite qualities for promoting the peaceful adjustment of political conflicts.

The Commission believes that the United Nations has not discovered the optimum balance between the public forum and the private conference table as instruments of pacific settlement. In general, the former has been emphasized to the neglect of the latter. The airing of disputes, the attempt to crystallize an international viewpoint, and the effort to mobilize the general opinion of the United Nations are useful and necessary functions, to which the General Assembly in particular lends itself. But, on the other side of the coin, we find the presentation of cases to the United Nations for propagandistic exploitation, the quest for parliamentary victories rather than diplomatic solutions, and the bitter speech-making and position-taking which often inhibit rather than promote compromise and adjustment. Too frequently, the parties to disputes are permitted to turn the organs of the United Nations into a battlefield. They should be required to enter the organizational chamber for a peace conference. The critical question is, who is master in this house? The answer is clear. The representatives of the international interest in a just and lasting peace, not the disputants, *ought* to be in command of the United Nations when it deals with explosive situations.

So far as this viewpoint can be translated into reasonably concrete recommendations, we think that it points to the desirability of introducing into the operation of the United Nations a substantially greater emphasis upon the role of independent mediators and intimate negotiating committees, functioning on behalf of the Organization. *We suggest that the United Nations develop the practice of dealing with a dispute or situation, either before or after preliminary debate, by referring it to private negotiation under the auspices of a rapporteur to be appointed by the Secretary-General in consultation with the President either of the General Assembly or of the Security Council. If the process of quiet consultation does not produce agreement, we recommend that a resolution proposed by the rapporteur should be given priority over any other draft resolution in the public debating and voting process.*

These proposals are designed not to accomplish the improbable and undesirable result of eliminating the open forum function of the United Nations, but to put the initiative in the treatment of political disputes where it belongs—in the hands of persons qualified to represent the international interest in making the United Nations an effective contributor to the peaceful settlement of disputes.

The Members of the United Nations have tended to neglect the judicial approach to the settlement of international disputes. While we recognize that not all controversies are susceptible to solution by judicial processes, we are confident that the World Court, symbolizing the rule of law in international affairs, can play a role of increasing significance. Therefore, *we urge the United States to take the lead in promoting resort to the World Court in contentious cases of appropriate nature. To this end it should modify the reservation attached to its ratification of the optional clause. We also urge United States leadership in persuading organs of the United Nations to make more use of the Court for advisory opinions.*

A political area which has assumed peculiar controversial importance in the United Nations is the broad field of colonialism. The clash between anti-colonial impatience and colonial obstinacy has persistently presented problems which fall along the blurred line between peaceful settlement and peaceful change. These problems are sufficiently distinctive to warrant special attention. While no formal arrangements can either guarantee the development of moderate and mutually trustful attitudes by the contestants over colonial issues or provide workable solutions to those issues in the absence of such development, the Commission believes that there are possibilities which have not yet been exploited for the promotion of constructive collaboration among those contestants.

The Commission believes that the provisions of the Charter relating to the government and development of non-self-governing territories (Article 73) constitute international obligations for Members of the United Nations and that the General Assembly is competent to inquire into the observance of those obligations. On this basis we believe that Member States administering such territories should accept the obligation of reporting to the United Nations on political progress as well as on economic, social, and educational developments.

We support the claim of the General Assembly that it has competence to decide what territories are non-self-governing and when they cease to be so because of changes in their constitutional status.

The Committee on Information from Non-Self-Governing Territories which, like the Trusteeship Council, has a balanced membership between administering and non-administering states, should be made permanent. The General Assembly should enlarge its functions so that it can make recommendations to Member States.

The Commission notes with regret the failure of Members of the United Nations to utilize the provision of Article 81 which authorizes the Organization itself to accept the responsibility of administering trust territories. International government of specific areas and populations poses many delicate and complex problems, but it is not an inherently unfeasible proposition. We are convinced that the United Nations ought to be engaged in expanding the limited body of experience in such matters which was provided by previous international organizations, and in learning to cope with the difficulties of international administration. The future of international relations is certain to present situations in which United Nations administration will prove desirable and perhaps even indispensable. The ideal merit of internationalization is that it provides political neutralization, removing an area from the sphere of competition among mutually distrustful states.

Moreover, the development of international administration under the United Nations, particularly in Antarctica and the ocean bed, offers the prospect of facilitating the exploitation for universal human benefit of major new food supplies and other economic resources, and of providing significant revenues to strengthen the programs of the United Nations. The ultimate usefulness of the United Nations may rest heavily upon its capacity to serve as governing authority in areas of various types. The development of this capacity is an urgent problem and a major challenge to the United Nations.

We believe that the United Nations is capable not only of administering territory, but of acquiring title under international law through cession by the state with title or through prior claim to territory or space to which no state has title. This is indicated by Article 81 of the Charter permitting the United Nations to administer trust territories, by the World Court's advice in the Reparations case, and by the delegation of responsibility to the United Nations in respect to Trieste and the Italian Colonies in pursuance of the Italian Peace Treaty.

We believe that the United Nations should undertake the responsibility of administering certain contested areas of international importance for water or air transport,[8] and certain uninhabited areas like Antarctica, at the request or with the consent of states having claim to such territories. With respect to the bed of the high seas beyond the continental shelf and to outer space, which are outside the jurisdiction of any state, we urge the General Assembly to declare the title of the international community and to establish appropriate administrative arrangements.

The most glaring of the political deficiencies of the United Nations is the one least susceptible to the ministrations of sympathetic

---

[8] In a statement on "Narrow Waterways and Strategic Bases" issued November 1951, the Commission stated:

"The first recommendation of the Commission to Study the Organization of Peace relates to the administration of strategic and narrow waterways connecting high seas and important for the shipping of all nations. The Commission has in mind particularly the threat to the peace arising out of the controversy over interferences by Egypt with international shipping in the Suez Canal. Threats to the peace might also arise in other places, such as the Turkish Straits. It is manifestly in the general interest of all nations that there should be no interference with international movement through such canals and straits by any one Power primarily pursuing its own national interest. Interference with the shipping of any particular country, or the transport of any particular commodity, should be permitted only in pursuance of action taken in the general interest by the United Nations. To permit particular countries to take advantage of territorial propinquity, as newspaper reports indicate Egypt is doing, will certainly provoke controversy and perhaps result in threats to the peace.

"The Commission to Study the Organization of Peace recommends, therefore, that an International Straits Commission be established under the authority and direction of the United Nations General Assembly for the purpose of controlling the administration of canals and straits currently of major strategic importance."

observers. This defect is the ultimate incapacity of the Organization to cope with deliberate and determined refusal by states to respect their international legal obligations, or to accede to the will of the international community as expressed, however imperfectly, in resolutions or recommendations of United Nations organs. Flat defiance of the United Nations is an uncomfortably familiar phenomenon. It is likely to become more rather than less frequent if the Organization increases the range of its activities and acquires more significant decision-making authority. When recalcitrant states act in contempt of the United Nations, public opinion tends to regard international organization as an exercise in futility. States which are injured or disadvantaged by such action are tempted to abandon their loyalty to the Organization. The danger grows that the whole enterprise will founder on the rock of the sovereign power of states to do as they please. What can be done about the refusal of states to comply with recommendations of United Nations organs? What can be done about flagrant violations of general international law, treaties, and binding decisions of international agencies? What can be done about the illegal and arbitrary use of armed force by one state against another, or about the more subtle forms of aggression which are in vogue?

With respect to the problem of non-compliance with resolutions which do not relate to charges of violation of legal obligations, and, being merely recommendations of the United Nations, have no binding effect, the only proper solution would appear to be the redoubling of efforts to achieve a judicious balance between the application of persuasive diplomacy and the mobilization of moral pressure. These methods are fundamental also to the treatment of the problem of illegal behavior by states, although in this case it would seem possible and eminently desirable to take additional measures. The Commission cannot conceive of the Organization's being either able or willing to resort to military sanctions against a state which violates international obligations without using armed force in its international relations, nor would we suggest that the United Nations should recommend or condone independent military action by states which feel themselves aggrieved by such violation. The hard reality is, however, that violence will ultimately break out in a situation in which states are encouraged to believe that they can commit illegal acts with impunity.

In order to prevent the emergence of situations of this kind, and to promote the ideal of international justice, which is inseparable from the cultivation of law-abidingness, *we recommend that urgent attention be given to the development of United Nations sanctions against internationally illegal behavior likely to disturb international peace and security, but not involving actual hostilities.* The first requirement of such a program is confirmation of the allegation of illegal action. If such a charge is not referred by the parties to the World Court as a contentious case for its decision, the General Assembly or Security Council should investigate the facts of the situation and secure the advisory opinion of the World Court before making a formal finding against the offending state. However, in cases carrying an imminent threat to the peace or involving clear-cut refusal to comply with a mandatory decision of an international agency, a more summary procedure would be necessary. Next, the resources of peaceful adjustment and moral pressure should be fully explored. If finally necessary, the United Nations should bring into play the power of the General Assembly to recommend or of the Security Council to order, and of either organ to coordinate the application of, all possible sanctions short of the use of armed force. These would include economic sanctions and what might be called "institutional sanctions"—deprivation of the privileges and benefits which derive from membership in the United Nations system. In such manner, the United Nations may contribute to the development of the respect for international law which is essential to the ordering of international relations.

In case of actual hostilities, the Security Council, or if it cannot function, the General Assembly, should continue the practice of calling for a cease-fire and withdrawal of forces at the earliest possible moment. A presumption of aggression arises from non-compliance with such provisional measures, and is confirmed by the failure of a state to demonstrate either a necessity for self-defense or a genuine request for military intervention by the state in whose territory it is operating. Under the Charter, there can be no legal state of war, nor can there be belligerent rights or military self-help apart from justifiable self-defense. Continued recalcitrance of an aggressor state should be followed by all sanctions, even military, with due consideration of the primary purpose of the United Nations to avoid general war.

We recommend continuance of the practice of dealing with actual hostilities by provisional orders, calling for cease-fire and withdrawal, and of employing armed force only if hostilities are continued. While there is need for flexibility to meet the circumstances of each case, the Commission recommends that, apart from necessities of self-defense against armed attack, situations involving aggression should be dealt with by the United Nations, not by nations or collective defense agencies acting independently. The United Nations should call upon and coordinate the action of its Members and of such agencies when forces directly available to it are inadequate.

The problem of achieving the limitation and control of armaments is an important part of the broader problem of creating general international security. While war is fundamentally a product of political conflicts, and those conflicts are more generally the cause rather than the effect of armaments races, it is nevertheless true that the existence of massive national armaments tends to aggravate the conflicts and to heighten the tensions which disturb international relations. The world is faced with the cruel paradox that the control of weapons depends in large part upon a universal expectation of justice and security under dependable international arrangements, but the realization of such expectations is frustrated in some measure by armaments races. The United Nations will not be significantly strengthened until there is a measure of disarmament, while the latter waits upon a strengthened organization. But if the armaments race is recognized for what it is, a function primarily of political conflict, the control problem assumes more realistic dimensions. While a fool-proof armaments control system under present conditions is technically and politically impossible, a working control system might well be the natural result of political accommodation. Any control system must depend in the first instance on recognized mutuality of interest, and at least a modicum of mutual trust. These essential qualities may be developed not only in special disarmament negotiations, but also—and perhaps more significantly—in broader negotiations looking toward general political accommodation.

We recommend that negotiations for the regulation of armaments under United Nations auspices be pursued vigorously, though we recognize that agreement for armaments control will probably have to be linked with political accommodation. We believe that some forms of international control are feasible and would foster attitudes that would be conducive to political accommodation. Avenues to be explored include control arrangements in limited geographic areas, inspection to prevent sudden attacks, pilot projects to test the effec-

*tiveness of such inspection, limitation or elimination of nuclear ex-
plosions dangerous to human life and health, international control of
intercontinental ballistic missiles and space satellites, and balanced
reduction of military forces and limitation of military production.*

The United Nations can do—and has done—a great deal to
minimize the possibility of the outbreak of war. Most of what the
United Nations can do must be done well in advance of a crisis in
which peace hangs in the balance, to prevent the development of such
a crisis. The constructive work of an international organization dedicated to the maintenance of peace must be accomplished not on the
brink of war but well back from the edge of the precipice.

*Problem-Area III: The Economic and Social Functions of the United
Nations.*

The second major category of United Nations responsibilities includes the myriad of international activities which may be subsumed
under the general heading of "economic and social functions." This
is the realm of the so-called functional approach to world order, the
area of constructive collaboration to promote common interests
relating directly to human welfare and indirectly to the creation of a
world society capable of supporting the institutional structure of
world order. The deficiencies of the United Nations in this sphere are
not to be taken less seriously because they involve the loss of golden
opportunities rather than the failure to cope with grave perils.

In this area, as in the political area, a significant problem is posed
by the unsatisfactory performance of an organ charged by the Charter
with a major share of responsibility. The Economic and Social
Council, unlike the Security Council, has not suffered paralysis of its
resolution-passing faculties or withered away in inactivity. It has, however, shared the fate of the Security Council in failing to fulfill the
promise of its official status as a principal organ of the United Nations
and in being largely crowded out by the functional aggrandizement
of the General Assembly.

The diminished status of the Economic and Social Council is
evidenced by, and in part caused by, the tendency of governments
to send relatively low-level and frequently unqualified representatives
to its sessions. For a variety of reasons, including the unwillingness of
states to give weight to the decisions of a body in which they are not
represented, the work of the Council is largely disregarded by the

General Assembly, which blithely proceeds, in the Second and Third Committees and in plenary session, to debate issues and formulate policies as if it has forgotten that the Council has already covered the same ground. The Council has encumbered itself with a network of Commissions and Sub-commissions whose records of achievement are uneven. In sum, the United Nations mechanism for dealing with economic and social matters is in need of revision to promote its fullest efficiency.

We recommend that the Economic and Social Council examine the functional commissions and eliminate those not found to be essential. We suggest that the Council make greater use of experts, appointed in their individual capacities as required for temporary service. We urge states which are elected to the Council to give recognition to the potential importance of that body by delegating persons of high standing and outstanding competence as their spokesmen in the Council. Thus revitalized, the Economic and Social Council should provide dynamic leadership for the United Nations in the development of a genuinely international outlook upon economic problems, and vigorous initiative in the exploration of economic frontiers which give promise of offering new possibilities for raising the level of human welfare.

We believe that one of the greatest challenges which confront our generation is that of making the United Nations a powerful engine of economic development and human welfare. *We cannot urge too strongly the desirability of setting the United Nations to the task of promoting and operating bold programs of technical assistance and capital investment. It is particularly important that special high-priority programs be initiated to further the development of non-self-governing territories and to assist such new states as may require external aid in formulating and carrying out economic development projects.* The future of human civilization is involved in this magnificent opportunity for constructive cooperation as surely as in the contemporary peril of competitive annihilation.

At the present time the launching of bold United Nations programs in the vital area of economic development is inhibited primarily by the reluctance of the states best able to provide financial support— most notably, the United States—to make available the vastly expanded resources which would be required for this purpose. The arguments which have been advanced to justify this attitude are not uniformly impressive. The case against the administrative competence of the United Nations in operating a large-scale program is a strong one, but we would point out that administrative competence can be acquired only by the experience of bearing important responsibilities. In this realm the United Nations can develop as much institutional effectiveness as its Members, and particularly the United States, are willing to permit it and are determined to make it develop. We are not impressed by the persistent claim that bold economic initiative must be postponed until defense budgets are reduced in accordance with formal disarmament arrangements. America and other nations *can* afford to launch ambitious programs now. What they *cannot* afford is to waste the opportunity now existing for concerted and concentrated effort to build the economic and social foundations of a world fit for order and peace.

Nevertheless, the Commission believes that good sense as well as political realism is reflected in the unwillingness of the United States and other major powers to commit considerable sums to programs which would be operated under the ultimate direction of voting majorities in the General Assembly. We think it is both objectively desirable and politically necessary to provide safeguards against the domination of United Nations development programs by either the states which are the primary beneficiaries or those which are major contributors to them. To that end, *we recommend the establishment of a United Nations Development Agency as the central authority for coordinating the programs of technical assistance and capital investment carried out by the specialized agencies, and for the operational management of the present and future activities of the United Nations itself in the economic development field. This Development Agency should be clearly recognized as a part of the United Nations, but it should be sufficiently autonomous to make decisions concerning the use of funds by an appropriate form of weighted voting. Such a system should be designed to ensure that the major contributing states will have a degree of influence commensurate with their importance in the support of United Nations economic programs. The Development Agency might be so constituted that the major contributors of funds would always occupy seats and the beneficiary countries would have rotating regional representation. Provision might be made that projects be prepared by regional subsidiaries for presentation to the Development Agency and that all programs be approved by a majority of the major contributors.*

Given this arrangement, the Commission believes that the strongest possible case could be made for the proposition that the real interests of the United States and other major powers would best be served by channeling the great bulk of their investments in global economic progress through the United Nations. Moreover, such an agency as we have suggested would be in the best possible position to impress upon underdeveloped countries their responsibility for maintaining a favorable climate for development assistance, both by taking essential positive measures and by refraining from actions which might call into question their stability and respect for contractual obligations.

The growing family of specialized agencies is, and must continue to be, of major significance in the economic and social work of the United Nations. *We advocate the immediate establishment and the vigorous support of the International Atomic Energy Agency. Inasmuch as the principle of inspection has been incorporated in its Statute, the United States and other major atomic powers should bring their bilateral programs under the Agency.*

We emphasize the importance of giving increasingly vigorous support to the specialized agencies and of putting into effective operation the Inter-Governmental Maritime Consultative Organization and the Organization for Trade Cooperation. The United Nations should promote the coordination of the specialized agencies both through improved formal arrangements and through the development of more effective collaboration under the proposed United Nations Development Agency.

Emphasis upon the developmental role of the United Nations in what are inaccurately but conveniently designated the "non-political" fields should not be allowed to obscure the fact that there is important international work of other varieties to be done. International activity in these fields is essential not only because there are underdeveloped economies requiring external assistance, but also because there are highly developed economies requiring a system of coordination and regulation to bring order into their complex interrelationships. The more highly developed a country becomes, the more dependent it becomes upon the delicate balances and the intricate mechanisms of the world economic and social system, and the more it stands to gain from the stabilization and good management of that system. A properly balanced program of international economic and social activity will number advanced countries no less than under-developed countries among its direct beneficiaries.

The phenomenal development of multilateral conventions during the last century reflects the increasing recognition of the stake which nations have in the standardization or coordination of policies, in the maintenance of minimum international standards, and in the establishment of uniform regulations for international intercourse of every variety. The furthering of this process is a vital part of the work of the United Nations and its specialized agencies.

The greatest single expenditure of effort by the United Nations in the field of multilateral treaty-making has been devoted to the elaboration of Covenants on Human Rights. It now appears that this project was too ambitious. *We believe that the most fruitful approach to the task of developing legally binding standards of human rights would be to attack the problem piecemeal. A series of conventions dealing with single or small groups of issues pertaining to human rights should be negotiated. Persistent effort should be made to promote the moral influence of the Universal Declaration of Human Rights as a factor in shaping legal systems and determining governmental policies.*

In general, however, it cannot be said that the agencies of the United Nations system have displayed excessive zeal, or inordinate ambitiousness, in promoting the development of multilateral treaties. Rather, it must be said that the United States has manifested inadequate understanding and appreciation of the importance of this development, and undue reluctance to share in the process of establishing the ground rules for the interacting elements of an interdependent world. Our nation has justly prided itself on being a leading and intensely active member of the United Nations and its affiliated organizations. But in recent years we have dragged our feet and have now virtually resigned from an important sector of United Nations work—that is, from the making of general international conventions. This trend must be attributed in large measure to the political pressures generated by an articulate minority of Americans. The Commission strongly deplores this inclination of American policy. *We urge the United States to contribute to the development and codification of international law by encouraging the work of the International Law Commission, and by participating actively in making general treaties on topics suitable for international action. In par-*

ticular, we urge the United States to ratify the United Nations Convention on Privileges and Immunities.

We believe that the great majority of the American people are prepared to have their nation play its proper role in the development of an ordered system of international relations. More vigorous participation by the United States is a prerequisite for the resumption of progress by the United Nations in the important activity of promoting the formulation of multilateral conventions for establishing standards and regulating the intricate relationships among states in our shrinking world.

A fundamental requirement for the strengthening of the United Nations is the promotion of general public understanding of the Organization and its work within the Member States. For this purpose, *we recommend that the United Nations expand its programs of public information; develop more effective means for evaluating the impact of those programs; seek more adequate dissemination of United Nations news, literature, and broadcasts in the territories of Member States; and strengthen the relations between the Economic and Social Council and non-governmental organizations. We urge the United States to assist in this effort by demonstrating greater respect for freedom of movement by observers and correspondents covering United Nations activities, as well as by United Nations personnel.*

Problem-Area IV: *The Financial Support of the United Nations*

The progressive development of international organization since the middle of the nineteenth century has carried with it, and has been carried along by, a corresponding rise in the volume of financial resources which states have been willing to invest in the enterprise. International agencies have never been, and are not now free from frustrating limitations imposed by budgetary difficulties and uncertainties. It is easy to lapse into cynical pessimism when one compares the relatively trivial expenditures for the support of the United Nations with the vast amounts poured into the coffers of national military programs. However, it is a strikingly significant fact that the world is now making annual expenditures through the United Nations and the specialized agencies virtually twice as great as the total sum which was made available to the League of Nations in its entire lifetime.

Whatever encouragement we may draw from the trend noted above should be directed not into a sense of satisfaction with present achievement but into a sense of hopeful determination to meet the challenge of the future. For the clear implication of the Commission's recommendations for the future development of the United Nations is that the Organization must undergo a budgetary expansion of revolutionary proportions. Two proposals in particular—that for the creation of a permanent United Nations Force, and the initiation of bold new economic programs—involve the prospect of expanding the budget by hundreds of millions of dollars. We do not lightly toss out such a demand for a dramatic break with the budgetary traditions of international organization. We do it with sober awareness of mankind's overwhelming need to cope with the grave perils, and to exploit the great opportunities, of the age in which we live.

Where is the money to come from? We would note, first, that there are potential sources of direct revenues for the United Nations which have been barely tapped and by no means fully explored. In the short or long run, significant amounts might be derived (1) from fees for special services performed by international agencies in the interest of governments or private concerns, (2) from levies on the operation of governmental services having an international character, and (3) from revenues from the exploitation of the natural resources of areas, such as the bed of the sea (beyond the continental shelf) and Antarctica, which should be placed under international ownership and administration. *We urge the United Nations to promote continuous and intensive exploration of possible new sources of revenue to supplement governmental contributions and to take timely action to exploit such sources as circumstances permit.*

However, we recognize the primary role of national governments as the financial supporters of international agencies. We think it is not now possible to discard the traditional premise that intergovernmental organizations are dependent upon the will of governments to determine their programs and assume financial responsibility for them. Hence we believe that the Member States of the United Nations must be encouraged to give more generous support to the Organization.

We suggest that the United Nations develop a program budget, combining all programs—such as relief, welfare, and technical assistance activities—falling outside the realm of standard or normal operations, and clearly distinguished from the administrative budget.

For the present, the program budget should be supported by the voluntary contributions of Member States and by such other revenues as the Organization may receive, while the administrative budget should continue to be covered by assessments upon Member States. However, we urge that agreement should be reached as soon as possible upon an arrangement whereby the contributions of Members to the program budget will be made on the basis of a special scale of assessment. In order to provide reasonable protection for the wealthier states against inequitable demands upon their treasuries, it is essential that the program budget should be prepared and controlled by a suitable weighted voting process.

If this should prove to be an entering wedge for the general breaking down of the principle of equal voting power for all members of international agencies, we would welcome this result. We believe that the long-term development of an increasingly effective United Nations demands the abandonment of that principle. But we equally believe that the time is not ripe for more than limited additions to the qualifications already imposed upon the egalitarian concept. The introduction of weighted voting, however important, is peripheral to the plan. The vital importance of developing a scheme of assessments for the financial support of all United Nations programs lies in promoting the general recognition that the international community bears the heavy responsibility of sustaining permanently the large-scale expenditures required to carry out essential functions of the global society, and that *all* states must carry their equitable share of that responsibility.

CONCLUSION

The future development of the United Nations is subject neither to confident prediction nor to the firm direction and control of any group of finite men, be they dedicated supporters, hostile critics, or harried statesmen. What the United Nations will become is not rigidly determined by inherent potentialities to be found in its Charter or by inexorable laws operating in the political universe which provides its context. The future of the United Nations will be built by men, individually and collectively—men imperfectly emancipated from the fears, passions, animosities, and narrow allegiances which form the chains called "historic forces" encircling them; men burdened with the weight of contemporary anxieties and conflicts;

men endowed with the gift of eternal aspiration and the capacity for rational and imaginative striving after higher values. Our recommendations are offered as a small contribution to a great enterprise.

The really great requirements of the United Nations defy the formulation of recommendations or the elaboration of concrete proposals. We have in mind two fundamental needs of the world organization:

First, the United Nations needs to exploit the values of international statesmanship, wherever it may be found. This rare commodity may appear in the spokesmen for small or great states, in the Secretary-General and other leaders of the international civil service, in experts, military specialists, or mediators. The United Nations should bend every effort to give it scope, to allow it initiative, to open the way for its influence. It is necessary and proper that the varied voices of national policy should be loudly heard in the United Nations, but it is also essential that the voice of the international interest should ring out as clearly as may be possible.

Second, the United Nations needs the support of an enlightened and discriminating public opinion, spread as widely throughout the world as possible, and concentrated particularly in the nations where popular sentiment is significantly reflected in public policy. We have in mind the need for the kind of understanding which is equally impatient with imperfection and with perfectionism. The United Nations requires the backing of a public opinon which is cognizant of the persistent inadequacy of all human attempts to achieve ideal values through social institutions, and which therefore patiently refrains from expecting too much. It also requires the prodding of a public opinion which will not accept the failure of social institutions to tap the full resources of human creativity, and which therefore urgently demands more and more of international organization.

The successful functioning of the United Nations is heavily dependent upon the improvement of fundamental conditions within the world in which it has to operate—the breaking down of the world's bipolarized structure, the diminution of its tensions and conflicts, and the loosening of the bonds which confine its peoples within rigid compartments of allegiance and community-feeling. Yet, the task of strengthening the United Nations cannot be postponed until circumstances make it easy. The challenge of our time is to invest the United Nations with the capacity to operate more efficiently within the world as it is, and thereby to promote the creation of the world as it ought to be.

The following members of the Commission have signed this Report. Signature means approval of the general principles outlined in the Report, but not necessarily of all the details. Specific reservations in a few cases are noted below.

JAMES T. SHOTWELL, HONORARY CHAIRMAN
ARTHUR N. HOLCOMBE, CHAIRMAN
QUINCY WRIGHT, CHAIRMAN, DRAFTING COMMITTEE
INIS L. CLAUDE, JR., RAPPORTEUR

HENRY A. ATKINSON
DANA CONVERSE BACKUS
HARDING F. BANCROFT
G. HINMAN BARRETT
CYRIL J. BATH
CLARENCE A. BERDAHL
DONALD C. BLAISDELL
ROY BLOUGH
FRANK G. BOUDREAU
JAMES B. CAREY
HARRY J. CARMAN
DAVID F. CAVERS
WALDO CHAMBERLIN
DANIEL S. CHEEVER
BEN M. CHERRINGTON
JOHN L. CHILDS
BENJAMIN V. COHEN
J. B. CONDLIFFE
EDWARD A. CONWAY, S.J.
NORMAN COUSINS
ROYDEN DANGERFIELD
MALCOLM W. DAVIS
OSCAR A. DE LIMA
CLYDE EAGLETON[1]
ALBERT I. EDELMAN

CLARK M. EICHELBERGER
RUPERT EMERSON
CHARLES G. FENWICK
LAWRENCE S. FINKELSTEIN
EDGAR J. FISHER
DENNA F. FLEMING
WILLIAM R. FRYE[2]
RICHARD N. GARDNER
ARTHUR J. GOLDSMITH
CARTER GOODRICH
LELAND M. GOODRICH
FRANK P. GRAHAM
J. EUGENE HARLEY
DONALD HARRINGTON
H. FIELD HAVILAND, JR.
WALTER D. HEAD
MELVIN D. HILDRETH
WILLARD N. HOGAN
ERLING M. HUNT
SAMUEL GUY INMAN
ELMORE JACKSON
PHILIP E. JACOB
PHILIP C. JESSUP[3]
PETER KIHSS
HANS KOHN

[1] With reservations on Recommendation No. 12.
[2] With reservations on Recommendations Nos. 7, 9, 10, and 13.
[3] Does not agree with Recommendations Nos. 12 and 13.

Walter H. C. Laves
Brunson MacChesney
Gerard J. Mangone
Boyd A. Martin
Charles E. Martin
Herbert L. May
Hugh Moore
Laure Puffer Morgan
Forrest D. Murden, Jr.
Samuel J. Noumoff
Ernest Minor Patterson
James P. Pope
George L. Ridgeway
Leland Rex Robinson
Joseph J. Robinson
J. William Robinson

Eleanor Roosevelt
Irving Salomon
Stephen M. Schwebel
Paul C. Sheeline
Paul E. Smith
Louis B. Sohn
Eugene Staley
C. M. Stanley
Arthur Sweetser
Amos E. Taylor
Willard L. Thorp
Edgar Turlington
Amry Vandenbosch
R. W. Van Wagenen
James P. Warburg
Harris Wofford, Jr.

Richard R. Wood

part 2

REPORTS OF THE SPECIAL
STUDY COMMITTEES

I

Maintenance of International Peace and Security

1 REGULATION OF ARMAMENTS

In all probability the United Nations cannot be significantly strengthened until the armaments race slackens. At the same time there seems to be little prospect of establishing major armaments controls until international institutions become stronger. The dilemma is cruel. International stability, such as it is, is largely dependent upon a weapons balance. Yet the very weapons that are required to maintain the power equilibrium also exacerbate the conflict of interests that inevitably characterizes a world of "sovereign" states. Recent Soviet threats to the lesser NATO powers contemplating rocket armaments illustrate the point.

Although serious efforts to regulate armaments by international control date back no farther than the League of Nations, there has been enough experience to suggest the conditions that must be met. One is that neither the Soviet Union nor the United States can afford to be markedly inferior to the other in weapons development. Peace depends heavily on an equilibrium of power in which a weapons balance is an important element. It follows that one condition for armaments control, including "cut-backs," "freezes" or the "regulation" of production, is the maintenance of a weapons balance. In the past, however, states have usually not been interested in "disarmament" plans that did not seem to alter the balance in their favor. Some hope, however, may be derived from the fact that maintaining an armaments race with nuclear weapons may be less attractive than accepting a system of regulated armaments.

Experience in both League and United Nations also suggests that political accommodation is a condition of armaments limitation. That is, international agreement to limit the use of force seems to be beyond reach unless the principal powers have achieved a mutually acceptable *status quo*. While satisfactory arms control schemes can doubtless facilitate political agreement, it is doubtful that armaments control is really the *sine qua non* of political accommodation. A measure of control and accommodation, moreover, may be more likely in a limited geographical area than on a universal basis.

National security is also a factor in armaments regulation if not a condition of its effectuation. In theory at least some believe that states will not really be prepared to limit their right and means to utilize force unless there is an international force able to serve their security needs and interests better than their own force, utilized either unilaterally or in concert with other powers. Insecurity stems from the conflicts of interest that characterize international politics where power, including military force, is decentralized among "sovereign" units. There would appear to be no means of escaping this Hobbesian state of nature, or global "civil" war, short of world government.

Yet even in the "state of nature" self-preservation was understood to be the natural law obeyed instinctively by all mankind. The possibility that the instinct for self-preservation may lead to a mutual interest among sovereign powers to limit and regulate the use of force warrants serious exploration in an era in which uncontrolled armaments races imply that national destruction is as likely as national defense. The dilemma of force in international relations, however, is not easily solved even when war no longer seems to be a rational instrument of policy.

War is unthinkable in the nuclear age, President Eisenhower has insisted, but how are national interests and safety to be defended when the advantage so often lies with those powers bold or reckless enough to threaten or utilize violence? Are we to infer from the assertions of both Premier Bulganin and President Eisenhower, predicting the destruction of civilization in a total nuclear war, that nations are ready to abandon force in support of their interests? The answer would appear to be negative unless political accommodation can moderate outstanding conflicts of interest. If national aims can be moderated while control techniques are being investigated, it may not be inconceivable that despite past failures mutual interest will lead the way to a workable armaments control system.

There is little doubt that changes in weapons technology will inevitably lead to changing concepts of national and international security. But it is also true that the limitation of national arms certainly depends on a good deal more than a system of international control. Mutual interest in a controlled armaments scheme, for example, requires a more fully developed political and legal order than is now offered by the United Nations. Experience since the first World War has shown that the peace problem is far bigger than armaments control.

Under the League, for example, many roads to peace were attempted. Security in particular was often thought to be the most promising choice. A common interest in the peaceful settlement of all disputes would develop automatically, it was postulated, if all states entered into a universal system of collective security capable beyond any reasonable doubt of deterring aggression. If it is true that collective security was never really practiced under the League, the reason in all probability was that the attempt could not be made, for severe conflicts of interest developed when important powers resented the international order that collective security was to perpetuate. Collective security and armaments regulation both require constant accommodation to maintain an acceptable political order.

Thus the too-frequent debates in the League period on the unanswerable chicken-and-egg question of which was prior, disarmament or security, were footless from the start. The more fundamental question was how to establish in a world of sovereign independent states a universal interest in the renunciation of force.

To tackle the problems of peace and armaments limitation primarily through international control of weapons is to advance on too narrow a front. Mutual interest in an international system in which conflicting interests are to be adjusted without recourse to force is dependent on progress in several directions. International security, for example, will be advanced as we approach both a universal conception of justice and a reasonable expectation that justice can be achieved. Without a global organization of law and power to effect such an expectation, conflicting interests must tend to breed mutual insecurity and recourse to violence. Yet it seems clear that at this stage armaments control does not require immediate Charter amendment. When more fundamental obstacles, both political and technical, are overcome, any necessary Charter revision can be expected to follow without undue difficulty.

Broadly speaking, these somber generalizations imply three alternatives: Disarmament through world government, which in all probability is the only sure way of relieving national interests of their awkward and dangerous dependence on force; the abandonment of disarmament negotiations, save for their propaganda value, in favor of continued reliance upon the "balance of terror" as a means of escaping the unthinkable war; and, finally, political accommodation accompanied by proposals for armaments control that may well bear little resemblance to disarmament, at least in the early stages.

The first alternative can be hardly more than a vision in view of history's record, and it scarcely offers a guide for public policy in the short run. There is wisdom in Lord Keynes' reminder that in the long run we shall all be dead. Many will agree, however, that while politics is the art of the possible, the nuclear age requires bolder definitions of the possible. The argument is persuasive, but those eager to transform the United Nations into a world government resting on a monopoly of armed force would do well to heed Andrew Jackson's alleged and imperishable command to "elevate them guns a little lower."

The second alternative describes the present dilemma and is unsatisfactory on many scores. Even if it is granted that deterrent power has been useful in forestalling aggression that might have led to all-out war, deterrent strategy is now a two-way street and seems less capable of preventing those relatively minor armed clashes that inevitably threaten to become "all-out" wars. "Brinkmanship" from the United States point of view loses a good deal of its utility when played both by the Soviet Union and the United States, and its prospect seems intolerable when several powers, armed with atomic weapons, can join the game.

Whereas the United States was the first power privileged to announce its intention of deterring aggression, presumably of any magnitude, by the threat of "massive retaliation," the Soviet Union can now do likewise and lost no time in threatening Britain and France in November 1956 with "every kind of modern destructive weapon" including "rocket technique" when the latter were employing "conventional" weapons in Egypt. A week later General Gruenther in a farewell and scarcely coincidental address to his NATO Command declared that rocket war meant suicide and, more pointedly, that the Soviet Union would be destroyed were it to push the button first. Although mutual fear may have deterred the great powers from large-scale war to date, the future holds no such promise when several nations may well possess atomic capability and the "balance of terror" threatens to become progressively less workable.

The present strategic situation raises another danger, moreover, for it implies rearmament rather than disarmament in NATO and elsewhere including the arming of Germany, because massive retaliation, when it invites counter massive retaliation, is no longer a feasible counterweight to Soviet ground troops. Premier Bulganin underscored the danger in his proposals of November 17, 1956, to President Eisenhower by declaring that the situation in Western Europe had become:

even more favorable for the armed forces of the Soviet Union than it had been at the end of the Second World War when the fully mobilized and equipped Soviet Army was able to gain a firm foothold in all of Western Europe, had the Soviet Union set itself such aims.

The Premier's suggestions for new disarmament talks in the same note seemed incidental to his emphasis on *realpolitik* for the benefit of the European members of NATO.

The second alternative, in short, implies too many difficulties to merit confidence. A balance of terror is an uncertain safeguard against nuclear war when several powers possess nuclear weapons. A NATO build-up, particularly if it includes a significantly armed Germany, may rule out the basis for political accommodation required for the controlled reduction of armaments, for the Soviet Union has made a reduction in NATO strength the condition of any control scheme that would appeal to the western powers.[1] Even if mutual fear inhibits the resort to massive weapons, there seems scanty assurance that a "limited" war fought with tactical weapons, atomic or otherwise, would not lead to a total war as the side threatened with defeat will be tempted to turn to strategic weapons in desperation. Modern warfare does not provide a sufficiently unambiguous distinction between tactical and strategic weapons to make "limited" war an appealing means to safety. If, as has been suggested, "the only attainable safeguard seems to be the limitation of war to levels of destruction compatible with civilization," the future seems bleak indeed.[2]

In short the alternatives seem to boil down to one: political accommodation fortified by some degree of armaments regulation

[1] See the Soviet Proposals of November 17, 1956, in *The New York Times* of November 18, 1956.

[2] Limited war as a possible safeguard is analyzed by James E. King, Jr., "Nuclear Plenty and Limited War," *Foreign Affairs*, Vol. 35, No. 2, January 1957, p. 239.

through international control. This proposition rests on several assumptions. One is that no matter how anxious nations may be to make the attempt a foolproof system of international control of existing armaments is no longer technically feasible in a world already well-stocked with nuclear weapons soon to include intercontinental ballistic missiles. All parties in the United Nations Disarmament Commission agree that there are severe technical limitations in any imaginable control scheme even if inspection with both aerial and ground surveys is included. Any system of armaments regulation must therefore depend very heavily on mutual interest for its sanction as was pointed out in one of the papers supporting the Commission's Ninth Report.[3] Mutual interest, in turn, depends upon a shared conviction that an unregulated armaments race brings security to none and that diplomacy must buff the sharper points of international friction. No control scheme, unaccompanied by political accommodation, is capable of curtailing violence when conflicting interests exceed a level of intensity that is acceptable to at least the major powers. Mutual interest, then, surely depends upon political accommodation which can be fortified by control devices that would not of themselves be sufficient to rule out the use of force or to maintain national safety. To put the matter another way, the international control of armaments becomes feasible to the extent that there is little disposition to resort to weapons.

While the technical problems of control have always been grave in both League and United Nations deliberations, it is the political obstacles that have proved insurmountable. Disarmament negotiations, moreover, seem more dependent upon political accommodation than political settlement seems dependent on disarmament. Weapons were scarcely the primary cause of the welter of conflicting interests in the Middle East or the fight for freedom in Hungary. In fact these struggles, and the ensuing resumption of the cold war, followed a year and a half of somewhat encouraging negotiations in the Disarmament Commission Sub-committee. It is equally clear, however, that the present armaments race has made these conflicts immeasurably more dangerous. Even if some degree of arms control becomes possible as an element of political accommodation, how-

[3] See David Cavers, "Disarmament and the Charter," in the *Ninth Report of the Commission to Study the Organization of Peace, Charter Review Conference,* N.Y., 1955, pp. 147-151.

ever, force cannot be abandoned entirely as an instrument of national interest in the foreseeable future. Of necessity, a control plan aimed at the reduction of force levels would depend in large part on the careful balancing of military power. Theoretically at least, this state of affairs can be altered only to the extent national security is served by some acceptable system of international security. Despite the fact that the rapid evolution of weapons technique may well lead to new potentialities for weapons control, it may well be true that a combination of international security power and political accommodation is more important than international controls in limiting national armaments. The importance of arms control potentialities in fostering a set of attitudes that would be conducive to political accommodation, however, should not be overlooked.

The significance of a United Nations Guard Force now emerges in clearer perspective. If the pursuit of military superiority over the USSR no longer provides security for the United States, because both parties already possess sufficient nuclear stockpiles to inflict mortal wounds, and if smaller powers also conclude that there is only insecurity in the present armaments race, the object of policy should be to develop sufficient United Nations security power as soon as possible in the hope of achieving a level of security that is increasingly beyond everyone's reach.[4] Such a force will become acceptable and effective only as states recognize that their interests can best be served by strengthening the United Nations.

Unfortunately the experience of the United Nations Emergency Force in patrolling the Egyptian-Israeli frontier has not been entirely reassuring in this respect. Efforts to provide for its political direction tended to fall victim to the play of power between the Soviet Union and the United States, between Israel and her Arab neighbors, and between the various voting blocs in the United Nations. The Soviet Union, for example, supported Egypt's efforts to restrict the role of

[4] R. S. Leghorn has made convincing arguments to show that present United States security policies, including the objective military superiority, are leading in fact to decreased security at increasing costs in terms of economics, technology, freedom, and tensions. He proposes the progressive development of UN security power; the avoidance of arms inferiority with respect to the Soviet Union, and international controls on the *use* of arms and on weapons *development* and *production*. Strict controls on present weapon stocks are impractical. See his remarks on *The Approach to a Rational World Security System* at the World Brotherhood Conference on "Removing Roadblocks to World Peace," unpublished Ms., January 10, 1957.

UNEF. It is beyond dispute that efforts to establish armaments control and a United Nations Force will for a long time be sharply limited by the conflicts of interest that characterize a world in which the nation-state continues to be the master plan for government. Like armaments control, a United Nations Security Force can be a rational policy objective only if combined with efforts toward political settlement.

Such a force, however, might play a role in armaments regulalation. For example, it is reasonable to believe that it might be acceptable and effective in guaranteeing an Arab-Israeli armistice or peace settlement if both the Soviet Union and the United States insisted upon it. Intransigence of the smaller powers is dangerous in large measure to the extent that big-power conflicts are involved. With big-power agreement such a force has a chance of success. Without such agreement even the willingness of smaller powers directly concerned might not be enough. The problem then is to contrive circumstances in which the Soviet Union and the United States would be equally interested in a Middle East settlement. Presumably such a settlement would require the disentanglement of interests by outside powers, a process dubbed "disengagement," and which would require the acceptance by the Soviet Union and the West of Middle East neutrality.

Seen in this light American emphasis on the United Nations in the Suez crisis is not necessarily so unwise as some critics have supposed. It was not necessarily imprudent to be disassociated in some measure from British and French action in the area in the fall of 1956. A Middle East settlement undoubtedly depends on the minimization of great power interests and the maximization of United Nations authority. If this principle were accepted as the basis for political settlement, UNEF would gain power and prestige, and its relation to armaments control would become obvious since a key element in Middle East disengagement would be an enforceable agreement to halt arms shipments to the conflicting parties. Were such an agreement reached, it presumably would not present unmanageable control problems, and a United Nations Security Force would be an appropriate element in the control machinery. If it is to develop at all, confidence in international authority and arms regulation must grow from relatively modest steps.

The possibility just suggested provides some basis by which to judge the role of the State Department in formulating armaments regulation policy. If it is conceded that the problem is primarily political, the decision to bring the White House Disarmament Staff into closer touch with the State Department is probably wise, for the disarmament impasse in all likelihood cannot be broken by control schemes alone, however imaginative they may be. On the other hand, a shift from the White House would be unfortunate if it reflected a lack of high-level interest in disarmament negotiation or if it implied that military and defense policy were not closely linked to diplomacy.

Even though the political front is the more important, weapons control cannot be neglected. A feasible armaments control plan, even of modest proportions, will make political agreement more attractive if it promotes some sense of mutual security. This goal looms as a possibility as nations become convinced they are all in the same boat drifting rapidly toward an abyss. Urgency stems from the fact that the control problem will be even more difficult than it is now when several nations acquire stockpiles of atomic weapons of their own making, and as methods of long-range slaughter are improved. It is certainly arguable that nuclear weapons are now in more responsible hands than may be the case in the future.

Is there any likelihood that with growing experience and confidence a United Nations Security Force might supervise other settlements that are the consequence of a policy of disengagement? Far Eastern areas come to mind at once, and it is important to have no misapprehensions about the nature of such a force. In any period of time for which it is reasonable to plan, it could never match any national army that is strong enough to be of any military significance. A relatively weak force, however, can be strong enough both to *facilitate* and *enforce* international agreements. Where national armies would be suspect along the thirty-eighth parallel in Korea or in Indo-China, an international force will have a chance of success if it has the backing of the major United Nations Members. Its very existence buttressed by demonstrations of reasonable efficiency might do much to awaken mutual interest, the indispensable sanction, in both big-power disengagement from troubled areas and in enforcing limited arms agreements in such areas.

It becomes clear at once that political accommodation of revolutionary proportions is in order in the Far East if armaments are to be controlled, if disputed areas are to be demilitarized, and if big-power conflicts are to abate. No arrangements in the Far East will be anything but chimerical without the active support of whatever government controls China. Non-recognition and non-representation in the United Nations are scarcely sound bases for the accommodation upon which armaments control must depend. It is indisputable, moreover, that no control plan, whether limited to Far Eastern areas or whether universal in scope, can be effective unless China is fully obligated. To date, the members of the Disarmament Commission have been debating appropriate force levels and control agreements, not only for themselves, but also for China without that power being on hand to represent its own interests.

When Communist powers are mentioned in connection with armaments control and security forces, the Security Council veto inevitably, but not entirely justifiably, comes to mind. If the primary sanction for an arms agreement is recognized to be mutual interest, the veto problem recedes from the center of the stage. Whereas little can be done to enforce a control arrangement unacceptable to a major power, the veto is not likely to be used when control arrangements are mutually acceptable. The mere exercise of the veto need not prevent a state party to a control agreement from taking measures to protect itself if violations of the agreement become manifest or even suspect.[5]

Bearing in mind the importance in these matters of mutual interest among the larger powers which the unanimity rule was designed to foster, the Security Council would appear to be the appropriate body to provide policy guidance for a United Nations Security Force and to oversee any armaments control establishment that may develop even though the latter body may be authorized to take precautionary measures in the event of a reported violation of the regulation agreement. Conceivably, of course, there may develop situations in which either the security force or the control agency might be guided best by Assembly recommendations, but for reasons that are treated elsewhere, the assumption by the Assembly of the Security Council's functions presents many hazards. The cardinal principle, of course, is that the major powers must be equally resolute in their support of a security force or an armaments control plan for either to be effective. To put the problem another way, either the United States or the Soviet Union can prevent the effective performance of an arms control agreement and the same is true, if to a less crucial degree, of a security force. Certainly lesser powers will be reluctant to move in these direc-

[5] On this point see Cavers, *op. cit.*

tions without a working agreement between the two major powers.

The possibility of linking arms control to political settlement has been explored most fully with reference to Central Europe. Since its far-reaching proposals of May 1955, the Soviet Union has offered a price for several control features that are acceptable to the West including aerial inspection on a geographically limited basis. Ostensibly the price is the retraction and gradual diminution of NATO strength. In reality, however, the price is the continued division of Germany. In indicating its readiness in November 1956 to "consider the question of employing aerial photography within the area of disposition in Europe of the principal armed forces of the North Atlantic bloc and of the Warsaw Treaty countries to a depth of 800 kilometers east and west of the demarcation line between the aforementioned armed forces," the Soviet Union may not have sacrificed very much. Because the area was formerly under German control, it is already familiar to the West despite the iron curtain. While this application of the Eisenhower aerial survey plan would help to provide mutual protection against surprise attack with conventional forces armed with tactical weapons, it would do nothing to alleviate anxiety regarding attacks on Western Europe with massive strategic weapons. Despite aerial surveys, moreover, the principal means of Soviet control over East Germany would remain, and without free elections prior to such a control scheme, tempting though it may be on technical grounds, it is difficult to see how it could do more than to perpetuate a political *status quo* that is unacceptable to the West.

These consideraions explain why Chancellor Adenauer stressed to Premier Bulganin in February 1957 that while the Federal Republic attached great importance to disarmament, such a state of affairs could be arrived at "only if the causes of existing tensions in the political sphere are removed." The chief tension, the German leader went on to state, was the Soviet insistence upon "the fact of the existence of two German states," a conflict that could be relieved at once by early reunification on the basis of free all-German elections.[6] Short of such a political settlement, the full-scale rearmament of Germany in the NATO system appears to be inevitable, since the power vacuum in Germany must be filled to achieve some degree of military equilibrium.

The Soviets have also suggested, in their proposals of November

[6] News From the German Embassy, Vol. 1, No. 2, Washington, D. C. March 2, 1957.

1956, a one-third reduction during 1957 of all foreign troops on German territory, a reduction to be supervised by some form of control, and an unspecified ("considerable") reduction of both Western forces in NATO countries and Soviet forces in Warsaw Treaty countries. A further step would be the liquidation "within two years of foreign military, naval and air bases in the territory of other states."

These proposals are similar to those advanced in 1955. The most conspicuous change was the grudging acceptance of aerial surveys along the iron curtain line, although this feature was held to have no real bearing on disarmament and therefore to be unworthy of more extended application.[7]

The Soviet proposal of 1955 for ground control posts at big ports, railway junctions, motor highways, and air fields to warn against dangerous concentration of armed forces was repeated. So long as these proposals involve a rollback of NATO power prior to the unification of Germany, they are not likely to gain Western acceptance. A Europe devoid of United States military power, with the Federal Republic unsupported by NATO strength, would be a Europe in which the Soviet Union would be immeasurably the greatest power, and the effect would be to abandon Eastern Germany and the Satellite countries of Eastern Europe.

Clearly there will have to be a better political bargain. Is it inconceivable that the Satellites might be free and neutral in return for a neutral Germany reunited through free elections? Could the retraction of NATO power that would be involved be matched by a reduction of Warsaw Pact power? Such a step would be a significant disengagement of Soviet and American power, and it might well require *fortification* by a limited armaments control agreement, the technical details of which seem to be not insurmountable on the basis of the published record of the Disarmament Commission. That is, geographically limited aerial surveys and ground control posts might do much to relieve Soviet suspicions that the Western powers were seeking to project their power and interests into Eastern Europe and Western fears that the Soviet Union had designs on perpetuating its grip on the Satellites or Eastern Germany. Incidentally, a neutral belt in Central and Eastern Europe need not preclude membership, by the

---

[7] Leghorn, *op. cit.*, considers this control feature proposed by President Eisenhower at Geneva in July 1955 important to verify arms information in order to prevent arms inferiority by one power in relation to another, i. e., to preserve a weapons balance.

powers involved, in the United Nations so long as that Organization is a universal organization and not a particular instrument of one of the "super powers."

A united Germany need not necessarily be a completely disarmed Germany. It is surely not without significance that the Soviet Union is seeking primarily to roll back NATO power with little mention made of German rearmament. German policy is more important than German arms, and an armaments verification system should be able to substantiate the fact of German neutrality.

Such a settlement, of course, implies an acceptance by Germany and the Soviet Satellites of a system of international control not traditionally acceptable to sovereign states. The advantage gained, for Germany, however, is reunification and perhaps economic well-being that, it must be admitted, could of itself be a source of international friction. The armaments burden on the United Kingdom and the retrenchment policies to cope with it that were adopted in 1957 illustrate the point. For the Eastern European countries, the advantage gained in return for international supervision of armaments and for neutral foreign policies would be freedom—or at least an increased measure of freedom.

While it must be admitted that the possibility of such a degree of political accommodation is at best a long shot, it is hard to see how else to smooth out the most acute political sore in contemporary international relations. The assumption that there is sufficient agreement on the *means* of armaments control to enforce such a political settlement seems justified on the record. Certainly it is no less than prudent to pursue with the utmost vigor control negotiations despite the fact that a really disarmed world lies well beyond the limits of practical policy planning. Looking at the record of the United Nations Disarmament Commission, without reference to the underlying political issues involved, one is tempted to feel cautiously optimistic about the agreement that appears to have been achieved.

What is lacking to date is exploitable mutual interest in the already recognized technical feasibilities. Really vital interest in armaments regulation, however, will emerge largely as some degree of political accommodation is achieved. This is not to say that every opportunity for accommodation at the control level has been exploited as fully as may have been desirable. It is hard to see what the United States could have lost had it taken up the two-year-old Soviet proposal for ground control posts in view of the fact that the West would appear to have been able to learn more about the Soviet Union than the latter would have learned about the West. It is difficult for the layman to be convinced that it is unwise to enter an "uncontrolled" agreement to cease weapons testing above a certain magnitude of destruction in view of the self-enforcing features of such an agreement and in view of the tremendous appeal that the Soviet offer has for other powers.

But the layman must forbear at times when technical matters are involved. There is disagreement among the experts as to the degree of self-enforcibility of a weapons-testing ban. The layman can help the policy maker in his task, however, by helping to define for the citizen what the disarmament problem is all about, and the first point to underscore is that the problem is primarily political. Without political accommodation disarmament must remain the "pipe dream of peace."[8]

Would a limited political settlement supported by an arms control program in one of the troubled regions that have been mentioned have any bearing on the United Nations? Undoubtedly that Organization would be strengthened by the relaxation of tensions that could be expected to ensue. More to the point, the control mechanism involved would benefit by becoming a United Nations element, for it is reasonable to suppose that a universal system is necessary in order to gain the confidence of all nations. Although only a limited number of states may be involved in some control agreements, others will be suspicious of power "deals" unless all control systems are supervised by a universal organization such as the United Nations. A strengthened universal organization for peace would doubtless follow the regulation of national armaments.

DANIEL S. CHEEVER, CHAIRMAN
DAVID F. CAVERS
RICHARD N. GARDNER
PHILIP E. JACOB*
C. M. STANLEY**

* COMMENT AND DISSENT BY PHILIP E. JACOB

1. The major military conditions for armaments regulation, as set forth in the report, no longer correspond to the realities of inter-

[8] The title of a work on the League Disarmament Conference by J. W. Wheeler-Bennett, N. Y., 1935.

national relations. The tremendous technological strides toward weapons capable of delivering total destruction anywhere in the world render obsolete the concept that security can be found in a "balance" of weapons, or an "equilibrium" of military power. To make arms control dependent upon the achievement and maintenance of such a condition is to turn the clock back to the fruitless negotiations of the 30's. The contemporary situation clearly indicates that *control itself* is the condition of security, not any particular balance, or ratio of national armaments.

2. Similarly, the report sets up unrealistic and unnecessary political conditions for armaments regulation. Given the present state of arms development, sober policy determination should conclude that no political objectives are worth a plunge into a major war. To insist on the accommodation of the principal political conflicts between the Soviet Union and the West before establishing at least some safeguards against unwitting acts which would lead to mutual destruction is to reverse the proper order of priorities. Arms control is the immediate requirement for self-preservation in this kind of an armed world. The political issues, important as they are, can be fought out by political means without the risk of blowing us all up, *once* essential international controls over armaments are operative.

3. The approach to arms control at least in the first instance must not be confused with the development of United Nations police functions. There is no alternative at the moment to establishing controls on the basis of *reciprocal self*-enforcing actions by the major military powers. The United Nations is in no position to impose controls against the will of heavily armed nations.

A United Nations Emergency Force has important tasks to perform but they do not include enforcement action. The United Nations would probably be the most appropriate agency to administer the international arms inspection arrangements which are generally admitted to be basic in any arms control system. But we must be clear that it would function here at the *behest* of the states voluntarily accepting control. It could insure that violations became publicly known, but it could not undertake to coerce a state. The ultimate sanction enforcing the control arrangement—and undoubtedly a fully effective one—would be the knowledge that deliberate violations would result in counter-action carrying the extremely grave risk of annihilative war.

** COMMENTS BY C. M. STANLEY

Secure and lasting peace undoubtedly requires substitution of world law for world anarchy. This process will compel a degree of disarmament far more extensive than the limited objectives of armaments regulation discussed in the report. Most likely nothing less than universal enforceable disarmament will be acceptable in a world of law.[9] Both will be necessary for a secure peace and neither can be fully achieved without the other. Therefore, the proposals of this report for armaments regulation should be viewed as "gateways" or "steps" toward a broader objective.

The experiences with disarmament attempts since the close of World War I seem to demonstrate that enforcement is a condition of appreciable progress in armaments regulation. No amount of "political accommodation" will long avoid the necessity of dependable enforcement. Certain limited phases of armaments regulation may be acceptable, or even desirable, without dependable enforcement provisions. But as armaments regulation encroaches on sovereignty, nations will increasingly be concerned with enforcement procedures. Hence, armaments regulation is not likely to progress far beyond advancement toward enforcement.

Certainly some degree of "political accommodation" is required before international agreements can be reached on any subject. However, the "political accommodation" needed to accomplish armaments regulation in a world of anarchy may demand a higher price than nations will pay. "Political accommodation" may be more achievable in the context of world law and enforceable disarmament than in the context of limited arms regulation. Only this broader approach offers the security which nations now seek with armaments.

In the face of the urgent threat of modern weapons, the fundamental requirement of a secure peace is an adequate supra-national organization. It is immaterial whether we call it a strengthened United Nations or a limited world federation, whether we give it "authority" or "sovereignty"; but we should not substitute armaments regulation with political accommodations for this necessary goal. Armaments regulation by fully sovereign nations may be a means to an end. It is not an adequate goal in itself.

[9] See C. M. Stanley, *Waging Peace*, New York, Macmillan, 1956. pp. 135-161.

2 ORGANIZING UN RESOURCES TO PRESERVE PEACE

In the final section of its Ninth Report, the Commission to Study the Organization of Peace observed:

> In a world in which "absolute war" or "limited war" are the alternative methods of settling inevitable conflicts, it is well to keep looking for further insights into the peaceful methods. We now know that these methods involve trust, understanding and predictability. Such a program (looking toward the effective use of international machinery as it now exists) would work at all three.

In other words, peace should be made secure by the development and greater use of methods of peaceful adjustment of international disputes, together with the employment of the opinion of mankind to check hostilities, and of strictly police methods to maintain the peace, once restored.

The Problem in Perspective

Discussion of the organization of UN resources to prevent or check aggression has to begin with a consideration of the nature and naturalness of social conflicts. It appears that such conflicts are "inevitable" in the sense that nations are sure to have differences of view about important matters; that these differences sometimes lead to serious disputes; and that the very steps taken to settle a particular dispute involve re-arrangements that may change previously satisfactory arrangements and so lead to fresh disputes. For our present purpose, *aggression* is defined as the resort to national armed force instead of peaceful methods to settle such a dispute by an attempt to impose the view of one party on the others concerned. Provision for the preservation of peace therefore involves provision for adjusting and, if possible, settling disputes peacefully, as well as for restraining resort to national armed force.

Some Remarks on Conflict

Since social conflicts are inevitable, it is important to accept that fact, and to proceed to consider methods of adjustment and of solution.

Acceptance of conflict as part of the natural experience of nations, as of the members of any other community, may help considerably in the development of means of preventing differences between nations from degenerating into war. This seems so obvious that one hesitates to mention it, until one reflects on the expressions of shocked disapproval with which the press and other organs of public opinion react to a particular conflict which attracts public attention. The dispute is often regarded as evidence of hostility, if not of peculiar wickedness. In that case, anything less than the complete success of one side (or the other, depending on the point of view) tends to be regarded as appeasement and evidence of betrayal; popular spokesmen may pander to this tendency of public emotion; and the chances of a workable solution are likely to be seriously diminished. On the other hand, if conflict is accepted as natural, it is easier to find—and get accepted—a mutually satisfactory adjustment of a particular conflict; the *quid pro quo* of such an arrangement can more readily be discovered; and the inevitable difficulties and delays in the the process are less likely to lead to the dangerous excitement that may preclude a solution.

On the Prevention of Conflicts

Although conflict is inevitable, it is possible to prevent or forestall many disputes.

The scope of such prevention is broad. For instance, the spread of knowledge about population control in a country whose population is pressing on its available resources might forestall a dangerous dispute between it and a less fully populated neighbor. Or the gradual dissolving of strong feelings of racial separateness, through education, might likewise reduce tensions. The development of arid lands, now the object of much effort by scientists and engineers, may result in reducing or eliminating many tensions; for example, in the Near East.

Prevention of conflicts by education can be accomplished by philanthropy and by private industry and investment, as well as by governmental and UN action. It might be an even more important function of the UN than it is now to expand the cooperation of private and public groups, of business and philanthropic agencies, while serving as a sort of chaperone—a protector of the reputations of the participating agencies against ill-founded accusations of imperialism and exploitation. As the acknowledged conscience of the international community the UN is well-fitted to serve in such a capacity.

Persistent international efforts to reduce barriers to international trade may remove or greatly reduce danger of conflicts over access to raw materials or other necessary commodities. When trade is restricted and a densely-populated nation has difficulty in obtaining foreign exchange with which to buy commodities it needs and cannot produce, there is danger that a policy of expansion will cause serious conflicts. A program of reducing trade barriers in such a case replaces the dangerous conflict over territorial boundaries by the more easily handled conflicts over the terms of trade treaties.

All of the specialized agencies of the United Nations may be said to be engaged in the work of forestalling conflicts. The more completely the nations are able to promote the general welfare by encouraging international trade, improving health, living standards, and respect for the dignity of the human person, the less probable are unsatisfied aspirations likely to lead to irreconcilable policies.

But there are limits to the possibilities of such action through the United Nations. Nationalism and self-determination are rampant forces that resist being directed into wholly constructive channels. Belief in the sanctity of the status quo is another force which fixes limits beyond which the UN can go only with difficulty. All Members must constantly keep reminding themselves that the UN is a place for "harmonizing the actions of nations in the attainment of common ends."

Disarmament and the Prevention of Conflicts

Disarmament deserves brief separate mention in a review of the prevention of conflict.

While national armed forces are intended for defense, their inherent tendency to competition results in the aggravation and complication of conflicts as a natural consequence of the development of national military power. Direct rivalry in military strength tends to produce tensions that intensify every conflict between nations that are arms rivals. Strategic considerations cause conflicts not necessarily related to the interests of nations but arising from the felt need for, or fear of, bases, strategic position, protection of lines of communication, prestige, or control of resources needed in time of war.

So great is the effect of military considerations in complicating and aggravating international conflicts that it might be said that "The chief cause of war is war." If resort to national armed force be accepted as a legitimate means of supporting national policies, then preparation for war tends to take priority over other programs for international relations. In this case, the resulting economic policies aimed at self-sufficiency in case of war, colonial policies aimed at acquiring convenient bases, and diplomatic policies aimed at gathering allies conflict with the policies that are aimed at forestalling conflicts by increasing the general welfare, by reducing trade barriers, and by improving the living standards and sense of personal dignity of human beings.

Disarmament is an important part of any UN program to prevent or check aggression. As amended by interpretation and usage, the Charter substitutes for war a collective resistance to aggression, if efforts to preserve peace by adjustment under UN auspices fail. As the opposite of armament, disarmament both affects and is facilitated by any strengthening of the fabric and procedures of peaceful adjustment of disputes.

ADJUSTMENT AND SETTLEMENT OF DISPUTES

Since disputes are inevitable and the difficulties in restraint of aggression are obvious, it is evident that there should be effective provision for peaceful settlement and thus avoid the necessity of dealing with aggression.

Methods of peaceful settlement are central to the problem of preventing aggression. Such methods may be of many kinds. Direct negotiation between the parties is the primary resource. Moreover, whatever contributes to an atmosphere of confidence and good will aids the effectiveness of direct negotiation. Hence it may be expected that, as the effectiveness of the United Nations increases, as progress is made toward regulating and reducing armaments, as the general level of welfare is raised, and as there is progress toward the general acceptance of a reasonably high standard of international conduct, direct negotiation over any particular conflict will tend to become easier, more effective, and more likely to produce satisfactory results.

In relations among individuals, many people who prefer settlement out of court to litigation find that such settlement by direct negotiation is aided by the fact that the law is adequate and is well known. So the development of a generally accepted body of law or equity for nations contributes to the conditions favorable to settlement by direct negotiation.

Behind the law stand the courts, not only to supplement direct negotiation when the aid of the disinterested third party is needed, but also to give authoritative—or at least widely accepted—interpretations of knotty points. But since international law is in a rudimentary stage of development, provisions for peaceful settlement cannot be based wholly on judicial processes. Direct negotiation needs to be supplemented by political and legal processes for invoking the aid of the disinterested third party.

Security Council

The architects of the UN Charter clearly expected that the Security Council would be the principal organ in the settlement of disputes, and it was given broad authority to deal with disputes at such a time and in such a manner as would be most likely to prevent them from endangering peace and security. The Security Council was thus given express power (1) to investigate any dispute or any situation which might lead to international friction, (2) to intervene at any stage of the dispute, (3) to recommend appropriate procedures or methods to be used by the parties, and (4) in certain circumstances to formulate and recommend its own terms of settlement.

Although a number of disputes have been settled under these provisions, and perhaps some small wars averted, the Security Council has been badly hampered by the veto provisions of the Charter. The qualification of the veto in respect to peaceful settlement, that is, the provision that a party to a dispute, even though a Great Power, shall abstain from voting, has been largely nullified by the "chain-of-events" interpretation written into the records of the San Francisco Conference and by the disposition of some Great

Powers, not themselves parties to a dispute, to use the veto on behalf of states within their orbit of interest or influence. Thus, the potentialities of the Security Council as a mediator, adjuster, conciliator between contending parties were greatly weakened from the early days of the United Nations.

It should be noted, however, that important steps have also been taken to clarify and make easier these procedures for peaceful settlement. The United States Senate, on June 11, 1948, adopted by a nearly unanimous vote (64-4) the Vandenberg Resolution, which included express approval of "voluntary agreements to remove the veto from all questions involving pacific settlements of international disputes and situations"; and the General Assembly, on April 14, 1949, by an overwhelming vote (43-6-2), approved the report of the Interim Committee (Little Assembly), which proposed among other things that questions in respect to pacific settlement should not be considered subject to the veto. It does not seem completely impossible, in view of these and other developments, that the Charter may be revised or clarified in this respect.

If formal revision or interpretation cannot be secured because of USSR or other obstruction, it would be possible to accomplish the objective in some measure through a multilateral treaty, in which those states that desire these more effective procedures for peaceful settlement could agree among themselves to renounce the veto, to accept a majority vote of the Security Council, and otherwise to make the intent of the Charter provisions easier to carry out.

The General Assembly

It is clear that disputes may also be brought before the General Assembly, and this has increasingly been done, in view of the difficulties noted above in respect to the Security Council. However, the General Assembly is hampered in dealing with disputes by its large size and to some extent by the inexperience and consequent irresponsibility of some of its members. What is particularly necessary, in view of these considerations, is the power of investigation, including the right of access to the territory of the parties in dispute and the right to acquire full and complete information about any situation that is determined to be endangering peace and security. If this right is limited, the General Assembly cannot act responsibly in the settlement of disputes.

The exclusion of United Nations investigators and even of the Secretary-General himself from Hungary is a case in point, and the right of Hungary to exclude these officials or to determine when and under what circumstances they may enter Hungary should not be admitted. The Charter provides (Articles 104, 105(1)) that the Organization shall enjoy in the territory of each Member such legal capacity, privileges, and immunities as are necessary for the exercise of its functions and the fulfillment of its purposes. In formal resolutions with respect to Hungary, the General Assembly has clearly expressed its view that United Nations officials and observers ought to be freely admitted into a Member's territory for purposes of investigation. The United States has strongly supported this view. It seems not only logical but quite probable that there will soon be established the principle that any country which refuses to permit investigations within its own territory may be judged by the UN as having failed to live up to its Charter obligations.

The Peace Observation Commission established by the Uniting for Peace Resolution in 1950 was expressly limited by the General Assembly to making its investigations only "upon the invitation or with the consent of the states into whose territories the Commission would go"; but the Commission to Study the Organization of Peace, in its Seventh Report, strongly urged that the Peace Observation Commission's authority be broadened so that it might also act on its own initiative. Some such continuing body, with complete right of access, is necessary in order that the UN may take cognizance of disputes or situations that may occur at any time and to determine whether there is danger to peace and security. Ad hoc commissions, with special instructions and authority, will still be needed for particular disputes.

The International Court of Justice

It must be admitted that thus far Nation States have been very reluctant to resort to the legal means which now exist for the settlement of international disputes.

Until now governments which have accepted the jurisdiction of the ICJ have accepted it, in theory, over a wide field, and have then specified reservations over specific cases and circumstances.

If there is to be a progression from politico-diplomatic methods to legal means for the settlement of international disputes, then it seems essential that a new, indeed an opposite, approach be made to gaining the acceptance by nations of the compulsory jurisdiction of the International Court of Justice.

Realism dictates that to arrive at the desired objective, the progression must be initiated in the current circumstances, and the new means for settlement must be developed gradually while making the fullest use of methods now available. Realism also suggests that a pragmatic approach to acceptance of Court jurisdiction may yield some fruitful results.

Certain disputes between nations urgently require settlement. Negotiations between the parties, diplomatic intercession, particularly by the UN Secretary-General, and the collective opinion of the UN General Assembly must be brought to bear as opportunity affords to reduce such problems as Suez, Palestine, Kashmir, etc. If and when agreed settlements of these disputes are reached, there should be included in each agreement an undertaking by the parties to accept the compulsory jurisdiction of the International Court of Justice over any future differences which may arise out of the settlement.

A second procedure might be for the signatories of treaties to review them and seek agreement to accept the compulsory jurisdiction of the Court in the event of any infringement of, or dispute over, the provisions of such treaties.

Both these suggested procedures, one affecting future settlements and the other affecting existing treaties, have the advantage of giving the nations involved a clear knowledge of the actual scope of the jurisdiction they would be conferring on the International Court. They would be accepting Court jurisdiction over the particular with no commitment to the general, rather than accepting the general and reserving the particular, as is the current practice.

One additional word needs to be included about peaceful settlement. An important additional resource would be recognition of the importance of *living with tensions or conflicts that are not yet ripe for solution.* There are occasions when either the technical knowledge for the solution is not available or the conflict is so sharp that neither side is able to make the concessions necessary for a final solution. In such cases the effective course may be to keep it under observation— meanwhile restraining resort by either party to the use of armed force —until there has been time for feelings to calm or for the necessary change of conditions to occur. This, it must be insisted, should not be allowed to serve as an excuse for avoiding the effort involved in timely dealing with an important difficulty.

The progressive change from political and diplomatic methods to binding and just legal methods is an essential part of the organization of methods for preventing and stopping threats to the peace and acts of aggression. Even among nations of good will, threats to the peace and acts of aggression are likely to remain as the ultimate recourse of national policy, unless reliable means are provided for the just and peaceful solution of disputes with other nations.

THE PROBLEM OF RESTRAINT OF AND RESISTANCE TO AGGRESSION

In addition to an atmosphere of reasonable good will, an orderly, harmonious international community needs not only means available for effective cooperation in the search for mutually satisfactory adjustment of problems but also provision for discouraging and restraining resort to the use of national armed force to impose, one-sidedly, a solution desired by one party to the dispute.

Despite their obligation to settle disputes peaceably and to refrain from the threat or use of force, Members of the UN are still tempted, human thought patterns being what they are, to use or threaten to use their own military forces to impose settlements rather than to work them out by peaceful means. Therefore, the necessity remains to consider provisions for dealing with the resulting situation on behalf of the community of nations in the interest of maintaining order in the community.

An Imprecise Instrument of Policy

There is a strong residue of naive assumption that the threat or use of military power is the final practical means of settling international disputes. The development in this century of total war, with the resulting direction of all the resources of the nation—economic, human, mental as well as military—into the war effort, has had the result of making war as an instrument of national policy so expensive and so far-reaching in its consequences that it is no longer the precise tool that statesmen of the eighteenth and nineteenth centuries hoped it would be. The effort and resources being devoted by the United States to rebuilding the former foes it defeated at such great cost in the Second World War indicates the incompatibility of modern war with long-range policy. But the recent experiment in Suez shows that the temptation to try to use war as an instrument of policy still survives.

Many students doubt whether collective security as envisaged in the League of Nations Covenant and again in the United Nations

Charter will ever be attained. In a sense it is doubtful whether it ever was possible. In the League, with the United States of America absent, there were not enough great powers who were members to make it possible, even in theory, for the League to work as an effective collective security organization. In the case of the UN, the position of the Great Powers has been too prominent and the elaborate superstructure provided by the Charter proves to have had no foundation in political fact. The UN has never been an organization capable of providing each Member with security from attacks by any other Member.

The nature of modern war as well as political reaction made the UN less than the ideal security shield. Even before the development of nuclear weapons the destructiveness of war was so terrible that the result of an attempt to restrain by military force the resort of a powerful nation to war would have been a remedy almost as bad as the disease. Yet a sense of assurance that a nation relying on peaceful methods would not be left to face alone a powerful aggressor has been thought to contribute in an important way to the development of the confidence that is necessary if peaceful methods are to replace reliance on the use of military force. And even though it would be costly, the restraint or defeat of a war-maker by a coalition acting under the direction of the international community might be expected to decrease rather than increase the likelihood of increased tension and future war growing out of the action, whereas war between two groups of nations, when carried on exclusively for national interests, tends to prepare the way for future conflicts.

Also dangerous is the surviving belief that readiness to make war is a chief defense against war. From this arises the situation we can now observe, of the "Communist" and "Western" groups of nations threatening each other with weapons of incalculable destructiveness while their clients, e. g. Taiwan and the two Koreas, calmly propose to use armed force to support their local policies in the hope that their larger patrons will back them up if they get into trouble. Here lies serious danger of a third world war.

Restraint of aggression by client nations could be accomplished by the patrons, if the larger members of each group—or, for the sake of reducing danger of involvement in unlimited liabilities, the "Western" group alone—were to make clear to their smaller clients that they will not support them in using war as an instrument of national policy. A restatement of this principle by the United Nations might have a certain value, at least as education about the unsatisfactory nature of the results of the resort to aggression. This is implied in the UN Charter but seems to need restating.

Collective Measures

Collective measures to check aggression have three features:

1) To counteract resort to the use of armed force instead of peaceful methods for settling a dispute;

2) They should be directed by the United Nations, not by any single nation against a rival;

3) They should be used to halt violence, not to impose settlement. These three features help greatly to distinguish collective measures for restraining aggression from alliances and other arrangements by one nation against a rival. This distinction may be important; many current arrangements, like NATO, that are claimed to be collective security measures, lose much of their effectiveness because they are so set up that they are not clearly distinguishable from alliances against a rival and so fail to convince that they are not a threat to the rival's security even if the rival does not initiate an aggression. The need is for an increase in security of *all* nations, not merely that of a select group. Alliances, by failing to do this, tend to become an aggravating factor in the arms rivalry that makes security through national armed forces so hard to attain.

The Decision

The decision to apply collective security measures presents certain difficulties. Nevertheless, the fact of a dispute is generally well known. Despite the instantaneous striking power of modern weapons, war is so costly that there is pretty sure to be a period of argument before an actual clash occurs. Nations will attempt to gain their objectives by discussion backed by threat. Every Member of the UN has the right to call attention to any serious dispute. The Secretary-General can make use of the right given him in Article 99 of the Charter to call attention to any matter which may threaten the peace. The Peace Observation system foreshadowed in the Uniting for Peace Resolution, and the arrangements for observation in such places as Israel and Korea, might be brought into play and applied to additional tension areas.

If the concept is accepted that the UN as a security agency is useful primarily as a mediator between opposing points of view and a stopgap of small wars, rather than a superstate capable of coercing the largest and most powerful members of the international community, it follows that collective measures must be designed accordingly.

It is not necessary to undertake a new exploration of the technical arrangements needed for concerted diplomatic, economic, and even military measures. The Collective Measures Committee of the General Assembly has already done this work. While some re-thinking and re-evaluation of its recommendations should be made, in the light of the recent Middle East and Hungarian situations and the experience of the UNEF, the UN General Assembly should again call on all Members to consult the Collective Measures Committee's reports. Members should be requested to heed the General Assembly's recommendations to adopt the necessary legislation to permit full use, on a moment's notice, of all pledged diplomatic, economic, and military measures. Especially, Members might inform the Secretary-General and the General Assembly of the military forces earmarked for use in case the necessity arises of resisting aggression collectively.

The direction of collective military measures raises difficulties. Perhaps most of the resentment and dissatisfaction with which the rudimentary attempt at collective military measures in Korea is regarded results from the failure adequately to meet these difficulties. Generals in the field were left to make policy decisions that the UN should have made. They were inadequately informed of the difference between the objective of war, which is to win victory, and of collective measures, which is to restrain attempts to impose a solution by force.

Simultaneously, the United Nations needs a police force. It should not be a force of a size, organization, and equipment to be a combat force, but a force so designed as to carry out strictly police functions. The outbreak of organized international violence in 1956 in the Middle East brought such a force into being. Although this force was hastily improvised, the circumstances of the case and the Members' reaction to it made possible the creation of a UN force based on sound principles.

The Big Five were expressly prohibited from participation in the Force. It was set up directly under the UN Secretary-General, who was provided with an Advisory Committee of the General Assembly.

The responsibilities of the force were fixed by the General Assembly. The UNEF (United Nations Emergency Force) did not go to the Middle East on the side of the victim, but on the side of law and order. It was not a military force, but a lightly armed police force, and its real power was derived from what it symbolized. Its greatest weakness stemmed from the Assembly's failure to insist on its right to send the UNEF to the territory of Members in the Middle East and station it there as long as necessary. It was necessary, under the Assembly resolution, for the UN to secure permission from the victim to send this force into Egyptian territory. Its functions and effectiveness were conditioned by the will of the Egyptian government.

In order that a UN police force may realize its full capabilities, it should be organized on a permanent basis. In modern times, no force, national or international, can act as a deterrent unless it is continuously in being.

If UNEF were to be made permanent, and continued to enjoy the power of world moral opinion, it might become a deterrent to local hostilities or to the spread of such conflicts into global catastrophes. It should remain lightly armed, and would in no sense be a combat force. It could not be used to fight a war to stop a war, but it would have certain peace-preserving functions.

A permanent force of this kind could be used for observation, patrol and guard duty in troubled areas. It could patrol cease-fires, armistice demarcation lines, and demilitarized zones, maintaining a separation of the parties and preventing breaches of the truce. This Force could guard sites, such as international waterways, for the mutual benefit of the nations concerned, and could oversee the carrying out of agreements when lack of confidence between the parties gives rise to dangerous tensions.

If UNEF is to be made permanent in order to carry out such peacekeeping functions, it must be developed further on the present basis, with the inclusion of certain new principles underlying its nature and use.

1) It should be clearly conceded by all UN Members that a standing force of this kind must be an equitably shared charge upon them all, and its cost should be incorporated into the regular UN budget.

2) At the direction of a substantial majority of the Assembly (two-thirds of the Members present and voting) it should be entitled to enter troubled areas without obtaining the permission of nations involved.

3) In order to capitalize the fact that it symbolizes the international community, it should be put into UN uniform.

4) As rapidly as possible, the members of the Force should be recruited from the smaller nations. Some members, at least, should be recruited individually by the UN, as its top-ranking officers are now, in order to assure their qualifications and their allegiance to the UN.

5) Experience with the actual use of such a Force would determine its size. For the present it should not be less than 2,000 nor more than 10,000. It should have its own equipment and its own means of land, sea, and air transport, for it must be constantly prepared and highly mobile.

6) Finally, such a Force should have the right to arrest and hold for proper disposition by UN authorities, individual raiders, saboteurs, vandals, etc. It must be able to hold lawless individuals if it is to carry out its duties in full.

If UNEF were made permanent on the basis described, it would be possible to develop it further as national arms were reduced.

The most important requisite of an adequate UN system for preventing and checking aggression is what might be called a consumer demand for it—recognition by the citizens and their governments that in this age of interdependence and nuclear weapons, peace is the first need of every nation and that the UN can aid and supplement the individual efforts of nations to settle disputes peacefully and to prepare for the adjustment of disputes that may arise in the future. This consumer demand might be stimulated in this country and elsewhere by the holding, after a fully adequate period of public preparation, of the Charter Review Conference voted by the Tenth UN General Assembly. The United Nations seems capable of developing, even without Charter amendment, either its existing agencies or new ones set up to meet more effectively the special problems of finding mutually satisfactory solutions of disputes, and so becoming a real safeguard to the security of nations by the process of preventing normal conflicts from leading to the destructive use of military force.

RICHARD R. WOOD, CHAIRMAN
CLARENCE A. BERDAHL
DONALD C. BLAISDELL
DENNA F. FLEMING
DONALD HARRINGTON
ELMORE JACKSON

3 PUBLIC OPINION AND COMMUNICATIONS

It is too seldom realized that the source of political authority, whether national or international, whether autocratic or democratic, is the opinion of the public subject to that authority, and that the opinion of the public depends upon the system of communication among its members and from the governing authorities to the members. President Lincoln once said:

Public sentiment is everything. With public sentiment, nothing can fail; without it, nothing can succeed. Consequently, he who molds public sentiment goes deeper than he who enacts statutes or pronounces decisions. He makes statutes and decisions possible or impossible to execute.[1]

The roots of political power can be discussed in four categories: the power of the sword, the power of the purse, the power of the law, and the power of the word.[2] Lincoln spoke of the last two—the capacities to legislate and to mold opinion—but he would undoubtedly have recognized that both of these powers are influenced by the capacities to kill and to bribe, the capacities to punish and to reward, or more generally the capacities to compel and to induce. Yet in a wider sense, the other three powers are dependent upon the last. No one can for long punish, reward, or legislate if overwhelmingly opposed by the opinion of the community, and the subtle influence

[1] Quoted by John W. Dafoe, in *Public Opinion and World Politics*, Quincy Wright, ed., University of Chicago Press, 1933, p. 3.
[2] Commission to Study the Organization of Peace, *Fourth Report*, December 1943, International Conciliation, January 1944, p. 62.

of opinion is itself a powerful force. Tyranny is checked by the potentialities of revolution. Wealth is inhibited by the demands of impoverished masses. Legislation is abortive if confronted by widespread determination to disobey. "As force is always on the side of the governed," wrote David Hume,

the governors have nothing to support them but opinion. It is therefore on opinion only that government is formed; and this maxim extends to the most despotic and most military government as well as to the most free and popular.[3]

The capacity of the United Nations to carry out its purposes might be strengthened by augmenting its power of the sword relative to that of its Members. This might be accomplished through a more effective military staff committee, a continuous development of the proposals of the Collective Measures Committee for earmarking and coordinating forces of the Members, and larger appropriations for technical field services or United Nations guards. Such measures lagged until the crisis of 1956 induced establishment of the United Nations Emergency Force for service in Egypt. But this force is not likely to become permanent and effective, nor is serious limitation of national armaments likely, so long as the average citizen of each Member Nation does not want his own country's power of the sword to be overshadowed by that of the United Nations.

The capacity of the United Nations to carry out its purposes might also be strengthened by augmenting its power of the purse, relative to that of its Members. At present, the national budgets of all the Members of the United Nations together amount to some 200 billion dollars a year, of which over half is for armaments. The regular budget of the United Nations is less than $50 million, and the combined regular budgets of all international organizations are less than $100 million, that is, less than one part in 2000 of the combined national budgets of the Members. The wealth of the United Nations is therefore minuscule compared to that of the governments of its largest Members, and is even less than that of the governments of most of its smaller Members. The General Assembly has the legal competence to increase the budget and to utilize these resources for services to the world's people who would then become more dependent upon the services of the United Nations and relatively less dependent on the services of their national governments. The nations might recognize

[3] Quoted Dafoe, *op. cit.*, p. 4.

the title of the United Nations to the bed of the sea or to the Antarctic continent, thus giving it a potential revenue as the resources of these areas become exploitable. The Charter might be amended, giving the General Assembly powers of taxation. These things, however, will not happen until there has been a reduction of the prevailing sentiment of nationalism which induces most citizens to prefer to obtain or to contribute governmental services through their national governments. With this sentiment, social and economic services of the United Nations or the specialized agencies tend to be limited to those deemed essential but which national governments obviously cannot perform.

The capacity of the United Nations to carry out its powers might also be strengthened by augmenting its power of the law. The Statute of the International Court of Justice might be amended giving the Court jurisdiction on application of one party in all international controversies of a legal nature that diplomacy has failed to settle. The General Assembly might make larger appropriations to the International Law Commission so that it could give more effective advice for developing and codifying international law, and the Charter might be amended giving the General Assembly both capability and authority to legislate on prescribed subjects. The Charter might also be amended to modify the voting procedure of the Security Council so that it could exercise its almost limitless formal powers to make the decisions necessary to preserve international peace and security. Obviously, however, such changes will not be made so long as most people cherish the legal sovereignty of their respective states and fear the tyrannical potentialities of a world legislature or a veto-free world executive council.

The basic problem, therefore, if the United Nations is to have greater capacity to achieve its objectives, is to modify the state of world opinion so that more people will be prepared to augment the relative military, financial, and legal powers of the United Nations compared to that of the states. In its Fourth Report, published during the war (1943), referring to an international air force such as that later projected in Article 45 of the Charter, the Commission to Study the Organization of Peace said:

An international air force could not operate in a vacuum. International political institutions to settle international controversies and to adjust international law to changing conditions and concepts of justice would be necessary in order to keep discontents from becoming dangerous. A sufficient sense of world solidarity would have to exist within the populations of all the important countries to enable such institutions to perform their functions. The development of such a world opinion involves all the factors which influence men to give a portion of their loyalty to larger social units. In the past, loyalties have moved from the clan to the tribe, from the feudal lord to the kingdom, from the city to the nation, from the State to the federal union. Numerous economic, social, technical, and other factors have contributed to these transitions. A transition from absolute national citizenship to partial world citizenship is in process in many minds as a consequence of the new means of communication and transport, disseminating universal moral and cultural ideas. Practical devices can assist the transfer of sufficient loyalties to the world order to permit the world authorities to function.[4]

The opinion of persons flows from many sources which may be classified as traditional (instinct, custom, and religion) or planned (education, information, and propaganda). Tradition has its greatest impact in early life, and results from face-to-face contacts of the rising with the older generation, within the family, local group, or church. This experience establishes basic attitudes that color the whole of later life and, among primitive peoples, in large measure determines it. Such peoples are said to have customary or static societies which change little from generation to generation.

Planned communication has its impact later in life, and results from formal education or communication at a distance of the written or printed word, or of verbal or visual symbols through the radio, cinema, or television. It proceeds through the development of ideologies, policies, and opinions of more flexible and less durable character than the attitudes acquired in very early life. Nevertheless, among civilized societies, differentiated from primitive societies by the use of writing, the influence of such methods becomes important. As civilization progresses through the development of symbol systems and agencies of mass communication, early attitudes tend to be increasingly influenced by these agencies. Societies cease to be "customary" and become "progressive," change occurs more and more rapidly, and people become more "opinion-directed" and less "custom-directed."[5]

[4] Commission to Study the Organization of Peace, *Fourth Report*, cit. p. 61. See also Quincy Wright, "The Mode of Financing Unions of States as a Measure of Their Degree of Integration," *International Organization*, Winter 1957, Vol. XI, pp. 30 ff.
[5] See David Riesman, *The Lonely Crowd*, Yale University Press, 1950.

Modern societies are of this type. In a generation American public opinion, reflected in the Senate, changed from opposition to the League of Nations to overwhelming acceptance of the United Nations, and from avoidance of "entangling alliances" to leadership in the creation of a system of alliances for defending the free world. Such changes of opinion have occurred in all countries, and they have been the fruit of symbolic transmissions through education, information, and propaganda, by means of the press, radio and telegraph, supplemented by rumor, travel, and group discussion. While such changes have taken place rapidly even in large populations, especially in periods designated as "revolutionary," conscious efforts to effect such changes encounter serious difficulties and may defeat themselves through arousing opposition movements. Basic beliefs, values, and loyalties established by tradition and imparted early in life to each generation are the essence of a civilization, culture, or nationality. Symbols, ideologies and rituals associated with these ideal entities become highly sentimentalized. Novel ideas which affect such social sentiments tend to be resented and resisted, and persons or organizations that attempt to effect changes of opinion on such matters may be branded as subversive. This is especially true of efforts to modify existing foci of political loyalty. Such efforts are almost certain to fail unless there is widespread information about events, such as defeat in war, or new conditions, such as nuclear weapons, which demand a change of ideas.

In the United States fundamental loyalties shifted from the state to the union during the century following the Declaration of Independence. The nationalism of Washington and Franklin, the constitutional interpretations of Marshall, and the oratory of Daniel Webster contributed to this change, as did the increased transportation, travel, and communication within the country. But the development of nationalism aroused a fighting states' rights sentiment at various times and various sections of the country, manifested for example in the Virginia and Kentucky Resolutions of 1798, the Hartford Convention of 1813, the South Carolina Nullification of 1832, the Dred Scott case of 1856, and finally the southern secession and Civil War which began in 1861.

Similarly, the initial success of Wilson and the League to Enforce Peace in developing the League of Nations idea in the United States, and the activities of the League during a generation in developing internationalism, induced nationalistic reactions manifested by the withdrawal of the United States into isolationism and the nationalistic reactions of Fascism, Naziism, Nipponism, and Sovietism. Similarly, the initial enthusiasm for the United Nations at San Francisco aroused an opposing nationalistic reaction manifested in the United States by the Bricker Amendment movement, and exaggerated attacks upon the United Nations, UNESCO, and other international organizations by certain patriotic societies. Similar reactions have occurred in other countries.

Studies concerning public opinion about the United Nations indicate that it has been predominantly favorable but in some countries has fluctuated as United Nations action has affected particular national interests. In the United States there has been more interest than elsewhere and opinion has been temporarily stable and geographically uniform during the eleven years since the Charter went into force. Some 80 per cent of sampled opinions have been favorable, 5 to 13 per cent unfavorable, and the rest indifferent. Opinion has, however, been relatively uninformed. It has identified the United Nations with peace: unfavorable opinion has tended to decrease when the prospects of continued peace were good and to increase when those prospects were bad, without reference to the actual influence of the United Nations upon those changes of prospect. People have tended to be less interested and informed on the United Nations and international affairs generally than on national or local affairs, in spite of the development of nuclear weapons, of the existence of cold or hot war, and of the multiplication of general and regional organizations during the period. A sampling of leaders in the United States indicates that they are much better informed on the United Nations than the rank and file, and that a smaller proportion are unfavorable or indifferent. Because of the low level of public information, governments have been relatively free to take a positive initiative in developing policies within the United Nations and gaining support for the recommendations of United Nations agencies by relying upon the generally favorable opinion about that institution. This appears to have been more true of public opinion than of Congressional opinion in the United States, perhaps because of the almost neurotic absorption of the latter in the problem of Communism.

Both favorable opinions about the United Nations and accurate information about it have been correlated with higher education, economic and social status, urbanism, and foreign travel. More public information about the United Nations would therefore probably increase the favorableness of opinion, the activity of the interested public, and the capability of the United Nations to achieve its purposes. However, it appears difficult to induce the public to absorb information offered it unless an active interest is first aroused, and this in turn depends to some extent upon the extensiveness and effectiveness of United Nations activity. Because of its technical assistance programs there appears to be more interest in the United Nations and the specialized agencies in some of the underdeveloped countries, where people benefit directly by such programs, than in the more developed countries.[6]

Because their effects are so fundamental, and reach so deeply into the structure of societies, conscious communications to modify political attitudes and opinions constitute an art which must be conducted with great subtlety and caution to be successful. Even the most successful political leaders, such as Franklin D. Roosevelt, have been aware that they cannot successfully urge proposals much in advance of existing public opinion. This was illustrated in the adverse public reaction to President Roosevelt's Chicago Bridge speech in November 1937, suggesting that aggressors be quarantined.

Communications intended to make the public more interested in and favorable to the United Nations may proceed (1) from individuals, (2) from private organizations, (3) from governments, or (4) from international organizations, and they may take the form of *education, information, propaganda,* or *instruction.*

Education seeks to impart knowledge to the student concerning the meaning of symbols and the characteristics of the values and objects to which they refer; to develop in him attitudes favorable to

[6] Robert H. Cory, Jr., *Communicating Information and Studies About the United Nations to the American People,* New York, Carnegie Endowment, 1955; Elmo Roper, "American Attitudes on World Organization," *Public Opinion Quarterly,* Vol. 17, No. 4, 1953; Joseph E. Johnson, "The United Nations and Public Opinion," Norman Wait Harris Memorial Foundation, 32nd Institute, *United States Foreign Policy and International Organization,* University of Chicago, 1956, *Proceedings.* William Scott and Stephen Withey, *Public Reactions to the United Nations, 1945-54,* Survey Research Center, University of Michigan, Ann Arbor, Mich., 1956. The Carnegie Endowment has initiated some twenty national studies of the United Nations, of which those in Denmark, Israel, Switzerland, Canada, and Sweden had been published by the summer of 1957. It is also supporting a comprehensive study of the level of information about the United Nations in the United States and the effectiveness of United Nations public information facilities.

the beliefs and values of his culture and nation, enabling him easily to adapt himself to the society in which he lives and assuring that the culture and national character will be carried on by the rising generation; and to develop skills in a practical craft, trade, or profession, so that he can earn a living. Its purposes are, therefore, both informative and indoctrinating. It lies between *information*, which seeks to impart objective knowledge, and *propaganda*, which seeks to indoctrinate in order to influence behavior in a particular situation. Information, however, is often selective and directed, and consequently has propaganda objectives, though more subtly conducted. Governments prefer the term "information" for their public relations activities because this term arouses less suspicion and opposition, especially in trans-national communications than does the term "propaganda." *Instruction* refers to orders or recommendations from a superior to an inferior, though the term is also used as equivalent to education of the young, since that relation is supposed to exist between the teacher and the student with respect to knowledge. Information will be received by any audience which regards the source as reliable and the content credible. Education will be received only by audiences which share the beliefs and standards which it supports. Instruction is only possible to audiences which recognize the duty of obedience to the source. Propaganda is always received with suspicion, particularly by audiences that are fundamentally different in culture and government. Consequently, it is usually veiled. Its actual objectives are concealed, and the audience is induced to believe that it is being given objective information or is being educated in the meaning of its accepted beliefs and values.[7]

A public relations agency or other communicator must understand the normal resistance of people, who regard themselves as independent, to being told what they should believe or how they should behave, if trans-national communication is not to have an effect opposite from that intended.

Individuals can do much through conversation, writing, party participation and voting, to influence opinion about the United Nations. In democratic theory, such grass-roots initiation is the proper mode of changing public opinion. But the individual's attitudes are in large measure shaped by the prevailing culture and national character, and by the educational system which supports them. Only if

[7] On the meaning of these terms see Quincy Wright, *The Study of International Relations,* New York, Appleton-Century-Crofts, pp. 285 ff.

education at the university level rationally relates the needs of today's world to appropriate attitudes, opinions, and policies, can the educational system, the national culture, and individual attitudes be modified to a more internationalistic position. Freedom of opinion, freedom of speech and press, in both intra-national and trans-national communication, supported by the Universal Declaration of Human Rights, by the activities of UNESCO, and by the various programs of exchange of persons, tend to develop international-mindedness and to augment the influence of international-minded individuals. Such programs constitute an important part of the public relations activities of the United Nations, UNESCO, and other specialized agencies.

Private organizations, combining the influence of like-minded individuals, can augment the individual's influence upon public opinion. In democracies, such organizations are generally permitted to function freely, but the influence of those favorable to the United Nations tends to be opposed by those unfavorable. Out of such controversy, public opinion eventually emerges. Within autocracies, private organizations are generally not permitted to function except as agencies of government policy. Public opinion, therefore, proceeds in large measure from the government, rather than from the people. The United Nations by recognizing non-governmental organizations adds to their influence and their facility for acquiring information. Such recognition is generally accorded to those non-governmental organizations which are not in principle opposed to the objectives of the United Nations. Recognition of freedom of association, in the Universal Declaration of Human Rights, and the encouragement by UNESCO of international associations in science, philosophy, and the social sciences, add to the influence of associations devoted to internationalism.

National governments are in the most favorable position of all systems of action to improve world public opinion about the United Nations. Such governments, however, are inclined to fear that by utilizing their influence in this direction, they may weaken their own power and position. Autocratic governments, by controlling all means of national communication, can if they wish change national opinion rapidly. Democratic governments, committed to freedom of speech and press, are hampered in such activity. But a strong governmental leadership can influence opinion greatly without violating its own principles.

International law assumes that it is the obligation of all states to integrate national law with international obligations. Some states have done this by general constitutional prescription. The Netherlands has recently modified its Constitution to recognize the domestic effectiveness of decisions of international organizations of which the Netherlands is a member.[8] Recent constitutions of France, Italy, Germany, and Austria recognize the superiority of international obligations, whether of customary international law or treaty, to national legislation.[9] The United States Constitution recognizes the general competence of the courts to apply customary international law and treaties, the latter irrespective of state legislation. But more recent federal statutes are applied, even if in violation of treaties, and the federal system has operated as a practical inhibition against the making of treaties deemed to encroach upon the traditional rights of the states. The Bricker movement has sought further to limit the judicial applicability of treaties by constitutional amendment. Insofar as national law automatically incorporates international obligations of the state, the dichotomy between nationalism and internationalism in opinion tends to be reduced, and governments are in a better position to influence public opinion in behalf of international responsibilities.

In addition to supporting a legal theory identifying international obligations with national law, national statesmanship can contribute to a world opinion favorable to the United Nations in the political field by continually identifying the nation with the United Nations. This tends to nullify allegations of inconsistency between national interests and the United Nations, or other international obligations. If international peace and security is in the national interest, and a strong United Nations is essential for maintaining it, then a strengthening of the United Nations is in the national interest. Similarly, the harmony of United Nations activity in behalf of human rights and fundamental freedoms with constitutional bills of rights can be emphasized, as can the harmony between the national interest in national prosperity, and the activity of the United Nations for promoting world prosperity. If, on the other hand, national leadership emphasizes the occasional conflicts between United Nations decisions or recommendations and national interests as interpreted at the moment, and pursues a policy of utilizing the United Nations only when

[8] *American Journal of International Law*, Oct. 1953, vol. 47, p. 537 ff.
[9] *Ibid.*, July, 1955, vol. 49, p. 347 ff.; Oct. 1955, vol. 49, p. 451 ff.

it serves national interests so interpreted, it cultivates nationalism rather than internationalism. The presumption of the Charter is that each state ratified it in the national interest, and that the fulfillment of the Charter's objectives is in the national interest of each of its Members, even though occasionally short-run conflicts occur. It can be emphasized, however, that the long-run value to the nation of the United Nations more than compensates for these occasional short-run conflicts with government policies.

It is believed that a world public opinion in support of the United Nations can be better developed through this process of identifying the United Nations with the national interest than by suggesting any superiority of the United Nations to the national interest. The United Nations should be conceived, not as something apart from and superior to the Member Nations, but as a manifestation of the continuing national interest of all the Members in facilitating cooperation for the realization of values to which all have subscribed in ratifying the Charter.

Efforts of international organizations themselves to influence world opinion, while important, have to be conducted cautiously to avoid nationalistic reactions. While all organizations, and particularly political organizations, need active support of their members, and to obtain such support have to conduct public relations activities, there is a danger that such activities by the United Nations will tend to emphasize the differences between United Nations agencies and the governments of its Members. So far as possible the United Nations should seek to utilize the public relations activities of its Member Governments and of private organizations.

However, the United Nations has an obligation to collect, analyze, and disseminate information about the state of the world, the conditions relevant to its purposes in the territory of its Members, and the activities of its agencies. Such information has been provided by the United Nations in year books and official documents and should be made available by all means of public intelligence, including United Nations local offices and broadcasting facilities.

Furthermore, the forums offered by the General Assembly and the conferences of the specialized agencies provide an opportunity for discussion and the focussing of world public opinion upon the policies and values of the United Nations. The services of technical assistance, health, respect for human rights, and development of self-government and self-determination, offered to people all over the world by the United Nations and the specialized agencies, tend to create a favorable opinion toward the institutions, especially in the underdeveloped areas where people have more to gain from such services. The long-run effect of more abundant trans-national communication favors international-mindedness, though the immediate effect is likely to be nationalistic reaction and hostility when such communication is first established between peoples of very different culture. The Universal Postal Union, the International Telecommunication Union, the International Civil Aviation Organization, UNESCO, and other specialized agencies are engaged in the facilitation of trans-national communication, both among governments and among peoples. These efforts undoubtedly have a long-run effect favorable to internationalism through breaking down barriers to communication, but it should not be overlooked that sometimes the short-run effect is in the opposite direction.

The activities of international organization described above are all indirect approaches to the problem of increasing international-mindedness. The question can be asked, "Can the United Nations do anything more direct to improve its status in world opinion?" Radio and television broadcasts from the United Nations to the people of the world, if carefully devised with reference to the particular audience and with major emphasis upon the integration of national interests and international organization, of national and world opinion, can undoubtedly do much. Such programs have been discussed in the United Nations since 1946, but the difficulties of finance, of technique, of content, and of national cooperation have hampered their development. The Ninth Report of the Commission to Study the Organization of Peace in 1955 on Charter Review declared that "in principle, it would seem that member states should be obliged to make decisions and recommendations of the principal organs of the United Nations available to their publics."[10] A supplementary treaty among Members of the United Nations might be negotiated, obliging them not only to make such materials available, but to cooperate with the United Nations in such communications. The town meeting of the world should be brought to every family by modern technology. The influence of such broadcasts if made both interesting and informing might be very great, but the willing-

[10] Commission to Study the Organization of Peace, *Ninth Report*, p. 33.

ness of national governments to cooperate would undoubtedly depend upon their general conviction that strengthening of the United Nations is in the national interest.

Such programs to be effective require expert programming agencies, clear signals, and a large budget. The report to the Commission in 1955 by General Frank Stoner on the United Nations information requirements indicates that the United Nations programs and listening audiences have not improved since 1950 and leave much to be desired.[11]

No less important than telecommunication is the press. A large corps of correspondents from the press of the world is established at the United Nations headquarters and documents are made available to them. A more adequate practice of press conferences by high officials and of providing explanatory materials might improve press coverage.[12]

It would appear that a much more extensive activity in the entire field of United Nations public relations is essential if the capability of the United Nations to perform its functions is to be increased. Such activities should be geared to that of private agencies and national governments in order continually to integrate the development of the United Nations with the national interest of each Member State.

Conclusion

No modification of the Charter seems necessary in this field, but existing activities should be extended and facilitated by increased financing, encouragement of activities by private organizations and Member Governments, and by supplementary treaties among Members. A better theoretical understanding of the subject, continuous collection of data on the trends of national and world opinion, and the utilization of private projects followed by appraisal of their effect is essential if extensive programs are to be effective.

1) The establishment of an agency to conduct a continuous qualitative and quantitative survey of the foci of attention and the state of opinion throughout the world would be desirable. Such a survey should include the changes of public opinion within the

[11] *Ibid.*, p. 212.
[12] William R. Frye, "Press Coverage of the United Nations," *International Organization*, May 1956, vol. 10, pp, 276 ff.

principal nations, including the United Nations and its policies; the processes within the principal nations of integration or differentiation of national and United Nations interests; the changes of opinion within each of the principal nations about the others; and the changes in the general tension level in the world and in the level of tension between selected pairs of states. The general influence of trans-national communication activity, and the effectiveness of particular programs in this field cannot be appraised objectively without such a background of information. Official national or international agencies would be seriously handicapped in preparing such a survey because, aware of its potential political and diplomatic influence, they would tend to make it either tendentious or uninforming. Some private agencies such as the Carnegie Endowment for International Peace and the Hoover Library at Stanford University have done pioneering work in this field. An adequately endowed private organization to make continuing studies and surveys should be established.[13]

2) Every effort should be made by the Member Governments, through constitutional provision or legislation, to identify the purposes and principles of the United Nations and the specialized agencies with their national interest and law. It should be emphasized not only by the national law but also by the declarations of the national leadership that achievement of the purposes and general respect for the principles of the Charter which all have accepted, and strengthening of the United Nations to assure such achievements and respect, is a major national interest of each, essential both to its security and prosperity in the present shrinking world. Consonant with such identification of the United Nations and the Member States, illegal behavior of the latter should not be alleged until it has been ascertained by due processes of law that a government has violated Charter obligations; even then the illegality should not usually be attributed to the state but to the government of the day. If sanctions are applied, the government should be considered the transgressor, and it should be deemed to have transgressed against the law of its own state and the interests of its own nation, as well as against the United Nations. Identification of the United Nations with its Members does not mean that every action of a United Nations organ is necessarily in the national interest of

[13] Quincy Wright, "Project for a World Intelligence Center," *Conflict Resolution*, March 1957, vol. 1, pp. 93 ff.

every Member or that it is consonant with Charter purposes and principles. While such actions if made by proper procedures deserve respect, they should not be deemed exempt from criticism. The United Nations cannot function unless the Members take positions and seek to influence decisions. Vigorous debate and the effort to achieve consensus is the life blood of the United Nations.

3) The United Nations should develop more vigorously its programs of economic and social service to peoples, of promoting respect for human rights, of assisting people to self-government and self-determination, of facilitating trans-national communication and exchange of persons, and of encouraging international associations in fields of philosophy, science, the arts, sports, etc., as a means not only of carrying on direct Charter purposes, but also of indirectly improving the public relations of the United Nations and the specialized agencies with the peoples of the world. Care should be taken, however, to conduct such programs in cooperation with the national governments whose people benefit, in order to avoid opposition between international and national activities in these fields.

4) The United Nations should invigorate its direct public relations activities more adequately to inform the world's public of the decisions and recommendations of its organs, and the activities of both the United Nations and the specialized agencies. Such activity should include distribution of printed material, radio, cinema, and broadcasting, and efforts should be made, perhaps by initiating a general treaty, to assure the cooperation of all Members in admitting such communications to their territory and cooperating in distributing them to their people. To achieve such cooperation, the United Nations communications should never have the character of concealed propaganda but should give comprehensive and accurate information about activities undertaken, results achieved, and the values which the activity is designed to promote. Only if a government has been found to have violated obligations under the Charter should communications have the character of "psychological warfare," and, in such cases, care should be taken to direct adverse comment against a defaulting government, not against the state or nation whose obligations and interests it has betrayed.

To improve its public relations the United Nations should develop not only its own publications and their distribution and its own broadcasting systems but should increase its efforts to facilitate and induce broader coverage by the press, broadcasting companies, and other private agencies. To these ends the public relations activities of the United Nations should be better coordinated with similar activities of the specialized agencies. A survey of these activities in the Member States might be initiated by the General Assembly and agreements might be negotiated by the Secretary-General to increase their adequacy. Finally, the relations of the Economic and Social Council with non-governmental organizations should be extended.

QUINCY WRIGHT

II

Protection of Human Rights and Fundamental Freedoms

4 HUMAN RIGHTS

INTRODUCTION

The Commission to Study the Organization of Peace has dealt with human rights on three previous occasions. It discussed the problem briefly in its Third Report, published in February 1943. Its Fourth Report, published in May 1944, considered in Part III the "International Safeguard of Human Rights." In it the Commission proposed "that measures be taken to safeguard human rights throughout the world by: (1) convening without delay a United Nations Conference on Human Rights to examine the problem; (2) promulgating, as a result of this conference, an international bill of rights; (3) establishing at the conference a permanent United Nations Commission on Human Rights for the purpose of further developing the standards of human rights and the methods for their protection; (4) seeking the incorporation of major civil rights in national constitutions and promoting effective means of enforcement in each nation; [and] (5) recognizing the right of individuals or groups, under prescribed limitations [and after exhausting local remedies], to petition the Human Rights Commission in order to call attention to violations."

In 1946 a "Bill of Human Rights" was drawn for the Commission by the Executive Committee of its Committee on Human Rights, which was established in February 1945 and was under the chairmanship of Dr. James T. Shotwell. This Bill enumerated in nineteen articles not only such classical human rights as "the right to protection of life and liberty under law," but also such new rights as the

105

"right to education" and the "right to social security." The provisions of the Bill were to "be deemed fundamental principles of international law and of the national law of each of the signatory States to be realized by appropriate action of international and national agencies."

In the meantime the United Nations established a Commission on Human Rights which prepared a Universal Declaration of Human Rights, following quite closely the pattern of the Bill of Human Rights mentioned in the previous paragraph. This Declaration was approved by the General Assembly on December 10, 1948, as "a common standard of achievement for all peoples and all nations." Later the United Nations Commission on Human Rights drafted two Covenants on Human Rights, one dealing with civil and political rights, and another one dealing with economic, social, and cultural rights. The two Covenants were considered by the General Assembly at its Tenth Session in 1955, but the discussion bogged down on the article relating to the right of political and economic self-determination of peoples and nations.[1] The Third Committee of the Assembly made better progress during the Eleventh Session, and it expects to submit the final text to the Assembly by 1958.

Though United States representatives have participated actively in the drafting of the Declaration and of the Covenants, in 1953 the United States Government announced that it "reached the conclusion that we should not at this time become a party to any multilateral treaty such as those contemplated in the draft Covenants on Human Rights, and that we should now work toward the objectives of the Declaration by other means" (U.S. Department of State Bulletin, Vol. XXVIII, pp. 579-81). The United States then proposed: that the United Nations appoint rapporteurs to study various aspects of human rights throughout the world (e.g., freedom of religion and the right to a fair trial); that annual reports on developments in the field of human rights be prepared by each Member Government for study by the Commission; and that the United Nations establish advisory services on specific aspects of human rights (e.g., send experts to countries requesting such services,

---

[1] It may be noted that the right of self-determination is being considered by another Committee of the Commission to Study the Organization of Peace, together with other questions relating to the protection of the rights of inhabitants of trust territories and other dependent territories.

provide scholarships for study abroad, and arrange for seminars). The last point was approved by the General Assembly in 1955, which authorized the Secretary-General to make provision for technical assistance in the field of human rights. The other United States proposals were approved by the Economic and Social Council in 1956, which requested that Members submit every three years reports on developments and progress in the field of human rights, and authorized a special study of "the right of everyone to be free from arbitrary arrest, detention and exile."

It may also be noted that, even before this resolution, the United Nations conducted special studies of particular human rights, such as forced labor, slavery, women's rights, and trade union rights. On the basis of these studies several international conventions have been prepared either directly by the United Nations or by the specialized agencies concerned, and in some cases special commissions were established to assist in the protection of the rights in question. The United Nations has also dealt with specific human rights problems in various countries, such as the trials of religious leaders in Bulgaria, Hungary, and Romania; the right of Russian wives of foreign nationals to leave the Soviet Union; the kidnapping of Greek children during the invasion of Greece; and the treatment of Indians in the Union of South Africa and the race conflict in that country. The discussion of these questions in the General Assembly helped to focus the public opinion of the world on the issues involved, and in some cases—that of Greek children and Russian wives—it led to positive accomplishments. In others it warned the accused Government that its behavior was subject to international scrutiny, and, in some instances at least, it probably prevented the repetition of the acts complained of. Even better results have been obtained with respect to the treatment of colonial peoples. In particular, many petitions from trust territories have been considered by the Trusteeship Council and the General Assembly, and the recommendations of the United Nations have usually led to a considerable improvement in the situation. In general it may be said that most Governments have proved to be quite sensitive to the pressure of world public opinion, and they have dared to oppose it only in cases where there was a serious doubt about the right of the General Assembly to deal with the situation.

HUMAN RIGHTS AND CHARTER REVIEW

If a Charter Review Conference is held, the problem of human rights is likely to be discussed in the following contexts:

1) On the one hand, an attempt might be made to strengthen the provisions of the Charter which now deal with this subject. In particular, some States might wish to make clear that the United Nations can deal with such violations of human rights as "shock the conscience of mankind," or with violations of human rights guaranteed by an international treaty even if that treaty does not provide explicitly for United Nations jurisdiction.

2) On the other hand, attempts might be made to broaden the exception of domestic jurisdiction, contained in Article 2, paragraph 7 of the Charter, in order to prevent the United Nations from considering any violations of human rights by a state.

3) Additionally, the problem of guaranteeing human rights against interference by the United Nations itself might arise, if, for instance, the United Nations should be given broad powers of inspection in the field of disarmament and the right to punish directly any violators of disarmament regulations.

It does not seem probable that it will prove possible at a Review Conference to obtain either a general agreement on increasing the United Nations competence in the field of human rights or even a more limited agreement defining more precisely the existing competence of the United Nations in this field. In particular, it seems very doubtful that anyone would seriously consider the possibility of granting to the United Nations the power to adopt covenants on the subject which would be binding on Member States without their ratification. Nor can it be contemplated that Members will confer on the United Nations the power to discuss petitions from individuals complaining about violations of their rights, though such power now exists in the limited area of petitions from inhabitants of trust territories.

In any case, it may be stated at the outset that no formal amendments are needed in the Charter to enable the United Nations to "promote" human rights by any means which might be put at its disposal. Thus the United Nations can sponsor multilateral conventions on the subject, adopt model provisions to be inserted in national constitutions, exercise such additional powers as States by bilateral or mulitlateral conventions agree to confer on it, and establish subsidiary agencies to deal with the problem in various ways—by methods similar to those adopted by the International Labor Organization in the labor field. While it cannot be said that the Charter, without further agreement, authorizes the United Nations to do more in this field than to study the problems, to discuss them, and to make recommendations on the basis of such studies and discussions, there is no doubt that States by agreement can broaden the powers of the United Nations in respect of human rights.

Present Problems

Assuming, therefore, that there are no constitutional obstacles to further United Nations action in the field of human rights, the question immediately arises as to the direction such action should take. The following problems will be considered here:

1) What can be done to promote human rights by international legislative instruments, such as the Covenants on Human Rights?

2) How can international standards be enforced?

3) Is there a need for special measures to protect the rights of minorities?

International Treaties on Human Rights

After the United States withdrew its support for the Covenants on Human Rights, the attempt to prepare a detailed and comprehensive treaty defining the rights to be protected internationally lost some of its momentum. Nevertheless it is probable that the General Assembly will finally adopt the two Covenants despite American non-participation. It is also conceivable that many Governments will find it difficult not to accept the Covenants, and under the pressure of their public opinion will ratify them, with or without reservations; others may ratify them in the belief that the Covenants are innocuous enough and contain enough loopholes to permit them to accept them without any need to change either their domestic law or their behavior. Once the Covenants come into force, it will be difficult to disregard them and they are likely to be quoted even against those who have not ratified them. The United States may thus find that it will be advantageous to it in the long run to accept the Covenants, and the climate of public opinion in the United

States may change sufficiently to enable a future administration to do it. This would happen, in particular, if there should be several Covenants and if the wording of one of them should follow closely the provisions of the United States Constitution on the subject. If the other nations would be willing to go so far to accommodate us, we might find it very difficult to reject a document trying to universalize our own constitutional principles.

If our Government does not want to be placed in the unenviable position of being the major opponent to a general course accepted by the other Members of the United Nations, it must come out in the immediate future with an effective substitute which will be attractive enough to draw away from the present bandwagon of the Covenants a sizable group of the main supporters of the human-rights movement. Perhaps the main attack should be on the fact that the more comprehensive the Covenants are the more foes they are likely to encounter and the less likely they are to be ratified. The disputes with respect to the desirability of inserting in the Covenants guarantees of the right to own property and of the right to self-determination are striking illustrations of difficulties inherent in either inclusion or exclusion of too many important rights in the Covenants. From every point of view, the present effort in this field appears too ambitious; the interests to be reconciled are too diverse and the area of agreement is too limited. There is, therefore, a constant danger that an agreement on the contents of the Covenants will be reached at the price of accepting the lowest possible denominator, and that the Covenants will not constitute any improvement on the standards already applied by the Governments willing to ratify them. The list of permissible exceptions to the rights included in the Covenants has been constantly growing and threatens to extend beyond the limits accepted by the jurisprudence of the United States and other Western countries.

The I.L.O. Method

Perhaps the chief mistake in the current approach to the problem is that the draftsmen of the Covenants have not followed the example set by the only international organization which over a period of thirty-five years has successfully promoted human rights, namely the International Labor Organization. Despite occasional grumblings and a few minor failures, the record of the I.L.O. is considered as satisfactory by both labor and business organizations, and has met with complete approval of almost all governments of the world. The basic reason for this success is that the I.L.O. has not tried to solve all problems at one fell swoop, but has proceeded very carefully and patiently from one problem to another, removing one social difficulty after another until an International Labor Code of more than a hundred conventions has been approved by a large number of States.

By analogy, the United Nations may limit itself at this point to the adoption of a few conventions dealing only with those human rights the protection of which is most urgent or which are almost universally accepted, such as equality of women, freedom from slavery, prohibition of *ex post facto* laws, protection against arbitrary arrest, etc. If such conventions should, for instance, be limited to those human rights which have been clearly recognized in the Bill of Rights to the United States Constitution, many of the difficulties about the American ratification of the Covenants would immediately dissappear. With respect to each new convention, the I.L.O. method of careful investigation of the state of national laws on the subject should be followed, and as in the I.L.O. the preparation of the draft conventions with an exhaustive commentary should be primarily the responsibility of experts in the Secretariat rather than governmental commissions. The first drafts should be sent for comments to all governments and second drafts should be prepared by the Secretariat on the basis of these comments. Only after this stage, an intergovernmental commission, having a status similar to that of the Governing Body of the International Labor Organization and selected in a similar fashion, would decide whether a particular convention merits submission to a Human Rights Conference for final approval, or whether the draft should take the form of a recommendation only. The Human Rights Conference should be composed in a similar manner to the International Labor Conference: each State which has ratified at least one of the previous human rights conventions should be entitled to four delegates; two of these delegates should be governmental delegates; the other two should be selected in agreement with the principal majority and minority parties in the national legislature. It may be hoped that agreements and recommendations adopted by a two-thirds majority of such a Conference would prove acceptable to States and would slowly establish an

International Code of Human Rights, equal in importance to that developed by the I.L.O. While this proposed machinery needs to be sufficiently autonomous to safeguard the rights of States which have accepted the special obligations against those Members of the United Nations which have not done so, no specialized agency should be established in this field and the new Commission on Human Rights and the Conference should continue to be served by the Human Rights Division of the Secretariat.

The Regional Approach

Simultaneously, a regional approach may be adopted. The nations of Europe, under the auspices of the Council of Europe, adopted in 1950 a Convention for the Protection of Human Rights and Fundamental Freedoms. Together with a Protocol of 1952, the Convention provides protection for a large number of human rights, defined more carefully than in the UN Declaration. This Convention has been accepted by almost all the members of the Council and seven of them have even accepted and put into force an optional clause granting to individuals the right of petition to a European Commission of Human Rights. Five states—Belgium, Denmark, Federal Republic of Germany, Ireland and the Netherlands—have also accepted the jurisdiction of a European Court of Human Rights, but three more ratifications are needed to bring the Court into existence.

As differences between regions are often more pronounced than differences within regions, especially if regions are carefully delineated for that purpose, the European approach might be followed in other regions, and attempts have already been made to map out such a program for the Americas. There is no reason why a convention on human rights, taking account of special needs of each region could not be adopted also in Southeast Asia, the Middle East, Latin America, and even North America. For instance, the United States might find it easier to reach an agreement with Canada, as well as Mexico, than with some countries of Asia or Eastern Europe. In particular, it may be noted that the three states of North America have in common a federal structure and thus can avoid the difficulties inherent in an agreement on human rights between federal and unitary states. Once a complete network of regional systems is established, further action might be taken to diminish differences between regional approaches, e.g. between North America and

Europe, and finally global coordination may be achieved through the United Nations.

ENFORCEMENT OF INTERNATIONAL STANDARDS IN THE HUMAN RIGHTS FIELD

The two draft Covenants envisage different methods of enforcing the standards contained in them. The Covenant on Economic, Social and Cultural Rights envisages a slow, gradual approach to the problem of implementation. It proposes that each State Party take steps "to the maximum of its available resources, with a view to achieving progressively the full realization of the rights recognized in this Covenant by legislative as well as by other means." It provides also for a system of periodic reports concerning the progress made and the difficulties encountered in fulfilling the obligations under the Covenant.

The Covenant on Civil and Political Rights, on the other hand, calls for immediate implementation. It requires each State Party: "to adopt such legislative or other measures as may be necessary to give effect to the rights recognized in this Covenant"; to ensure that any person whose rights are violated shall have "an effective remedy," including a judicial remedy; to ensure that "the competent authorities enforce such remedies when granted"; and to submit reports on the measures taken to fulfil these obligations. An international Human Rights Committee would be empowered: to deal with complaints by any State Party that another State Party is not giving effect to a provision of the Covenant; to ascertain the facts and "make available its good offices to the States concerned with a view to a friendly solution of the matter"; and, if a solution is not reached, to draw up a report stating "its opinion as to whether the facts found disclose a breach by the State concerned of its obligations under the Covenant." Any of the States concerned may appeal further to the International Court of Justice.

In addition, there is before the United Nations a Uruguayan proposal for the appointment of a United Nations High Commissioner (Attorney-General) for Human Rights, who would be entitled: to "receive and examine complaints of alleged violations of this Covenant which may be submitted to him by individuals, groups of individuals, national and international non-governmental organizations and intergovernmental organizations"; to investigate each case and, if necessary, "to conduct an inquiry within the territory under the jurisdiction of the State Party concerned"; and, if the complaint cannot be settled through negotiation and conciliation, to "seize the Human Rights Committee of his accusations" and to participate at all hearings which the Committee may hold on the complaint.

Under the European Convention on Human Rights, a European Commission of Human Rights has already been established. That Commission can deal with complaints by any State Party alleging breach of the Convention by another State Party. In addition, with respect to seven States which have accepted an optional clause to that effect, the Commission may receive petitions from "any person, non-governmental organization or group of individuals claiming to be the victim of a violation" by one of these States of the rights set forth in the Convention. The Committee of Ministers of the Council of Europe is authorized: to decide by a majority of two-thirds of all its members whether there has been a violation; prescribe measures to be taken by the State concerned in order to remedy the situation; and, if satisfactory measures have not been taken within a prescribed period, to decide by the same majority "what effect shall be given to its original decision." All these decisions of the Committee are to be regarded by the States Parties "as binding on them." The Convention also contains provisions for a European Court of Human Rights having jurisdiction over appeals from the findings of the Commission, but these provisions are not yet in force.

It is clear that some States are willing to go quite far in the direction of enforcement of human rights provisions through an international commission, entitled to deal not only with complaints by States but also with petitions by individuals and organizations. It seems desirable to encourage this approach on both global and regional scales. Any agreement adopted should, therefore, embody optional provisions enabling any State willing to take such a step to accept, in whole or in part, the jurisdiction of a Human Rights Commission to hear complaints brought by: other States which have accepted the same obligation; citizens of such other States; citizens of the State exercising the option; or national or international non-governmental organizations fulfilling such criteria as the State making the option shall prescribe.

In addition, any agreement on the subject should provide for periodical reports on the observance of obligations and the difficulties encountered in their execution. Even those States which have not ratified a particular agreement, but have accepted a basic convention on human rights (either global or regional), should be bound: to submit each agreement adopted by the group to which they belong to their legislative bodies; to report at appropriate intervals what further action they intend to take to have the agreement ratified, specifying the difficulties which prevent or delay the ratification; and to report the position of their laws in regard to the matters dealt with in the agreement, showing the extent to which effect has been given to the agreement, despite its non-ratification, by legislative, administrative, or judicial action. These proposals are again modelled on provisions in the I.L.O. Constitution which have proved to be quite effective in stimulating governmental action.

PROMOTION OF HUMAN RIGHTS BY OTHER MEANS

The Tenth Session of the General Assembly accepted an American proposal for "advisory services in the field of human rights." It authorized the Secretary-General to provide Governments, on request, with: advisory services of experts, fellowships, scholarships, and seminars. The Governments interested in such services will have the right to determine the kind of service to be rendered to them and will make proposals to the Secretary-General concerning persons who should be given scholarships and fellowships. Each requesting Government will be expected "to assume responsibility, as far as possible, for all or a considerable part of the expenses connected with the assistance furnished to it." It cannot be expected that there will be any real demand by States for this sort of aid; at best, limited assistance might be asked for with respect to relatively unimportant matters.

Studies of particular subjects by special rapporteurs might be useful as a preliminary step for further action, such as adoption of conventions on those subjects, but if such studies are entirely divorced from any action, they will prove to be of little practical value. The United Nations is trying at this point to eliminate studies which are designed as substitutes for, rather than preliminaries to, action. There seems to be no reason for applying a different principle to the studies in the human rights field.

Annual reports by each State on current developments with respect to human rights might prove of assistance to compilers of Yearbooks on Human Rights, but as long as there are no means for checking their accuracy and exhaustiveness, they are likely to contain paeans of praise for national accomplishments in some fields and no accounts of tragic shortcomings in other fields. Such reports may be, of course, extremely useful as an indication of standards which are actually observed by States, and they are absolutely necessary for follow-up studies of implementation of formally adopted standards as they provide a practical check on their adequacy and effectiveness. As long as there are, however, no clear standards to be implemented or revised, such reports can be only of limited value as checks on the adequacy of governmental behavior. Their only value in such a case would be to keep alive the interest of Governments and of public opinion in the promotion of human rights.

As it has been pointed out earlier in this chapter, the results of discussion in the General Assembly of violations of human rights by particular States have only sometimes led to positive results. It is not clear whether the General Assembly has actually any jurisdiction to adopt resolutions on specific violations and its recommendations have in any case no binding force. They have been flouted with impunity by some of the States concerned, and there seems to be little profit in the current tendency to enumerate in the preamble to a new resolution the many past resolutions which have been disregarded. It is the first refusal to execute a recommendation that matters, and if there seems to be no chance that the State concerned will change its attitude, it might be better for the General Assembly to put the matter on the shelf until a more propitious time. Continuous castigation through ineffective resolutions has often the opposite effect to the intended one and the policy of the culprit is likely to become worse rather than better. While the majority in the General Assembly can claim repeated propaganda victories and the defeated State can only retaliate by vastly publicized walkouts, the lot of the people involved is seldom improved as a result of these antics and quite often even deteriorates considerably. Until the General Assembly is given sufficient powers to enforce the execution of its decisions in this field, the present approach to the problem is not to be commended for future repetition. In the meantime, the majority in the General Assembly should adopt a more enlightened policy with respect to the many complaints brought before it; it should be willing to abandon propaganda victories for more moderate but more positive results. The situation might improve considerably if the art of compromise were practiced more skillfully in place of the present tendency to pseudojudicial condemnation.

On the other hand, certain general recommendations of the General Assembly have had marked impact on local developments. In particular, the Universal Declaration of Human Rights has influenced national legislation and governmental policy in many countries. Though it is generally recognized that this Declaration has no binding character, such an authoritative pronouncement has proved to be of more value than originally expected. Even if the Covenants should fail to be generally adopted, the Declaration might become the turning point in the attempt of the United Nations to improve the standards in the field of human rights. While much has been done to popularize the Declaration, further efforts by the United Nations and the United Nations Educational, Scientific, and Cultural Organization seem to be called for. It is not enough to concentrate on generalities; very often important differences are concealed under general phrases. The Declaration is being interpreted in various ways in various countries; in particular, Soviet interpretations of various rights differ considerably from those of the Western nations. These differences need to be explored and elucidated, and they should be brought to the attention of all those young nations whose practices have not yet fallen into a stultified pattern. As many of these nations have copied in their constitutions and laws many provisions of the Declaration, it is important that their practice should follow the most enlightened interpretation of the Declaration and that they should be well acquainted with the long-range implications of adopting one or the other method of implementation of various rights. Much can be accomplished in this field, at relatively small expenditure of money and effort.

PROTECTION OF MINORITIES

Before entering into a discussion of the current problems connected with the protection of minorities, it is necessary to define the term "minorities." For present purposes, it may be sufficient to adopt the definition approved by the United Nations Sub-Commission on Prevention of Discrimination and Protection of Minorities in 1954 (E/CN.4/703, p. 72), which reads as follows: ". . . the term minority shall include only those non-dominant groups in a population which possess and wish to preserve ethnic, religious, or linguistic traditions or characteristics markedly different from those of the rest of the population . . ." The Sub-Commission added that while there are some special groups which "need to be protected by special measures, national and international," some groups having minority characteristics prefer to have no special protection and are satisfied with receiving identical treatment with the rest of the population. No international action should hinder "spontaneous development of minority groups towards integration with the rest of the population of the country in which they live, which takes place when impacts such as those of a new environment, or that of modern civilization, produce a state of rapid racial, social, cultural, or linguistic evolution"; and "nothing should be done that is likely to stimulate their consciousness of difference from the rest of the population." Account must be also taken "of the circumstances under which each minority group has come into existence, for example whether it owes its existence to a peace treaty or to voluntary immigration." Though these ideas of the Sub-Commission were not endorsed by the Commission on Human Rights, they constitute a measure of agreement on this difficult question and can serve as a point of departure for further studies.

The problem of safeguarding the rights of minorities can be divided into two principal segments: (a) preventing discriminatory treatment of the members of such groups—i.e., prohibiting policies which relegate them to the status of "second-class citizens" because of the differences which distinguish them from the ethnic majorities in the States of which they are nationals—and (b) assuring to minority groups the enjoyment of the "positive" rights—linguistic, religious, and cultural—which are essential to the preservation and development of their distinctive ethnic and cultural attributes, in so far as such groups wish to maintain their identity.

With respect to (a) above, the Charter, the Declaration of Human Rights, and the two draft Covenants reflect the broad theoretical consensus that basic human rights should be enjoyed equally by all individuals. Many States do discriminate against members of minorities, but few would reject the ideological tenet of non-discrimination which has a major place in the modern human rights movement. Hence, there would appear to be no serious political obstacle to the inclusion in all international treaties concerning human rights— global or regional, comprehensive or specialized—of clauses prohibiting unequal treatment of members of minorities on the ground of their ethnic, religious, linguistic, or cultural peculiarities. Such clauses, supported as far as possible by the development of effective international guarantees, are of vital importance to all national minorities.

With respect to (b) above, the situation is quite different. By no means all national minorities, or all members of particular minorities, wish to have or to use special rights conducive to the perpetuation of ethnic distinctiveness. However, some minorities are characterized by fervent belief in the legitimacy and fundamental importance of the demand for such rights, and are dedicated to resistance of efforts to impose assimilation upon them. This viewpoint does not now command such general support as it did at the end of World War I, when the League of Nations undertook to serve as guarantor of positive minority rights in a number of European States which were bound by special treaties and declarations. For several reasons, the United Nations has not sought to reproduce the League system for safeguarding special minority rights; one of those reasons is that the nations of the world are far from an agreement that minorities are entitled to possess, or that States can properly be expected to grant, special rights designed to impede assimilation and to promote ethnic pluralism within the State. The right against assimilation has no such assured standing in the human rights movement as the right against discrimination.

In 1953, the Commission on Human Rights ostensibly approved the concept of positive minority rights by inserting the following provision in Article 25 of the draft Covenant on Civil and Political Rights: "In those States in which ethnic, religious or linguistic minorities exist, persons belonging to such minorities shall not be denied the right, in community with the other members of their group, to enjoy their own culture, to profess and practise their own religion, or to use their own language." There is considerable evidence that this action represented only a token victory for the advocates of such rights, not a genuine reversal of the well-established tendency of the United Nations to abstain from endorsing the proposition that all states possessing ethnic minorities should permit those groups to nourish their corporate identity if they so desire. In general, the Organization is committed to the view that non-discrimination is adequate and that the granting of positive minority rights should lie within the discretion of States containing ethnically diverse populations. It cannot be expected now to do more, but it must at least help and not hinder those who are willing to chart new paths in this field. The United Nations must be prepared, however, to take into account the increasing demands of colonial peoples for the recognition of their right to autonomous development. In the long run, it will have to develop a more positive approach to the claims of distinctive cultural groups, whether governed as colonies or as minorities within national states, to the right of cultural self-determination.

Under the circumstances, it is suggested that the most practicable methods of promoting the enjoyment, by those minorities which desire them, of rights going beyond the negative right of non-discrimination are as follows:

1) A convention dealing with positive minority rights should be drafted in accordance with the plan outlined earlier in this Report, and opened to ratification by all States willing to do so, with the proviso that any State may make its ratification contingent upon reciprocal action by another State or States which it designates;

2) The United Nations should stand ready to accept as a part of the human rights legislation to which the enforcement mechanism should apply any bilateral or regional treaty which States might adopt to regulate the treatment of minorities in which they are reciprocally interested because of ethnic affinities.

These suggestions accept as their point of departure the fact that the United Nations has completely abandoned the ambitious effort the League of Nations to remove the minority problem from the domain of bilateral relations between "Host States" and "Kin-States" into a multilateral arena. The League did not succeed in eliminating the minority problem as an irritant in the relations between States, and critics have suggested that it even added fuel to a dying flame. The United Nations has decided to try another approach to the subject and is concentrating its efforts on non-discrimination. This does not mean, however, that positive minority rights cannot be protected by other means. If some States should be willing, either unilaterally or on the basis of bilateral bargaining, to establish a regime of special rights for particular national minorities, the United

Nations should put its implementing machinery at the disposal of these States. It cannot be expected to do more, but it must at least help and not hinder those who are willing to chart new paths in this field.

Louis B. Sohn, Chairman
Eleanor Roosevelt
Henry A. Atkinson
Inis L. Claude, Jr.
Arthur J. Goldsmith
Amry Vandenbosch

5 THE COLONIAL PROBLEM

INTRODUCTION

It has been said that the United Nations Charter is a pre-atomic instrument. The UN's response to the problems posed by the existence of "territories whose peoples have not yet attained a full measure of self-government" might be called pre-Bandung.

When the San Francisco conferees, in 1945, proposed the inclusion in the UN Charter of Chapters XI, XII, and XIII to reflect international concern for all non-self-governing peoples and the special responsibilities of the United Nations for those territories which had a special international character which brought them under the trusteeship system, they were taking an historic step, measured by all previous experience. The trusteeship system provided for in Chapters XII and XIII of the Charter was, it is true, based largely on the experience of the League of Nations mandates system which preceded it. But the Charter went a great deal further in elaborating the supervisory powers and jurisdiction of the United Nations organs charged with responsibility over the administration of trust territories. And Chapter XI, regarding non-self-governing territories, was a unique statement of international concern in colonial areas not having a special international character, which carried with it an unprecedented recognition by the colonial powers of responsibilities to the international community, limited and carefully defined as they were.[1]

[1] Article 23 (b) of the League of Nations Covenant was a broad undertaking by the members "to secure just treatment of the native inhabitants of territories under their control."

122

However, these arrangements were the product of experience which could only be retrospective and of the particular world climate in which the Charter evolved, was formed, and ratified. It is not easy after so much history has intervened to recapture successfully the mood, predominantly optimistic and rationalistic, and the political influences which conditioned the formulas on which the participants at San Francisco agreed. The delegates, sobered by the statistics of the greatest war in history, still expressed faith in the possibility of human progress toward a better world. The UN was to be the institutional framework in which the great powers of the time would take the lead to bring about that vision and within which the problems that would arise could be dealt with on the basis of reason, fortified by memory of the high cost to mankind of its past failures to apply reason successfully to its affairs.

With respect to the colonial areas in particular, the effort was to institutionalize the trusteeship mission of the colonial powers, despite the marked uneasiness of some of them, and to provide for supervision to make sure that they would not backslide in what was expected to be the very long range but inexorable march of human progress. Both the philosophic thought and the actual political reality were expressions of an essentially European-American outlook. There were Asian countries represented, to be sure, notably China, India, and the Philippines, and a highly articulate Arab bloc representation. Europe had relatively less weight than in previous major conferences. Nevertheless, the occidental great powers dominated the conference. And it was their accommodation of views on the colonial problem which prevailed. Although the dimensions of the problems were vast, involving some 800 million colonial peoples in Asia, Africa, the Pacific and the Caribbean, the predominant expectation was that they could be controlled by the colonial powers, if only because of their superior military capacities. In part, this expectation was falsified by the lack of intelligence available to the colonial powers concerning some of the former colonial areas, as events in the Netherlands East Indies would soon prove. The colonial powers recognized that the old colonial structure was subject to separatist and nationalist stresses; wartime collaboration with the Japanese had been both an expression of colonial impatience and a stimulus to nationalist desires, while the example of Japanese military prowess stirred self-confidence among Asians. And so the trusteeship system and the more limited obligations under Chapter XI were devised as a means of channeling colonial aspirations in an orderly and peaceful fashion toward a solution defined for territories under Chapter XI as "self-government" and in the case of the trust territories as "self-government or independence as may be appropriate to the particular circumstances of each territory and its people and the freely expressed wishes of the peoples concerned."

In fact, the present that has emerged is vastly different from what it was expected to be. Rational change and orderly progress have been denied by the realities of emotional nationalism. In a decade, the colonial peoples who occasioned Chapters XI, XII, and XIII of the Charter were reduced to less than 200 million by the process of emancipation which has taken place. In terms of population, the dimensions of the problem have been vastly reduced. On the other hand, the example set by the newly independent countries has served as a vast stimulus to the aspirations of peoples who are still in colonial status; the pace of change in these areas has been much swifter than the Charter provisions assumed. Moreover, since 1945, the independence of new states and the admission of thirteen of them to the society of nations as members of the UN have effectively altered the old balances of power and representation so that the western heritage of civilization and philosophy no longer dominates the field as it did in 1945. The voting balances in the organization have shifted so that peoples who have experienced colonialism heavily outnumber the colonial powers and the other representatives of European civilization.

Finally the assumption that colonial problems could be dealt with on their merits in an international atmosphere which was ordered by the dominance of the great powers in combination has obviously been erroneous. Quite the reverse has been true. The tension between the Soviet Union and its allies, on the one hand, and the western democracies, on the other, has diverted the strength of the colonial powers from the tasks of colonial management and has had the result of embroiling problems of colonialism in the larger political and strategic struggle not only directly as in the case of Indo-China but indirectly as well. Moreover, the broad political contest has focused attention on colonial problems in ways which were unforeseen in 1945.

In these circumstances, it is fortunate that Article 109, paragraph

3 of the Charter has automatically stimulated a review of the provisions of the basic instrument and of the workings of the organization. In order to take the greatest advantage of this opportunity, however, it is important to make more than a formal approach to the language of the Charter. It is necessary to examine Chapters XI, XII, and XIII, not just as legal instruments, but also as mechanisms by which existing and anticipated political forces may be effectively expressed with the object of finding the best and most stable resolution of them.

In order to achieve this end, it is necessary to understand the United Nations in its bearing upon the complex and subtle set of relationships which exist among the peoples of colonial territories, the governments and peoples of the metropolitan powers, and the other members of the international community. Certainly, the UN's machinery influences this set of relationships, but what that influence is and how it works is not an easy thing to understand and it varies from case to case. One thing is sure, namely that this set of relationships and the UN's influence on it are affected far more by the attitudes and policies of member governments and the peoples concerned than by the institutional arrangements of the UN Organization.

The Problem of the Acute Cases

As much as the provisions of Chapters XI, XII, and XIII and the UN machinery created to implement them on the whole represent a considerable advance over anything which has preceded them, it is a striking fact that neither the Charter provisions nor the machinery have provided the United Nations with a basis for dealing with most of the critical colonial situations which have arisen since 1945. The Indonesian struggle for independence, the advance of Morocco and Tunisia to independence, the Algerian case, and, in different categories, the Cyprus and West New Guinea (West Irian) cases, and the solution of the postwar problem of disposing of the Italian colonies—all these have come to the attention of the United Nations, but not under Chapters XI, XII, or XIII; either they have come under the General Assembly's general power of discussion and recommendation under Articles 10, 11, and 14 or they have come before the Security Council under Chapters VI and VII. This fact reflects two important things, namely, the inadequacy of the San Francisco expectations about the orderly procession which colonial evolution would follow and, secondly, the practical necessity to find ways around the limits which the recognition of the sovereignty of the colonial powers imposed on the United Nations' powers under Chapter XI.

The acute cases which have come before the United Nations as issues affecting peace and security have highlighted many facets of the colonial problem and the relationship which the UN has to it. These cases illustrate, in a focused way, some of the dilemmas and problems of principle, philosophy, and politics which recur in virtually all aspects of the colonial problem before the United Nations. They reflect the conflicting claims and aspirations of the colonial powers and of the colonial peoples. They reveal in stark outline the sharply conflicting views, often diametrically opposed to each other, which members hold on the UN's role and functions.

Self-Determination

Article 1 of the Charter speaks of the principle of "self-determination of peoples." This phrase reappears in Article 55. But it is conspicuously absent from the chapters which specifically relate to colonial matters. Nevertheless, this principle has been at stake in each of the "acute cases" and underlies much of the controversy in the UN over Chapters XI, XII, and XIII.

Simply stated, it is an assertion that a people should be free to decide its own destiny. Although few, especially in the United States, would deny this principle, it seems to raise as many issues as it resolves. Some of these issues are:

1) How should "a people" be defined? Should the definition limit the application of the principle to units described by national political boundaries? But it is an unfortunate fact that political boundaries, especially in Africa, have been arbitrarily drawn and do not necessarily reflect ethnic, economic, and historic affinities and realities. Should the principle apply to lesser, homogeneous groups, for example, tribal groupings, such as the Ashanti in the Gold Coast or the Ewe in Togoland and the Gold Coast? Or, carried to its logical conclusion, should the principle of self-determination apply to any group, of whatever size, that chooses to exercise it? Doesn't this raise the spectre of "fragmentation" or "Balkanization" of the world into a multitude of tiny units to the probable detriment of the peoples themselves and certainly to the disadvantage of world stability?

2) How does the act of self-determination take place? Colonial societies tend to have fairly rudimentary equipment for government and decision-making at what might be called the national level. How does one know what is actually represented by the assertion that the people of a colony want to be free? Is this the belief of all the people or most of them, or is it the view of a dominant majority or minority, or merely of an entrenched leadership group?

3) When is a people ready for self-determination? Is it possible to define criteria which will ensure that only those peoples will exercise the right who have the qualifications for viable autonomy—experienced leadership, a sound constitutional structure, capacity to defend the national territory and integrity and to maintain law and order, the ability and will to protect the legal rights and interests of foreign nationals and enterprises within the country, the basic economic capacity to provide for the needs of the people? Otherwise, will not self-determination mean the creation of autonomous units which, because of their weakness, poverty, and disorder, will generate instability and be a source of danger to their neighbors, not to mention the harm which might be done to their own peoples? On the other hand, do not these questions imply a point of view which may be out of step with current realities? Witness the following remark by a former Governor General of Nigeria: "The nascent nations of Africa do not accept Western time-tables of the proper or prudent timing of independence, and when we talk of premature grant of self-government, the adjective presupposes a point of view which is not admitted by Africans ..."[1]

4) Is there a legal right to self-determination? It has often been claimed in UN debates that the language of Article 1 of the Charter, i.e., "respect for the principle of equal rights and self-determination of peoples" established or recognized a legal right and created for the colonial powers a legal obligation to permit the peoples under their control to exercise this right. The colonial powers, of course, while recognizing the principle, have denied the existence of such a *right*. In the extended debates on the Human Rights Covenants, they have sturdily resisted efforts to include a self-determination clause and presumably they will not ratify Covenants which contain such a clause, at least not without nullifying reservations. How can such a right be

[1] Lord Milverton, G.C.M.G., "Thoughts on Nationalism in Africa," *Corona*, Dec. 1955, p. 446.

enforced, in any event, against a colonial power which is unwilling to recognize it? No international tribunal is accessible, in the existing legal order, to a colonial people which seeks juridical confirmation of its attempt to exercise the right. There are some who believe that advisory opinions by the International Court of Justice might help to clarify the legal aspect, especially if they deal with the conditions which have to exist before a right of self-determination may be said to exist. But such opinions would be more political than legal. It may be significant that, although there has been more than one suggestion that an advisory opinion be sought, the states which claim the existence of a legal right have not supported the proposals. It seems doubtful that there is a legal right to self-determination. In any case, it would seem that the problem is not one which can be resolved in legal terms and that efforts to assert a legal right serve only to force the issue to political decision by the UN's normal processes of political controversy.

5) Who decides these matters? This question raised in sharp form by the acute cases, goes to the heart of the controversy over the role of the United Nations and is considered in the next section of this report.

The Role of the UN

The sustained effort of the anti-colonial bloc in the UN, comprising the states from Africa, the Middle East, and Asia, some Latin American members, and the Soviet bloc, to employ the UN as a forum for bringing pressure against the colonial powers in behalf of nationalist movements has raised in acute form various questions about the role of the UN on colonial issues.

Domestic jurisdiction. There is no escaping the fact that the domestic jurisdiction question, and the opposite side of the coin, the question of the UN's competence, have been the focus for considerable passion in the UN. It is on this issue that the main battles over the acute cases have been fought, both in the Security Council and in the General Assembly. Several considerations deserve recognition:

1) For the colonial powers, the question of the UN's competence to intervene in what they consider to be family matters is regarded as of the utmost importance. This question, perhaps more than any other, influences the view which the colonial powers, France and the Union of South Africa in particular, have of the UN and of

their relation to it. France's walk-out during the tenth General Assembly, because of the decision to include the Algerian question on the agenda, was a dramatic and accurate reflection of the importance that France attaches to this question.

2) The anti-colonial faction, on the other hand, does not agree that disputes between the colonial powers and nationalist forces, especially when they threaten violence, lie outside the proper jurisdiction of the organization.

3) There has been marked reluctance on both sides to seek juridical advice by means, for example, of advisory opinions from the International Court of Justice, on various formulations of the domestic jurisdiction question as it has arisen. Advisory opinions might not eliminate conflict on the issue but might serve to narrow the areas of controversy and point the way to workable practices and procedures. One question on which an advisory opinion might well be sought is whether or not the inclusion of an item on the agenda of a UN organ constitutes intervention in the meaning of Article 2, paragraph 7.

4) While the legal issue is by no means easily resolved as to whether Article 2, paragraph 7 limits the freedom of UN organs to deal with colonial questions, especially those which threaten peace and security, it nevertheless seems unlikely that discussion should be interpreted to constitute "intervention" in the meaning of Article 2, paragraph 7. In any case the practice of the colonial powers, supported by the United States on several occasions, to oppose inclusion of colonial questions on the agenda of the General Assembly and the Security Council seems an unwise one. For one thing, this effort does not foreclose debate, which takes place (in the guise of debate on the issue of inclusion) with equal vehemence and equal effect on the relations between the colonial power and the nationalist movement. Secondly, this policy gives to the decision to include an item on the agenda a significance which is unwarranted.

By implication, the colonial powers have often admitted that to include an item on the agenda is to recognize the competence of the organization. This does not have to be so. Their position would be a much stronger one if the question of competence were raised in connection with actions proposed for the UN organs rather than in connection with inclusion and discussion of an item. It would be much sounder to revert to the original practice, which the United

States warmly favored at the time, of opening the agendas of organs widely to proposed items. If all items were included on the agenda automatically, or nearly so, there would be no presumption that the inclusion of any specific item implied that the question was not one within the domestic jurisdiction of a member, thereby lying beyond the UN's power to take action comprising "intervention." An incidental desirable consequence would be to spare the UN, especially the General Assembly, many time-consuming and tedious debates on competence. The non-administering states could contribute to order in this area by exercising restraint in debating issues on which constructive action is not possible.

5) It is improbable that an easy resolution of this issue can be found. Majorities in the General Assembly will continue to assert their interest in dealing with colonial problems; and the colonial powers will continue to resist this assertion. No rule of thumb exists by which to measure the usefulness or the harmfulness of having UN debates on all colonial questions. There are, however, two useful guidelines which can be applied in reaching a judgment on individual cases when they arise: a) The cooperation of the colonial power is desirable in each case if colonial issues are to be resolved peacefully and constructively in the mutual interest of the colonial people and the colonial power, and of the world community. There are hopeful signs that the General Assembly, confronted by the French walk-out, came closer to recognizing this fact during the tenth General Assembly than at any previous time. b) It is by no means certain that debate of a colonial issue will in all cases and at all times facilitate a solution. The decision whether or not to deal with a colonial question should take into account the anticipated consequences, in terms of the state of negotiations or other relations between the nationalist movement and the colonial government, the state of domestic opinion of the two parties, the domestic political situations of both sides, and the wider requirements of the region in which the colony is situated and the world as a whole.

The effect of UN action. In estimating the effect of UN debate and action on evolving colonial situations, there is one necessary starting assumption, i.e., that, although determined nationalist movements commanding sufficient popular support invariably achieve their ends, the colonial power controls whether the process will be peaceful and constructive or bloody and debilitating to the new nation in the making. It is true that the metropoles have not, in several of the recent acute cases, commanded anything approaching a monopoly of force in the territories concerned. But they have disposed of enough military power, in Indonesia and Morocco to cite but two examples, at least to prolong hostilities after they have broken out, to deny to the nationalist forces control of the key urban centers and communications networks, and, in general, to prevent the nationalist forces from immediately achieving their goals. In the territories, at least the acquiescence of the colonial powers is necessary before nationalist movements can attain their ends.

That is not to say that nationalist forces cannot bring about the reluctant acquiescence of the metropoles by the attenuating application of military pressure. But it is presumably the interest of the United Nations to bring about accommodation by means other than encouragement of nationalist military action against the superior and more concentrated military power of the metropole.

In the United Nations, the situation is analogous to the situation in the field. Decisions of UN organs can have no binding effect *vis-à-vis* the colonial powers, and, even if they did, the colonial powers would be unlikely to acquiesce in decisions to which they did not agree. The governments of the colonial powers control the extent to which they implement the decisions, in whatever form, of the UN organs, assuming, not unrealistically, that the UN will not use force to impose its decisions on the colonial powers. Hence, a UN majority can achieve its objectives *vis-à-vis* the colonial powers only when its behavior is such as to persuade the governments of the colonial powers that they should cooperate. The converse is also true, that nationalist movements need to have assurance that their legitimate aspirations can be served by a restraint on their part which allows solutions to be sought by negotiation and conciliation in which the UN plays a part, if they are to be dissuaded from forcing issues by violent means.

Other considerations to be considered include the following:

1) Acute cases, practically by definition, are situations in which mutual confidence and the will to proceed jointly toward an agreed solution in the common interest have broken down. Usually, force is being used or threatened. In such situations, passions on both sides are high and easily excited to further heights. Behavior in the UN which exacerbates the disagreement and heightens the passions

is unlikely to contribute to the kind of peaceful resolution of the issues, in the interest of both sides and of the international community, for which the organization should strive.

2) The colonial powers, whether realistically or not in the long run, tend to believe that they have the competence and the ability to resist colonial rebellion and to bring about a resolution of colonial problems within the frameworks which they have themselves set. Hence, they regard UN interest as an interference in their affairs, an offense to their prestige, and a liability with respect to achievement of the ends they seek. The nationalist movements, on the other hand, look to the UN as a source of outside strength and as a means to limit the freedom of the colonial powers to resist the nationalist forces. The fact of this imbalance in perception of the UN's role tends to fortify the resistance of the colonial powers to UN "interference" and to limit their willingness to cooperate with the UN majority.

3) The colonial powers are not monoliths. Moreover, they vary considerably among themselves in their approaches to colonial problems, in their domestic political processes and situations, and in numerous other ways which affect decision-making on colonial issues before the UN. In each of the colonial powers, there are forces, of varying potency, willing to encourage colonial advance and the peaceful solution of colonial problems. There are, of course, forces at the opposite extreme of the spectrum. The effectiveness of UN action may depend considerably on whether such action fortifies the "liberal" elements more than it does the "conservative." In general, UN pressure upon the United Kingdom is more likely to be effective than upon the other colonial powers. The history of UN attempts to deal with the Southwest Africa question, and, in situations that are not colonial, the Indians in South Africa, and the racial policies of the Union of South Africa, demonstrates how UN pressures can strengthen the "conservative" elements in a domestic political situation and contribute to results the reverse of those hoped for, at least in the short run. There is another consequence of this variety among the colonial powers, namely, that some of them may often be willing to bring pressure on the others to move toward the UN majority. The United States, for example, has often been in the position of working behind the scenes and sometimes openly to persuade France and Holland to

show greater flexibility in dealing with acute cases. The application of such influence is probably encouraged by moderate behavior by the majority and discouraged by extreme behavior which pushes the colonial powers toward a united front, in the face of what they regard as a common danger.

4) What is true of the colonial powers is equally true of nationalist movements. There is no reason to doubt that much the same domestic political considerations are at play. Nationalist leaderships in a real sense are acting as "governments" which face the same problems of decision-making, of selecting the action courses which will achieve their objectives, as do the governments of the metropoles. And in facing these decisions, they confront much the same constellations of domestic pressures, interest groupings, political parties, personal ambitions. In nationalist movements, there are moderate factions, which, although devoutly patriotic in their nationalism, nevertheless see benefit for their countries in peaceful progress toward national autonomy, be it as independent nations or in some constitutional relationship with the metropoles, in collaboration with the latter, and with end results which allow both the metropoles and the former colonies to carry on relationships that promise to contribute to the benefit of both. The use of the UN as an instrument to influence the course of events in acute cases should take into account the desirability of strengthening such moderate elements in nationalist movements. They will not be strengthened if the UN is resorted to in ways which encourage the belief that it offers greater gains to the nationalist movements than will serious negotiations with the colonial powers when the latter are willing. Similarly, the UN can be used to strengthen their positions if pressures are sensitively and discreetly applied to lead the governments of colonial powers toward a greater willingness to negotiate. Resolutions condemning the colonial powers or setting forth high sounding but extreme principles and objectives are less likely to be useful than behavior which, by taking into account the sensitivities of both sides, creates a climate in which genuine efforts to reach agreement become possible.

5) The anti-colonial majority in the UN is also a diversified grouping. Many of its members are motivated by high purposes, often stemming from their memories of colonial rule. In other cases, the colonial issue offers the opportunity for personal aggrandize-

ment or political advantage for UN delegates and national leaders. For the Communist states, the colonialism issue is a classic opportunity to fish in waters troubled by the clash of European colonial interests and nationalist forces. Some of the members of this grouping have close ties of interest with the United States and with the very European colonial powers whom they oppose on this issue. In general it may be said that the cohesiveness of this group is in direct proportion to the obstinacy of the colonial powers. It is in the interest of the latter, measured in terms of the colonial problem itself or in a broader setting, to behave in ways which will encourage independent thought and action by these states and provide a moderate center toward which some of them may be attracted.

Some Conclusions:

This Committee does not presume to have "the answer to the colonial problem." If anything is clear from the evidence of the acute cases, it is that there can never be a fully satisfactory solution to human problems of such intensity and importance and that the best one can expect to achieve is a climate in which men of good will can strive for accommodation, test that accommodation against emerging conditions and needs, and make new adjustments as situations call for them. The Committee can make no categorical recommendations about the role of the UN in achieving such a climate or in taking advantage of it should it come to pass. The Committee recognizes that colonial problems are as diverse as the colonial societies and relationships from which they stem. The resolution of each colonial situation has to be tailored to its particular circumstances. If the Members of the UN who dominate its proceedings on colonial issues recognize this overriding fact, then the organization may be able to contribute constructively to the resolution of individual colonial problems as they arise.

Nevertheless, and subject to the above qualifications, there are certain general considerations which seem worth setting forth here.

1) The drive among colonial peoples for national self-determination must be dealt with as a reality of the modern era. Moreover, the lesson of history is that colonialism of the traditional kind is in process of liquidation. The problem today is how to accomplish the transition peacefully and with the greatest advantage to all concerned.

2) Although the colonial powers and the colonial peoples are the principally interested parties in colonial disputes, the world as a whole, through the United Nations, has an interest in the peaceful and just solution of conflicts which may threaten peace, regionally or universally, and which certainly affect the achievement of the purposes of the UN, set forth in the Preamble and Articles 1, 55, and 73 of the Charter.

3) In confronting acute colonial problems, the UN, as well as the colonial powers and the nationalist leaders of colonial peoples should strive for viable resolutions which recognize that the mutual benefit of the colonial peoples and the colonial powers is not incompatible with national dignity and self-respect for colonial peoples. Such resolutions should:

a) Allow colonial peoples to exercise the full degree of freedom of which they are capable.

b) Provide for constitutional arrangements, including not only independence but also continued autonomous association with the metropole, or affiliation with neighboring countries, which best meet the needs of the country concerned, its neighbors, and the metropolitan country concerned.

c) Permit the continuation of those aspects of the colonial relationship which are freely accepted by and serve the interests of both the colonial people and the former colonial power, such as: sharing of technical skills and capital resources which colonial peoples require and which the colonial powers are able to give; mutual contributions to security; free intellectual and cultural exchange.

4) The UN will contribute to such resolutions of colonial problems only as the anti-colonial majority recognizes that colonial progress will benefit from the willingness of the colonial powers to cooperate. Ill-considered use of the means of pressure available in the UN will more often than not make it more difficult for metropolitan governments to cooperate in the United Nations to attain this end. On the other hand, the UN can be discreetly used, according to the circumstances of individual cases, as a means of encouraging the colonial powers and the nationalist movements to reach agreement in their mutual interest on progressive steps toward new relationships in accordance with reasonable time-tables.

Particularly, more emphasis should be placed on the UN's potential as a means of mobilizing the resources of all its members to contribute to the essential prerequisites of viable independence for colonial areas. There should be a special emphasis on non-self-governing territories in the UN technical assistance program. The anti-colonial majority has a special responsibility to contribute materially to the achievement of the objectives which they so vigorously proclaim. Their contributions to such a program would properly be regarded as a measure of the sincerity with which they advocate the principle of self-determination. The cooperation of the colonial powers is particularly important in this connection because their consent is needed before assistance programs can go forward in a colony.

5) The colonial powers should recognize, and be encouraged to recognize, that the issue of self-determination is the chief obstacle to the rational achievement of colonial solutions which preserve their vital interests in their colonial relationships. While the Committee recognizes that the principle of self-determination may not resolve any particular cases, it nevertheless believes that an assurance to colonial peoples that they can exercise the right under specifically defined circumstances, when, for example, a UN organ decides that the time is right, would:

a) Diminish the passion and encourage reason in nationalist movements.

b) Strengthen the moderate factions within nationalist movements which are inclined to seek national status in fruitful collaboration with the metropolitan powers.

c) Increase the chance of reasonable time-tables for progress toward self-determination.

d) Widen the opportunities for constructive contributions by the colonial powers and the United Nations to the viability of emerging new units.

e) Encourage agreement on constitutional relationships which best serve the needs of the emerging national community, its neighbors, and the metropole.

f) Provide greater guarantees than now exist that the nationals and economic interests of the metropole will have a continued place in the new relationships that emerge.

g) Increase the likelihood that the act of self-determination will take place responsibly, with adequate preparation and awareness of the new responsibilities being entered into.

h) In general, heighten the chances for viable solutions of colonial situations.

6) Such a guarantee of the right of self-determination would not eliminate all hazards. Some peoples might still opt for national freedom who are not objectively prepared for it. Such a guarantee would certainly not solve the problem of what is a people. It would certainly not resolve the problems of multi-national societies. But a declaration of this character would provide the colonial peoples and their nationalist leaders with the greatest opportunity to face their futures responsibly. And it is the unmistakable lesson of recent colonial history that the doubts of others do not deter a colonial people from pressing for self-determination. The acute cases, which have cost the colonial powers heavily and will continue to do so even after they have been resolved, have resulted from the passionate conflict which ensues when the right of a colonial people to self-determination is contested by the metropole.

7) With respect to the problem of deciding when an act of self-determination has taken place, consideration should be given to the device of UN supervised plebiscites, recently used with some success in Togoland under British trusteeship.

8) It should be frankly acknowledged that new states will emerge that are not qualified for statehood. An example is Somaliland under Italian trusteeship which will be independent, by decision of the General Assembly, in 1960. For such states the problem is to supply the prerequisites of independence to the extent possible after political independence has been achieved. In this, the United Nations can and should play a key role by mobilizing the resources of all its members through a special United Nations program of technical and capital assistance, directed especially to new nations emerging from colonial status.

9) In general the UN can contribute to colonial progress only if all concerned display a greater spirit of accommodation than has been evident in the past. The colonial powers should acknowledge the interest of the world community in the satisfactory resolution of colonial issues and welcome the material contributions of which the UN is potentially capable. The anti-colonial majority should recognize that the colonial powers have interests in the colonies which they consider vital to their national existence and prosperity and should exercise with discretion the pressures which it can exert.

THE DECLARATION REGARDING NON-SELF-GOVERNING TERRITORIES

Chapter XI of the Charter, the "Declaration Regarding Non-Self-Governing Territories," is a statement by the states administering "territories whose peoples have not yet attained a full measure of self-government" that they will abide by certain principles in their government of the non-self-governing territories under their jurisdiction. Among the obligations they accepted was the undertaking of Article 73e "to transmit regularly to the Secretary-General for information purposes . . . statistical and other information of a technical nature relating to economic, social, and educational conditions in the territories . . ." No special machinery was created by the Charter and there was no definition of the territories to which the provisions of Chapter XI would apply.

The Chapter obviously was a compromise, the most on which agreement could be reached at the time, between the reluctance of some of the colonial powers to subject their administration to international scrutiny and the desire among many participating states to incorporate in the Charter the concept that colonial powers should be accountable to the international community for their administration. The advocates of Chapter XI tended to regard it as desirable for the international toehold it established in the terrain of national sovereignty over the colonies rather than for the uncertain contribution it might make to ameliorating conditions in non-self-governing areas. While the Declaration had its formal origin in the preamble to the British proposal on trusteeship, most of the colonial powers viewed with undisguised misgiving the efforts at the San Francisco Conference to expand the brief statement of principle in the British preamble into a thoroughgoing and detailed set of standards to govern colonial administration. The resulting compromise involved acceptance by the colonial powers of a broadly couched set of principles, including the principles that administration of non-self-governing peoples should "ensure, with due respect for the culture of the peoples concerned, their political, economic, social and educational advancement, their just treatment, and their protection against abuses" and should also "develop self-government, . . . take due account of the political aspirations of the peoples, and . . . assist them in the progressive development of their free political institutions, according to the particular circumstances of each territory and its peoples and their varying stages of advancement." Presumably, the interest of the international community was acknowledged by including the Declaration in the Charter and also by the clause providing for submission of information. In the latter connection, it should be noted that the obligation specifically does not cover political information, a source of considerable subsequent controversy.

The limits of the Declaration, the directions in which it has developed, the controversies which have arisen are all determined by the conflict between: 1) the inescapable fact that the non-self-governing territories fall either under the sovereignty or some other form of exclusive jurisdiction of the metropolitan powers; and 2) the equally inescapable fact that a majority of the UN's members believe that, because the territories do not govern themselves, they are entitled to a special measure of international interest and protection, with emphasis on progress toward self-government. It seems that these two propositions set the limits within which future progress may be possible and, at the same time, point the directions for such progress.

First, what have been the main issues of past contention?

1) What is a non-self-governing territory? Article 73 speaks of "territories whose peoples have not yet attained a full measure of self-government." Beyond this, the Charter does not define the territories which come under the provisions of Chapter XI. Confronted with this lack of precision, the UN General Assembly at the outset acquiesced in the determination by the administering authorities themselves of the territories which they considered as falling within the language of Article 73 and on which they would supply information under Article 73e. No definition of what comprises a non-self-governing territory has ever achieved official sanction in the United Nations.

This lack has given rise to two major difficulties in the short history of the United Nations. For one thing, several of the colonial powers, notably Belgium, have come to resent what they regard as the discriminatory pattern under which their "colonies" come under international scrutiny and their administration is subjected to what they regard as uninformed and unfair criticism, while other territories in comparable stages of development, whose peoples have also not "attained a full measure of self-government," do not. This so-called "Belgian thesis" emphasizes the well-known "salt-water fallacy," i.e., that discrimination results between different forms of colonialism, because the territories which are familiarly known as "colonies" are separated from their metropoles by international bodies of water, while areas that should properly be considered colonial but are contiguous to the metropoles or included within the national boundaries escape this designation. The advocates of the Belgian thesis devote particular attention to Soviet colonialism, but they refer also to the hinterland of Brazil and other areas inhabited by peoples who "have not yet attained a full measure of self-government."

The second major difficulty has been over who decides when a territory is "non-self-governing" in the meaning of Article 73 and, particularly, who decides when a territory on which reports have been submitted ceases to come under the reporting requirement. There have been a great number of instances of territories achieving constitutional advances which have led the administering authorities to cease reporting on the grounds that the territories concerned were no longer non-self-governing in the meaning of Article 73. In such situations, the administering authorities have insisted that they alone, because of their exclusive jurisdiction, can decide when a territory ceases to come under Chapter XI. A strong contingent of UN members, however, has insisted, in effect, that if Chapter XI means anything at all, it must mean that the UN has an interest in this question and that, consequently, the administering authorities should not be free to cease reporting on a territory without the General Assembly having a role in the decision. One consequence of this controversy has been the adoption by the General Assembly of a list of factors which should be taken into account in deciding whether a territory is or is not a territory whose people have not yet attained a full measure of self-government. Since the list was adopted, there has been a seemingly acceptable compromise pattern for treating cases involving the determination of administering authorities to cease transmitting information for territories under their jurisdiction. While the administering authorities have continued to contend that the question lies within their sole jurisdiction, they have in fact submitted full information on the changed constitutional situations leading to their decisions. The General Assembly, basing its action on the list of factors, has in each case accepted the propriety of the decision. In the long run, however, the situation may not be so satisfactory. On the one hand, the administering authorities may succumb to the temptation to create constitutional situations which, while falling short of a reasonable definition of "a full measure of self-government," may nevertheless comprise effective barriers to the further transmission of information. There have already been cases where changed constitutional circumstances have genuinely restricted the ability of the administering authorities to continue submission of information. On the other hand, a General Assembly majority might decide at any future time that the decision of an administering authority to cease transmission of information was not justified, thereby precipitating a deadlock which could only be frustrating to all concerned and especially unsettling for the people of the territory.

2) What arrangements should be made to handle information submitted under Article 73e? The slender beginnings of the Charter requirement that certain types of information be submitted, subject to careful limitations, have been developed into a far-reaching UN system for handling this information. Summaries and analyses of this information, supplemented by materials available from other official sources, are prepared and published by the Secretary-General. The information itself is based on a "Standard Form," approved by the General Assembly, which is more comprehensive than the League of Nations' questionnaire on the mandated territories. A Committee on Information from Non-Self-Governing Territories, created for successive three-year terms over the opposition of the administering authorities, promises to become a standard feature of the UN's machinery. This committee, composed equally of administering and non-administering states, annually considers the summaries and analyses of the Secretary-General. The practice has developed of devoting detailed attention to economic, social, educational conditions in turn in a three-year cycle. The Secretary-General's reports are made available to the specialized agencies whose representatives participate in the discussions of the committee on information. In addition, the General Assembly's Fourth Committee each year considers the reports of the committee on information.

Despite the fact that the discussions of the Committee on Information are general rather than particular, that is, they are concerned with economic, social, and educational conditions in all non-self-governing territories but not with any single territory, several of the administering states have consistently opposed any substantive functions whatever for the committee and have opposed its continued existence. In fact, Belgium has not participated in the Committee since 1953.

3) Submission of political information. The obligation to provide

information does not encompass political information among the categories covered. This omission was deliberate and reflected the compromise which was possible at the San Francisco Conference. Ever since, the administering authorities have been under strong pressure to submit political information. They have resisted these pressures, although some of the administering authorities have voluntarily supplied political data and although information is, for the most part, readily available from other sources, many of which are official publications of the colonies or the metropoles. Primarily, the resistance of such governments as France, Belgium, and the United Kingdom is designed to hold the line agreed on at San Francisco and to avoid opening doors for loose interpretation, to their discomfort and disadvantage, of the agreements recorded in the Charter.

4) Efforts to extend the arrangements. This concern of the administering states over the possibility that the original outlines of the Charter system might be extended to their disadvantage finds some corroboration in various efforts which have been made both to broaden the functions of the UN and to add dimensions to the existing structure of obligations. For example, there has been a concerted effort, which some of the administering states have been resisting, to bring about representation in the UN for the inhabitants of the non-self-governing territories. On at least two occasions, the General Assembly has commended to the administering states the practice of some of them whereby inhabitants of the territories are included in UN delegations. Another example involves the suggestion that the General Assembly be empowered to send investigatory missions to territories for which the administering authorities intend to cease transmission of information. One purpose suggested for such missions was to ensure that the principle of self-determination had been adhered to in the process of change.

Some Conclusions

In thinking about the UN's role with respect to non-self-governing territories, several considerations seem to have great significance:

1) Legally and in fact the administering powers are the responsible authorities in the non-self-governing territories.

2) Nevertheless, the world community has an interest, acknowledged by the Charter, in the welfare and progress of non-self-governing peoples. In a closely inter-connected world, especially one rent by

pervading political and ideological schism, the fact of national sovereignty or exclusive national jurisdiction in the affairs of a non-self-governing territory can not be allowed to interfere with the legitimate interest of the community at large in developments which are likely to affect it, politically, strategically, and economically. The Charter says in effect that the non-self-governing territories, because they are non-self-governing, comprise a special concern of mankind. This principle should be maintained. To maintain it is not to deny the merit in the "salt water" argument. Surely, the best answer is not to adulterate the principle already established but to launch new efforts to reach a new plateau of principles which apply to other peoples who "have not yet attained a full measure of self-government."

3) Since the Charter was adopted in 1945, there have been significant changes in the conditions affecting non-self-governing territories.

Considerable political change has taken place with the result that many former colonies have made considerable progress toward self-government and some have either achieved it or are about to. In this process, the colonial powers have often been willing partners. The debates in the UN have themselves been important stimuli to some of the colonial powers who have learned in the UN how strong are the tides of change and how important it is to swim with them. In short, the whole climate has changed since 1945 so that the question is no longer whether most non-self-governing territories will achieve self-government, but whether they will be adequately equipped to use it wisely and productively when it arrives.

4) As is true of the acute cases, progress for non-self-governing peoples can best be accomplished in collaboration with the administering powers who have not only material contributions to make and stores of experience to give, but who also have the capacity to impede progress, with results which, as recent history shows, are invariably harmful to the new entities when they have achieved their autonomous status. The most successful employment of the UN in the interest of non-self-governing peoples requires a fruitful collaboration among the administering powers, the peoples concerned, and other members of the UN.

5) The UN's potential contribution to the objectives laid down in Article 73 has only begun to be made. The processes which have developed for comparing information about different territories, for

considering broad economic, social, and educational problems affecting the territories, and for debating the questions in the UN organs have no doubt been an important contribution to the emergence of comparative standards for colonial administration. It has no doubt been useful and in the interest of the non-self-governing peoples that each administering power has had to test its practices against the practices of others as they are reflected in the information made available and circulated under the procedures that have developed. But an inordinate proportion of the time spent on non-self-governing territories has been devoted to wrangling over questions of form and procedure. For this, both the administering powers and the anti-colonial forces share the blame, the former for failing often to recognize that the majority interest is a legitimate one and that it represents real forces in the world which must be reckoned with, and the latter for frequent intemperance and failure to couch their proposals and demands in terms which recognize the importance of collaboration with the administering powers. If the two camps can meet on common ground, the UN has a real contribution to make in the future in mobilizing the ideas, skills, and resources of its wide membership for the development of the national fabrics without which the non-self-governing territories cannot enjoy to the full the new forms of political and constitutional status which they will certainly achieve. The first, and most important, prerequisite for an improved role for the UN in dealing with non-self-governing territories is that the organization must be transformed from an arena of combat into a workshop for experiment and collaboration in pursuit of shared objectives. To bring this about, both parties must be prepared to make concessions. Specifically:

a) The anti-colonial forces should credit the administering powers with good faith and should acknowledge the constructive achievements of the past decade. While not all the practices of all the administering powers are equally commendable, there are many creditable aspects of the recent record of colonial management. The anti-colonial states should, at the very least, display a high sense of discrimination in formulating and presenting their views.

b) The anti-colonial forces should recognize that, in the interest of the non-self-governing peoples as well as of peace and stability in the world, political progress should be linked with the other, non-political prerequisites for viable autonomy. Instead of concentrating on unrealistic formulas for independence time-tables, they might cooperate in elaborating constructive schedules for step-by-step progress in which economic, social, and educational development are linked with political and constitutional advance.

c) The anti-colonial forces should demonstrate their good faith by contributing to the UN's technical assistance program for the purpose of aiding the development of non-self-governing territories. In doing so, they should receive assurance that their contributions will be effectively employed toward this end.

d) The administering powers for their part should acknowledge that Chapter XI of the Charter is not only here to stay but that it reflects the legitimate interest and concern of the international community. They should agree to the permanent constitution of the Committee on Information from Non-Self-Governing Territories and should participate in its activities. In deciding to cease the transmission of information about any territory, they should proceed in step with the UN organs, inviting the collaboration of the latter in determining by suitable means whether a full measure of self-government has been achieved in the meaning of Article 73.

e) The administering authorities who do not do so should agree to submit political information, along with the economic, social and educational data now required. This acquiescence in the clear desire of the majority would be an exhibition of good intent and, as such, should contribute to an improved atmosphere. It would not substantially alter the information now available through other channels. If necessary, Article 73e of the Charter should be amended by the insertion of the word "political," hopefully with the concurrence of the administering powers.

f) The administering powers should agree to the proposition that they have the obligation to formulate and announce schedules for step-by-step and coordinated political, economic, social, and educational progress toward self-government. No set formula, obviously, can fit all colonial situations. But each administering power, taking into account the individual circumstances, potentials, and needs of the non-self-governing territories for which it is responsible, might set forth the steps which it proposes to take and the targets which it expects to meet for a beginning period of, say, five or ten years. It might also record the forms and quantities of outside assistance required for the attainment of these goals.

g) Both sides should be willing to have treatment of non-self-governing territories take place predominantly in the Committee on Information, where the emphasis can be on constructive contribution based on growing expertise and where the special interests of the administering powers are reflected in the balanced composition of the Committee. Recourse to the General Assembly and its Fourth Committee would be available in case of deadlock and should provide a special incentive to the administering powers to come to agreement in the Committee. However, this incentive will be effective only if the non-administering members exercise restraint enough to convince the administering powers that the advantage lies in continued cooperation rather than complete withdrawal or obstinate resistance.

The Trusteeship System

The UN trusteeship system, set up to provide an extra measure of supervision over the administration of territories with a special international status, is of diminishing significance. Its scope seems destined to shrink as the trust territories achieve new status. This year, Togoland under British administration became part of Ghana, thereby graduating from the system. Somaliland, administered by Italy, is scheduled to become independent in 1960. Other territories are moving toward new, autonomous status, in most cases if not all as parts of adjacent colonies.

Moreover, the original hope, reflected in Article 77c, that colonial powers might voluntarily place new territories under the system seems to have been overly optimistic. For one thing, the colonial powers do not seem to have acquired enough confidence in the working of the system to be encouraged to place additional territories under it. For another, the entire concept is being bypassed by events. The pace of change in the colonial world has been so rapid since the Charter was adopted that the transitional functions which the trusteeship system was designed to perform have in a sense become outmoded. It is certain that colonial peoples would not, in most cases, regard trusteeship as an advance over their present status. While it remains possible that trusteeship will be a convenient device for internationalizing disputed areas such as West New Guinea, or even for extending international jurisdiction into new zones such as Antarctica, on the whole it seems improbable that there will be many more customers for the system. A not unreasonable prognosis would be that two more decades should see the achievement of the system's primary aim, namely its own liquidation as a result of the achievement by the trust territories of the new status which it is the purpose of the system to facilitate. Some of the territories, to be sure, can probably never be viable, even in association with other political entities. But a system whose sole concerns were Nauru and the Trust Territory of the Pacific Islands would be a far different thing from what was visualized by the Charter.

If these speculations are valid, the best definition of the trusteeship problem today is: how may the system best be employed to facilitate the transition to their new status of those territories which remain under its jurisdiction? The following considerations seem relevant:

1. The special international status of the territories, because they were under the League of Nations mandates system or, in the case of Somaliland, because it was "detached" from Italy as a result of World War II, with the concomitant special responsibilities of the administering authorities and of the UN, provide an unusual opportunity to set standards worthy of emulation with respect to other non-self-governing territories.

2. The special responsibility of the UN should be taken far more seriously than it has been. To cite only the most obvious example, the General Assembly's decision to fix a ten-year time limit for the attainment of independence by Somaliland in 1960 was totally irresponsible unless it is matched, as it has not been thus far, by a commensurate willingness to supply the means to make that independence meaningful. There should be a special UN effort, either as part of the regular Technical Assistance Program or in some other form, to mobilize skills and resources as a positive contribution to the advance of the trust territories toward their ultimate status, be it "self-government or independence as may be appropriate to the particular circumstances of each territory and its peoples and the freely expressed wishes of the peoples concerned . . ." The UN should also recognize a special obligation to provide assistance to make the new status of its former wards meaningful, after it has been achieved.

3. There is considerable room for improvement in the techniques of supervision by the Trusteeship Council. Arrangements should be made to provide more adequate attention for petitions concerning trust territories. The volume of petitions received far exceeds the capacity of the Trusteeship Council committee which is charged with the

responsibility of screening them. Perhaps a proper solution would be to rely more heavily on the Secretariat in the initial screening process. Members of the Trusteeship Council should also take more seriously their responsibility to supply high level and experienced personnel for the Council's visiting missions. The Charter itself does not specify how the missions should be composed. The first visiting mission, to Western Samoa, included an independent expert, but the precedent has not been followed up.

4. The administering authorities should recognize that the trust territories are in a unique position entailing special responsiblities for them. The idea of intermediate time-tables, supported by a majority of the members of the UN, seems worthy of testing. Obviously, hard deadlines for the ultimate evolution of the trust territories to their new status would be arbitrary and might well create expectations that are too high. In other cases, such deadlines might actually postpone changes which will occur more rapidly in the natural course of events. But intermediate time-tables, or schedules, seem both more reasonable and more useful as a means of projecting the steps which should be taken in the next few years to speed the territories on their way toward full self-government or independence. In any case, it seems that the international community has a right to expect a special effort of this kind in view of the international status of the trust territories.

5. As in the case of non-self-governing territories, the cooperation of the administering authorities is important. One of the difficulties of the trusteeship system thus far has been the difficult relationship between the Trusteeship Council in which the administering authorities comprise half the membership and the General Assembly in which they are heavily outnumbered. As in the case of the non-self-governing territories, it would be a good thing if the primary consideration of trusteeship questions could take place in the Trusteeship Council, with the General Assembly, so to speak, held in reserve.

CONCLUSIONS

The temptation is great to conclude a report of this character with generally optimistic remarks, which would probably be banal. The conclusions which this Committee might wish to state are implicit throughout the preceding sections. Recapitulated, they are:

1. The original intent of chapters XI, XII, and XIII of the Charter was and remains valid, namely, that the status and progress of colo-

nial peoples are a proper concern of mankind, that the administering authorities have a responsibility both to the colonial peoples and the world at large for their administration, and that the international community has something to contribute to the process of colonial development.

2. Change has taken place in the colonial world far more rapidly than anyone could anticipate in 1945 and, as a result, the main problem is no longer to provide guarantees for the welfare of colonial peoples during an extended period of tutelage. Since self-government within a fairly short term is probable for most colonial peoples, whether or not they are adequately prepared for it, the need now is rather to devise effective means for helping to smooth the transition to self-government in whatever form.

3. Unfortunately, the potential contribution of the United Nations has not been fully exploited and is unlikely to be, if existing trends are projected into the future.

4. The opportunity is a challenging and important one to which the Members of the United Nations can and should respond by seeking means to collaborate in employing the instrumentalities of the United Nations to contribute constructively to the real needs of the colonial peoples.

5. The essential pre-condition for using the United Nations in this way is a willingness on the part both of the colonial and the anti-colonial members of the United Nations to pursue shared goals in an atmosphere of constructive collaboration.

That such far-reaching change will come about, no one can confidently predict. Perhaps there is ground for optimism in the knowledge that failure will be costly—in human terms, and in terms of the political and economic price that the freedom-loving world will have to pay for chaos in colonial affairs.

LAWRENCE S. FINKELSTEIN, CHAIRMAN
EUNICE H. CARTER
WALDO CHAMBERLIN
MALCOLM W. DAVIS
RUPERT EMERSON
BRUNSON MACCHESNEY

6 PRIVILEGES, IMMUNITIES, AND RIGHT OF ACCESS

Between the country in which an international organization is located and the organization itself many problems of relationship must inevitably arise. The international organization must be independent of control by the state, yet it engages in innumerable activities which bring it into contact with the laws and interests of the host government.[1] The experience of Switzerland with the League of Nations[2] provided many lessons for use in making arrangements for locating the United Nations in New York. These arrangements have on the whole worked well, but the scare over Communist subversion in the United States led to measures by its government which caused trouble with regard to the rights of United States nationals in the Secretariat, and with regard to access to the United Nations of persons from abroad. The controversy raised in the minds of other states questions, or open accusations, as to the good faith with which the United States was meeting its obligations as host state to the United Nations; it also

[1] Ideally, an international organization should have its own territorial base, independent of any state, but this would involve innumerable problems and great expense, for example, the security of the territory, the provision of public utilities, of law and police and courts, etc.

[2] See Martin Hill, *Immunities and Privileges of International Officials* (1947); Egon Ranshofen-Wertheimer, *The International Secretariat* (Carnegie Endowment, 1945); J. K. King, *The Privileges and Immunities of the Personnel of International Organizations* (1949); L. Preuss, in 41 *American Journal of International Law* (1947), p. 555; S. Schwebel, *The Secretary-General of the United Nations* (1952), pp. 72-74; same author, "The International Character of the Secretariat of the United Nations," *British Yearbook of International Law*, 1953, p. 71.

produced in the minds of some Americans apprehensions concerning danger to national security arising from the presence of the United Nations, which led to opposition to the United Nations itself.

Since the United Nations will presumably be in the United States for a long time to come, these questions, which affect the good reputation of the United States as well as the operation of the United Nations, deserve serious consideration.

LEGAL ARRANGEMENTS

The understandings between the United States and the United Nations are to be found in a number of legal instruments: (1) The Charter, (2) the General Convention on Privileges and Immunities (not yet ratified by the United States), (3) the Headquarters Agreement, (4) the International Organizations Immunities Act of 1945, a statute of the United States. There are other acts of Congress and executive orders which are relevant and help is to be found also in arrangements between international organizations and the countries in which they are located.[3]

The Charter. Article 104 of the Charter provides that

The Organization shall enjoy in the territory of each of its Members such legal capacity as may be necessary for the exercise of its functions and the fulfillment of its purposes.

The United Nations, by this Article, is given legal capacity, not only under the laws of the State concerned, but also under international law. It was so held by the International Court of Justice in the case of Reparations for Injuries Suffered in the Service of the United Nations.[4]

By Article 105:

1. The Organization shall enjoy in the territory of each of its Members such privileges and immunities as are necessary for the fulfillment of its purposes.
2. Representatives of the Members of the United Nations and officials of the Organization shall similarly enjoy such privileges and immunities as are necessary for the independent exercise of their functions in connection with the Organization.

---

[3] For these, see ST/LEG/2; and summaries in Repertory, Vol. V., pp. 346 ff.
[4] I.C.J. Reports, 1949, p. 174.

3. The General Assembly may make recommendations with a view to determining the details of the application of paragraphs 1 and 2 of this Article or may propose conventions to the Members of the United Nations for this purpose.

In accordance with the last paragraph of this Article, the General Convention on Privileges and Immunities and the Headquarters Agreement with the United States were approved by the Assembly.[5]

It is also important to note in this connection that the Secretary-General and his staff are bound "not to seek or receive instructions from any Government" (Article 100), and they take an oath to this effect; and, on the other hand, the Member States undertake "to respect the exclusively international character of the responsibilities of the Secretary-General and the Staff, and not to seek to influence them in the discharge of their responsibilities" (Article 100, paragraph 2). The Conference at San Francisco strongly emphasized the independence of officials of the United Nations[6] and this is obviously of the greatest importance. If the host country were able to control, through its territorial jurisdiction, the thinking and activity of United Nations officials, even those of its own nationality, the United Nations could hardly be regarded as international in character, and other states would be unwilling to participate in it.[7] The effort to work out the Charter principles in detail has resulted in several instruments which, taken together, can not yet be regarded as a systematic whole.

The General Convention on Privileges and Immunities[8] was intended to be ratified by all Members and to establish in more detail than the Charter provisions the rights of delegates and officials. Unfortunately, the United States, in which such situations would most often arise, has never ratified the General Convention. This was due primarily to objection to two provisions: (1) that officials were to be

[5] Other agreements have been made, such as the one concerning the Ariana site in Geneva; and the General Assembly has made some recommendations concerning the application of Article 105, e.g., for the International Court of Justice. See ST/LEG/2; Repertory, IV, p. 331.

[6] Recalling the furor occasioned, even in the non-member United States, by the efforts of Fascist Italy to instruct its nationals working in the League of Nations.

[7] It may be recalled that U.S. delegates withdrew from the International Institute of Agriculture in Rome, because of the domination exercised by Mussolini.

[8] Adopted on February 13, 1946. Attached to Resolution 22 (I), found in U.N. Doc. A/64, p. 25. By August 31, 1954, forty three members had ratified, six of them with reservations. See Repertory, Vol. V. pp. 327 and annex.

exempt from taxation and (2) that they were exempt from national (meaning usually military) service.

With regard to the former, the principle sought to be established was uniformity of payment to UN officials, in view of the fact that the takehome pay of an official subject to income tax in his own country would be much less than that of an official not subject to such a tax; in most countries, there is no income tax. The United States argues that this exemption would free these nationals from virtually all taxation, which would be unfair to its other nationals. To meet this situation, the United Nations decided to assess all its officials, and did so at a rate at least as high as that of the United States income tax. This was done in the apparent belief that it would satisfy the United States and lead it to accept the General Convention. This country, however, did not carry out whatever understanding there was supposed to be, with the result that nationals of the United States in the Secretariat were burdened with two heavy assessments. To relieve this situation, the United Nations returned to them what they had paid to the United States (or most of it) in income tax[9]; and this, naturally, produced complaints from other Member States, who objected to having their contributions used for such a purpose. This feeling led, at the Tenth Assembly, to adoption of a resolution on December 15, 1955, which penalizes those states for whom the UN must pay relief for double taxation by reducing the credits to which they are entitled in the Tax Equalization Fund.[10]

The objection of the United States to exemption of its nationals from military service has not occasioned so much discussion; it would be difficult to ascertain how many states would agree with this attitude of the United States and would draft into military service their nationals working in the Secretariat. Some questions of fundamental importance are raised by this situation. To those who see the world organization as a body working for peace in the world, the work done by a person in the Secretariat may appear to be as important as that which he might do in his own military forces. They would ask: how can the United Nations fulfill its hope of maintaining peace and order in the world if its promising young officials can be pulled out by Members for military purposes? To others, however, national

[9] An income tax would then be levied on this return, which would also have to be repaid by the UN and so on *ad infinitum!*
[10] General Assembly Resolution 973 (X).

security can be provided only through national military strength, and to this end, no citizen should be excused from making his contribution to that strength. It would, they would say, be unfair discrimination to exempt those who happen to work for the United Nations.

The problem can be reduced to the question, now theoretical: is security obtainable only through national military strength? There would be very few states in the world today which could provide such security. Or is the United Nations to be given the strength which would enable it to provide security for all states? The Commission to Study the Organization of Peace has consistently given an affirmative answer to the latter question. The weakening of the United Nations, through calling its officials to national military service, would be proportionately a greater danger than the weakening of national security through the exemption of Secretariat personnel from military service.

The failure of the United States to ratify the General Convention —whatever may be thought of its justification—leaves a large gap in the system which was intended to assure the independence of the United Nations in its work. For this, the responsibility clearly rests upon the United States and, within the United States, upon Congress.

The Headquarters Agreement[11] has been ratified by the United States which is thereby bound to grant certain privileges and immunities both to the Organization and to persons connected with it or doing business with it. These rights will be considered below, insofar as they relate to the purposes of this study. The importance of the Agreement was increased by the fact that it and the General Convention on Privileges and Immunities were supposed to be complementary documents, and the failure of the United States to ratify the latter leaves the Headquarters Agreement the only international instrument, aside from the general terms of the Charter, binding the United States in this respect.

The International Organizations Immunities Act of 1945[12] therefore becomes important. This Act was adopted by Congress to take care of the situation until the international agreements had been made, and its provisions do this generously enough. It must be kept in

[11] Adopted October 31, 1947; attached to Resolution 169 (II).

[12] Public Law 291, 79th Cong., 1st Sess. May be found in Senate Doc. No. 87, 83rd Cong., 2nd Sess: *Review of the United Nations Charter, A Collection of Documents*, p. 93.

mind, however, that it is a national statute, which can be repealed or modified by Congress; and that it gives to the President the right to designate the international organizations entitled to rights under its terms. This, from the viewpoint of the United Nations, is an insufficient guarantee of its independence of action and of the freedom of its officials to carry on its work.

There are other instruments which affect the relationship between the United States and the United Nations; some of these will be indicated in the following pages. Experience since they were adopted suggests that some improvement might be made by combining them all, revised and integrated, into one instrument. Such an effort, however, might be dangerous; in the current wave of nationalism, it might not be possible to achieve even so inadequate a system for protection of the independence of the United Nations as now exists; the example set by the United States on the plea of national security might well be extended by other states. At the least, however, the United States should ratify the General Convention on Privileges and Immunities, even with reservations, if it could not be done without them.

PRIVILEGES AND IMMUNITIES

By customary international law, a wide range of privileges and immunities are allowed to the diplomatic representatives of sovereign states. These were originally connected with the person of the sovereign, but the trend has been to limit them to those necessary for the performance of the functions of representation of the interests of the states. This principle was clearly stated, and carried somewhat further, in the Charter of the United Nations. There are, however, gaps and overlapping between the instruments above noted which give rise to some uncertainty.

Delegates. According to Section 16 of the General Convention, the expression "Representatives of Members" includes "all delegates, deputy delegates, advisers, technical experts and secretaries of delegations." The privileges and immunities accorded to them by Section 11 of the Convention are:

(a) immunity from personal arrest or detention and from seizure of their personal baggage, and, in respect of words spoken or written and all acts done by them in their capacity as representatives, immunity from legal process of every kind.

(b) inviolability for all papers and documents;

(c) the right to use codes and to receive papers or correspondence by courier or in sealed bags;

(d) exemption in respect of themselves and their spouses from immigration restrictions, aliens registration or national service obligations in the State they are visiting or through which they are passing in the exercise of their functions;

(e) the same facilities in respect of currency or exchange restrictions as are accorded to representatives of foreign governments on temporary official missions;

(f) the same immunities and facilities in respect of their personal baggage as are accorded to diplomatic envoys, and also;

(g) such other privileges, facilities and immunities, not inconsistent with the foregoing, as diplomatic envoys enjoy, except that they shall have no right to claim exemption from customs duties on goods imported (otherwise than as part of their personal baggage) or from excise duties or sales taxes.

These rights are accorded "while exercising their functions and during their journey to and from the place of meeting," to Representatives of Members to the principal and subsidiary organs of the United Nations, and to conferences convened by the United Nations. They may be waived, and according to Section 14 they should be waived, by the Government of the Representative in any case in which immunity would impede the course of justice; since the immunity is granted not for the personal benefit of the individual but to safeguard the independent exercise of his functions, he should be allowed to claim immunity only where this independence would be prejudiced.

While the wording and principles stated in the General Convention manifestly are intended to set some limitations upon immunities, and specifically do so in some instances (e.g. excise and sales taxes), Subsection (g) of Section 11 leaves some uncertainty as to the extent of the difference between the usual privileges and immunities of an ambassador and those of the Representative of a Member State, who may in fact have the title of ambassador. This uncertainty is heightened by the terms of the Headquarters Agreement which of course is binding only for the United States and for the Headquarters area, but, on the other hand, sets forth rights to be accorded to delegates in that area. Section 15 lists those entitled to these rights; (1) the principal permanent representative to the United Nations (does this mean, to any organ?) or a permanent representative given by the Member

the rank of ambassador or minister plenipotentiary; (2) such resident members of their staffs as may be agreed upon between the
Secretary-General, the Government of the United States, and the
government of the Member concerned; (3) the principal permanent
representative of a member of a specialized agency with the rank of
ambassador or minister plentipotentiary at the headquarters of such
an agency in the United States; (4) other principal permanent
representatives of members of such specialized agencies and resident
members of the staffs thereof as may be agreed upon between the
executive officer of the agency, the Government of the United States,
and the Government of the Member concerned.

These persons are entitled in the territory of the United States "to
the same privileges and immunities, subject to corresponding conditions and obligations as it accords to diplomatic envoys accredited
to it" (Section 15). Similarly, the International Organizations Immunities Act mentioned above provides that such persons, insofar as concerns laws "regulating entry into and departure from the United
States, alien registration and fingerprinting, and the registration of
foreign agents" shall be entitiled to "the same privileges, exemptions
and immunities as are accorded under similar circumstances to officers
and employees, respectively, of foreign governments, and members of
their families." Also "Representatives of foreign governments in or to
international organizations and officers and employees of such organizations shall be immune from suit and legal process relating to acts
performed by them in their official capacity and falling within their
functions as such representatives, officers or employees, except insofar
as such immunity may be waived by the foreign government or international organization concerned." (Section 7).[13]

Thus, there are discrepancies as to privileges and immunities in
the three principal documents dealing with them. The Headquarters
Agreement apparently gives to delegates the rights accorded by
customary international law to diplomats; the General Convention
limits these somewhat; the International Organizations Immunities
Act leaves much control over them to the United States. This control
is checked by the Headquarters Agreement, but not by the General
Convention, which has not been ratified by the United States.

[13] However, as was noted above, Congress may modify this law; the President
may designate such organizations as he chooses to benefit from it; and the Secretary of State may (Section 8) deprive an organization of the benefits of the law.

In the usual practice of diplomatic intercourse between states, the receiving state has the opportunity, through *agréation* or otherwise, to refuse to receive a diplomatic agent sent to it, and, on the other hand, to declare *persona non grata* such an agent already received by it and to require him to leave his position. Such freedom, obviously, could not be allowed to the United States in regard to persons coming to the United Nations; if so, that Organization could be hindered or blocked in its work and could not claim independence. The obligation of the United States to receive these representatives extends to states not recognized by the United States, though they may be limited to the headquarters area and transit to and from it (Section 15 of the Headquarters Agreement).

The United Nations itself, though recognized as an international legal person, is not equipped or authorized to send or receive diplomatic persons. The Secretary-General may ceremoniously receive newly accredited delegates, but the United Nations has no executive head and no foreign office which can officially accept as the legally constituted representative of a Member a person sent by that Member; nor can it refuse to receive such a person. In practice, his credentials are examined by the Secretary-General who reports to the organ concerned; if there is a question concerning them, decision is made by that organ; there is no central office which can accept credentials for a representative to all organs of the United Nations. It will be recalled that the question of the representation of Communist China has been raised over and over again in each organ and sub organ. There is no present way by which the United Nations can decide this question for all organs. Provision is made in the General Convention for the protection of UN officials in various signatory countries, and for a *laissez-passer*, which is as near to a passport as the United Nations can issue; but it is only in exceptional cases recognized by Member States.[14]

Secretariat. The privileges and immunities of the staff of the United Nations are stated in the General Convention on Privileges and Immunities, not ratified by the United States. Under its terms, the Secretary-General and the Assistant Secretaries-General, with their spouses and minor children, were given the same status as diplomatic

---

[14] See Michael Brandon, "The United Nations *Laissez-Passer*," in 1950 British Yearbook of International Law, p. 448. Pakistan and the United Kingdom waive requirement of a visa for holders of a *laissez-passer*.

envoys, under international law. With the exception of these high-ranking officials—who seem to be given even more status than the representatives of Members—one can hardly speak of "diplomatic privileges and immunities" for the staff. The other members of the staff, excepting those recruited locally and paid by the hour, were by General Assembly Resolution 76 (I) given the privileges and immunities stated in Articles V and VII of the General Convention, limited in general to those needed for the performance of their official functions, including immunity from national taxation and national service. The influence of the United Nations has been toward reducing diplomatic immunities. The staff is aware that they are not entitled to speed or park in the wrong place.[15]

Under the Headquarters Agreement, to which the United States is a party, the headquarters area and persons therein are given immunity against official action by an agent of the United States, but the laws of the United States apply therein except insofar as superseded by a United Nations regulation made under Section 8 of the Agreement, and the courts of the United States have jurisdiction over illegal acts committed therein, when the matter is turned over to them by the United Nations.

The United States is given protection against persons, whether officials or delegates, who abuse their privileges of residence. Section 13 provides that no such person can be expelled from the United States except with the prior approval of the Secretary of State, who must consult with the Secretary-General or with the state concerned. In case of dispute, the matter is to be referred to arbitration. No dispute has gone so far; though, as will be seen below, there was some controversy, resulting in an agreed statement of principles. There have been a number of cases in which persons were not allowed to stay in the United States. Doubtless the best known of these was the case of Gubichev, who was accused of spying. The United Nations suspended him, saying that he had no immunity except for his official functions. And members of the Soviet delegation who attempted to repatriate five defecting seamen were withdrawn in response to representations by the United States.

[15] There have been surprisingly few cases involving the status of staff members. The first of these involved the Secretary-General himself, *Westchester County v. Ranallo*, 187 Misc. 777, NYS 2nd 31. In a later case, *Curran v. City of New York*, 119 NYLJ 16, it was held that the Secretary-General was immune from legal process.

ACCESS

Mention has been made above of Sections 11 to 13 of the Headquarters Agreement, and closer attention must be given to them in connection with the persons who are entitled to come and depart from the United Nations headquarters, and the rights given to them.

Five categories of persons are specified, in Section 11, concerning whom the United States "shall not impose any impediments to transit to or from the headquarters district":

1. Representatives of Members or officials of the United Nations, or of specialized agencies as defined in Article 57, paragraph 2, of the Charter, or the families of such representatives or officials;
2. Experts performing missions for the United Nations or for such specialized agencies;
3. Representatives of the Press, or of radio, film or other information agencies, who have been accredited by the United Nations (or by such a specialized agency) in its discretion after consultation with the United States;
4. Representatives of non-governmental organizations recognized by the United Nations for the purpose of consultation under Article 71 of the Charter; or
5. Other persons invited to the headquarters district by the United Nations or by such specialized agency on official business.[16]

It was intended by this text that the United Nations should be safeguarded against interference by the host state with transit to and from the United Nations of persons having business with that Organization. Difficulties with the United States have nevertheless arisen. The external danger from Communism was blown up into an irrational fear that some Communists might be able to enter the United States under cover of business with the United Nations. This national emotion facilitated adoption of the McCarran Act, which set severe restrictions upon entry into this country, some of which affected UN personnel. That Act is now being reconsidered by Congress which should not overlook its effect on United States obligations to the United Nations. By the McCarran Act,

---

[16] By Section 14, the Secretary-General shall confer with American authorities "as to methods of facilitating entrance into the United States . . . by persons coming from abroad who wish to visit the Headquarters District and do not enjoy the rights referred to" in Article IV.

subordinate consular officials are authorized to deny visas, and have apparently been afraid not to do so, in the case of persons suspected of Communist sympathies; and immigration officials have felt it their duty to refuse admission to such a person, even though he had a visa. In the exercise of these functions some persons were held up who, under the fourth of the five categories above listed, had a right to come to the United Nations.

In September 1950, a Frenchman named Fischer, representing the World Federation of Trade Unions, a Communist-dominated Non-Governmental Organization of Category A, was held on Ellis Island for three days, though he had a visa from the United States Embassy in France, and was then sent back.[17]

Complaints concerning the treatment of Fischer were made by the Soviet bloc, and the Economic and Social Council (to which non-governmental organizations are accredited by Resolution 340 A (VI) asked the Secretary-General to report on negotiations with the United States. The position taken by the United States was that she was obligated to admit NGO persons to the Economic and Social Council only, and this only after there was mutual agreement as to the purpose for which they came.[18] This disagreement was sought to be resolved by Resolution 606 (VI), adopted by the General Assembly, which authorized NGO representatives to attend meetings of the Assembly at which economic and social matters were discussed.

A number of cases were complained of at meetings, the most shocking being that of Mrs. Alva Myrdal, formerly Director of the Social Affairs Department of the United Nations, and at the time holding a similar post with UNESCO. She was on an official visit to the United Nations, and had a properly issued visa from the embassy in Paris, but when she arrived she was detained by immigration authorities and not allowed to leave until she had been given a "parole".[19] The delegate of Sweden protested against this failure on the part of the United States to observe its obligations, and later announced that the United States regarded her as *persona grata*; but

[17] There were early cases involving foreign press representatives, and there have been others, such as Reverend Michael Scott, who have been restricted to definite areas. No effort is made to cover all the cases of this type; indeed, full information is not available. See "Obligations of the United States to United Nations Persons," Proceedings of the *American Society of International Law*, 1954, p. 172 ff.

[18] UN Doc. E/1862; E/1921; *Repertory*, Vol. V. p. 343.

[19] A term usually relating to captives or criminals.

the United States itself has never issued an explanation concerning this incident.

The cases of Dessau and Luccock, who were refused visas to attend the fifteenth session of the Economic and Social Council, led that body to seek an explanation from the United States, and it replied that it had been found necessary to invoke Section 6 of the Joint Resolution by which Congress had authorized entry into the Headquarters Agreement.[20] This Resolution included the following statement:

Nothing in the agreement shall be construed as in any way diminishing, abridging or weakening the right of the United States to safeguard its own security and completely to control the entrance of aliens into any territory of the United States other than the headquarters district . . . and such areas as it is reasonably necessary to traverse in transit between the same and foreign countries . . .

The Secretary-General replied on April 10, 1953 with a memorandum[21] from the Legal Department which denied that this statement constituted a reservation to the Headquarters Agreement, as claimed by the United States, and maintained that the United Nations would not, even if it were a reservation, be bound by it, since it had never been accepted by the United Nations; and that in any case, the words quoted applied only to areas outside the district. In case of continuing disagreement, the Memorandum pointed out, the United States was obligated to arbitrate. However, negotiations were undertaken and at the 743rd meeting of the Economic and Social Council, Secretary-General Hammarskjold reported that a procedure had been established, based upon three principles: decisions by the United States would be taken at the highest level; they would be taken in time for the United Nations to give consideration to the matter; and the Secretary-General would be supplied to the fullest extent with information and evidence. Later, he supplied the Council with a progress report[22] which enumerated rights agreed upon as follows:

(1) The Headquarters Agreement should not be allowed to be used in such a way that persons could engage in activities outside their official functions:

(2) subject to the purpose of the Headquarters Agreement, the United

---

[20] Public Law 357, 80th Congress. The statement of the United States Representative, Mr. Wadsworth, is found in UN Doc. E/SR. 679.

[21] Doc. No. 2397.

[22] E/2492; see also E/2501.

States could grant visas valid only for transit to and from the head-quarters district and sojourn in its immediate vicinity; it could make any reasonable definition of "immediate vicinity," of the necessary routes of transit, and of the time and manner of expiration of the visa following the completion of official business; and it could carry out deportation proceedings against persons who abused the privilege of residence by engaging in activities in the United States outside their official capacity;

(3) in the case of aliens in transit to the headquarters district exclusively on official business of, or before the United Nations, the rights of the United States were limited by the Headquarters Agreement to those mentioned.

The United States has also denied passports to some of its citizens working for or with the United Nations to attend meetings abroad. Miss Ursula Wassermann, in the Secretariat, was denied a passport to attend a meeting in Geneva, though a compromise was effected through which she was allowed to go on a United Nations *laissez-passer*. Miss Elinor Kahn, representing an NGO (World Federation of Trade Unions) had her passport recalled and was unable to attend a meeting of the Economic and Social Council in Geneva.[23] These denials in reverse of right of access, though less apt to occur, would seem to be as clearly as those above an unwarranted interference by the United States with the work of the United Nations.

Such incidents as these demonstrate the need for clear statement of the rights of UN persons in relation to the host state. Most of the difficulties with regard to access to the United Nations have been the result of the emotional wave of American dislike and fear of Communism in the United States. As this outcry has died down, American officials have not felt so pressed to pursue persons connected with the United Nations.[24] It is to be hoped that clear understanding has been reached; on that assumption it might be felt that the episode, unpleasant as it was, did good in clarifying some of the obligations of the United States to the United Nations.

Access, however, is not merely a matter of the host state, and there have been other instances in which states have denied entrance to United Nations officials. Albania, Bulgaria, and Yugoslavia refused admission to the Balkan Commission during the Greek frontier

---

[23] See stories by Peter Kihss in the New York *Herald-Tribune*, August 22, 1948, and July 5, 1951.

[24] Though in 1956 a representative of WFTU to ECOSOC was denied a visa until too late to attend the session.

troubles; the Soviet Union denied access to North Korea, South Africa refused to admit a UN Committee; more recently, access to Hungary was denied to the Secretary-General; access to Egypt had to await permission from President Nasser; Israel asserted that it would not admit the UN Emergency Force in its territory; and India, that a UN force would not be admitted to what it alleges to be its territory.

It is of course true that there is no definite statement—such as those in the Headquarters Agreement—providing for access of United Nations officials into Member States. The Charter does, however, give authority to the Security Council to undertake investigations (Article 34) and the right of the Secretary-General to conduct his own investigation has been conceded. The Convention on Privileges and Immunities provides (Section 9) for UN communications in each Member State as favorable as that given the diplomatic mission to any state; and gives to its officials and experts on mission certain immunities in each Member State. (Articles V and VI.)

The value of such provisions and the effective performance of functions are much lessened by the alleged right, currently asserted, of each state to deny admission to the United Nations officials. While it is true that no state can demand of another state admission of diplomatic agents into the latter state, the United Nations stands on quite a different relationship with its Members. It is implicit in the Charter, and in other instruments, that Members should receive and cooperate with the officials of the United Nations; but in practice this right is sometimes denied, and the United Nations makes an arrangement for each such visit, or for attendance at a United Nations conference held elsewhere than at Headquarters.[25]

The question of access to, or representation of the United Nations in, Member States, is a different question from that of privileges and immunities. The latter are fairly well provided for, though in fact they depend upon the former. The activities of the United Nations will increasingly require representation, even permanent offices, in Member States; examples may now be found, such as information offices or the resident representatives for technical assistance. A right of access is important into Member States as well as to Headquarters in New York or Geneva.

It is not an unrelated or distant consideration that there should be more assurance of free exchange of knowledge among Members.

[25] See examples in ST/LEG/2.

The objectives of the United Nations can hardly be achieved if its experts can be denied admission by a Member because of his political beliefs.

The Problem of Loyalty

The emotional wave in the United States which produced the difficulties concerning access to the United Nations led also to efforts to interfere with officials of the United Nations who happened to be nationals of the United States. Article 100 of the Charter obligates the Secretary-General and staff not to "seek or receive instructions from any government or from any other authority external to the Organization"; and the Member governments are correspondingly bound, by the second paragraph of this Article, "to respect the exclusively international character of the responsibilities of the Secretary-General and the staff and not to seek to influence them in the discharge of their responsibilities."

These words of the Charter do not deprive a staff member of his national character and allegiance, but they do create for him two loyalties, and, while the boundary line between them would ordinarily be clear, he may occasionally have difficulty in choosing between them. We have noted above the problems of income taxation and national military service. The state to which the staff member belongs has a right to exercise jurisdiction over him for national purposes, but may not interfere with him in the discharge of his functions as an official of the United Nations. There is little doubt that those who made the Charter intended that, where conflict might arise between the duties of a staff member to the United Nations and his duties to his own country, his international duty must prevail.[26] The possibility of such a conflict is perhaps greater in the host country, which may for various reasons, including national security, be concerned with the activities of its own nationals in the Organization.

Share in Appointment

It was not intended that any Member State should choose, or influence the choice by the Secretary-General of, its nationals who might hold posts in the Secretariat. A Yugoslav proposal to that effect was defeated by the Preparatory Commission of the United

[26] Schwebel, loc. cit., pp. 98-100, who quotes the French delegate to the effect that the staff member must resign if he is unwilling to do this. The situation could rarely arise—e.g. if his State were determined to be an aggressor.

Nations (1945). When a Communist regime took over in Czecho-slovakia and sought to oust officials of Czech nationality in the Secretariat as "unfriendly" to their country, Secretary-General Lie firmly rejected the suggestion. Secretary of State Byrnes refused to supply information concerning United States applicants for jobs in the United Nations for fear of interfering with the independence of the Secretary-General. In practice, however, the Secretary-General may find it difficult to obtain information concerning an applicant (e.g. his police record) except through his government. In 1949, the Department of State, at the request of Mr. Lie, agreed to furnish information, not as to professional ability, but as to political behavior which might make the candidate a poor risk as an international civil servant. What was furnished to Mr. Lie was not information, but conclusions; and he complained that these were sometimes furnished to him in a single word, and with no evidence to enable him to reach a judgment.[27]

The purpose of the United States was not to help the United Nations to find capable employees, but to ferret out persons sus-pected of Communist sympathies, a procedure which does not seem to harmonize with the obligation in Article 100 of the Charter to "respect the exclusively international character of the responsibilities of the Secretary-General." The pressure by the United States in this respect put the Secretary-General in an embarrassing position. He could not consistently exclude a person for Communist sympathies when his staff contained Communists from Communist Members, but the pressure upon him was steadily increased. A Federal Grand Jury in New York in 1952 informed the world, without evidence to support the charge, that there was in the United Nations "an over-whelmingly large group of disloyal American citizens," a "menace to the United States." In 1953, Senator McCarran proposed a bill, fortunately never adopted as law, which would have penalized heavily any American citizen who took a post with the United Nations

---

[27] See UN Doc. PC/AC/54; PC/AB/66; Hearings before the Sub-Committee to Investigate the Administration of the Internal Security Act and other Security Laws, on Activities of United States Citizens Employed by the United Nations, 82nd Cong., 2nd Sess., Pt. I., p. 414 and 415. The views of the Secretary-General were stated in the Report of the Secretary-General on Personnel Policy (UN Doc. A/2364) and at the 413th meeting of the General Assembly.

On the general question, see also "Obligations of the United States to United Nations Persons," Report of the Committee for Study of the Legal Problems of the United Nations, Proceedings of the American Society of International Law, 1954, p. 164; Schwebel, as cited above, and citations therein.

unless he had been cleared by the Attorney-General of the United States. It was said that this bill was not intended to interfere with the discretion of the Secretary-General, but it would manifestly have delayed and limited his choice of applicants.

The Secretary-General discharged a number of United States nationals from the Secretariat, in most cases because they had invoked the Fifth Amendment before United States investigative organs which had questioned them concerning their possible Communist associations or subversive activities. They appealed to the Administrative Tribunal of the United Nations which sustained some of them who held permanent contracts, and awarded some $180,000 in total to them. This award outraged certain elements of opinion in the United States, and objections were raised in Congress to the use of American funds for the payment of these awards. The delegation of the United States to the United Nations felt constrained to ask the General Assembly to review the awards. Most delegations did not sympathize with this request, but they were reluctant to antagonize the United States. A way out was found by asking the International Court of Justice whether the General Assembly had the right to refuse to give effect to an award of compensation by the Tribunal. The Court replied that the Assembly had no such right and that the decision of the Administrative Tribunal was final and without appeal.[28]

The United States, still ruffled, asked the General Assembly to change the Statute of the Administrative Tribunal so that an appeal could be taken from the Administrative Tribunal. This the Assembly did in Resolution 957 (X), which set up a committee of the General Assembly empowered to investigate such appeals and to request an advisory opinion from the Court in cases in which it felt such a course justified.

CONCLUSIONS

The above survey demonstrates the need for definite legal statement of the rights of the United Nations in the host country. The failure of the United States to ratify the General Convention on Privileges and Immunities leaves this need unsatisfied, the more so that this Convention was intended to be complementary to the Headquarters Agreement. There may have been some reasonable cause for the hesitation of the United States to ratify the Convention,

[28] I.C.J. Reports, 1954, p. 47, 62.

but it is more difficult to find excuse for the ten-year delay in seeking adjustment which would facilitate ratification. Experience accumulated in those ten years suggests that it might be desirable to combine the various existent agreements into one uniform system, but in the present international situation, and in the wave of extreme nationalism which characterizes it, it is not recommended that the attempt should be made. The United States, however, should ratify the General Convention, even if it is necessary to attach reservations to this acceptance.

Some attention needs to be given to the diplomatic credentials of delegates to the United Nations. Section 15 of the Headquarters Agreement contemplates the rank of ambassador for permanent representatives to the United Nations. It has usually been held, in diplomatic practice, that a state may confer the rank of ambassador (or other diplomatic rank) upon a person, but that the receiving state may accept or reject him; his status depends upon both states. When a delegate is given the title of ambassador, however, there is no receiving state, unless the United Nations or the United States may be so regarded, and neither would seem to fit the role. Does the mere fact that the sending state has given to its delegate credentials as an ambassador require the United States, or the United Nations —or, for that matter, any state—to accept him as such? Is he thereby lifted from the provisions of the Headquarters Agreement or the General Convention and made entitled to treatment as an ambassador under general international law? There is a connection between this problem and that of the way in which the United Nations handles the credentials of its delegates, a problem which has never been solved.

The diplomatic status of the Secretary-General and the agents whom he sends abroad equally deserve study. It is surprising to find that the protocol list, in which the Department of State establishes precedence for ceremonious occasions, puts the Secretary-General far down the list; surely his status entitles him to rank at the very least with Ambassadors. Diplomatic status is given to him and the Assistant Secretaries-General—a title now abolished—but there is no provision enabling such status to be given by him to his representatives sent to various countries.

The emotional wave in the United States led to actions in the name of national security which injured the United Nations and did much more injury to the good name of the United States. It is of the greatest importance to the United Nations that access to it should not be prevented or embarrassed; and no one state, not even the host state, can be permitted to interfere with those who with proper reason wish to come to it. The methods employed by the United States to deny entry to certain suspected persons have, perhaps, been within the letter of law, but they were undoubtedly contrary to the spirit of the Charter and the Headquarters Agreement and inimical to the United Nations. At times the methods employed by the United States seem to have been characterized by childish petulance. The investigations of Americans employed in the Secretariat undoubtedly affected the independence and morale of that organ and were regarded by many as contrary to the obligations of the United States under the Charter. Reluctance to submit to the decision of the Administrative Tribunal and subsequent efforts to limit it tried the patience of our friends in other delegations.

Worse than the actions themselves was the procedure which, in un-American, arbitrary fashion, offered no evidence and made no explanation for the stopping of an entrant, even with a visa, or for a derogatory report to the Secretary-General concerning an American. Democracy, in its fight against totalitarianism, cannot afford to gain the reputation of being arbitrary itself. To overcome the reputation acquired through these episodes requires abandonment of such methods and a more sincere and mature attitude on the part of the host state.

It appears that working arrangements have been made between the United Nations and the United States through which the two situations have been brought under more satisfactory control. A great deal remains to be done in removing impediments, such as certain provisions of the McCarran Act or of regulations and procedures concerning loyalty tests. To insist that the United States must "clear" any American for work in the United Nations, or be able to bar access to a foreigner whose political views are distrusted by the United States, is to detract from the independence of the Secretary-General, his staff, and the United Nations as an institution.

CLYDE EAGLETON, CHAIRMAN
EUNICE H. CARTER
J. EUGENE HARLEY
PETER KIHSS
STEPHEN M. SCHWEBEL

III

Development of International Cooperation

7 REGULATION OF INTERNATIONAL COMMERCE

INTRODUCTION

The general purpose of this report is to examine those activities of the United Nations and the specialized agencies that are concerned with economic problems other than those that are most directly related to economic development. This area includes questions of commercial policy, monetary policy, and transportation and communications. The report also considers the effectiveness of the United Nations organizational structure to deal with these questions.

FUNDAMENTAL ASSUMPTIONS

There are three main assumptions that have guided the Committee's deliberations. The first is that the major economic and social goals of the United Nations and the United States remain, in the words of the Charter, "higher standards of living, full employment, and conditions of economic and social progress and development." The second is that the achievement of these objectives requires maximum coordination of national policies on a universal basis. Finally, it is believed that, although there is no simple or generally accepted formula for determining the pace, direction, or financing of this economic development, the process by which such a formula is devised should be as broadly cooperative as possible.

COMMERCIAL POLICY

A Glance at the Past

The development of postwar trade policy has been dominated from the beginning by the interests and plans of the most powerful trading nation, the United States. Briefly put, the initial plan of the United States was to commit all of the major trading nations, and particularly the United Kingdom, to accept the general objective of a progressive approach towards freer trade and to seek that ideal by means of mutual trade concessions based on the United States tradition of the reciprocal trade agreements program which had been launched in 1934 under the leadership of Cordell Hull. The fact that this plan remains only partially fulfilled is due to a number of circumstances, the most significant of which would appear to be the unexpected magnitude and difficulty of the reconstruction process, the growing reluctance of both business and labor leadership within the United States to give full support to the plans of its government, the age-old desire of underdeveloped countries to ultilize trade barriers to shelter the growth of "infant" industries, and certain short-term economic and political crises, particularly the Korean conflict, that have had the effect of reinforcing protectionist sentiments.

Those trade concessions that have been achieved have been negotiated chiefly within the framework of the General Agreement on Tariffs and Trade (GATT), and the Organization for European Economic Cooperation (OEEC). This report will focus primarily on the former which is most closely associated with the United Nations. The GATT is an agreement that was negotiated in 1947 both to approve a large number of immediate trade concessions and to obligate its signatories to accept certain long-range principles and procedures in the interest of freer trade that were expected to be organized eventually under the proposed International Trade Organization. Because the latter has never been approved, the signatories of the GATT have resorted to maintaining and strengthening that instrumentality in an attempt to fill the vacuum.

Since the first negotiations in 1947, there have been several tariff negotiating sessions that have resulted in substantial concessions on approximately 60,000 items or about 60 per cent of the world's trade. As a result, the United States tariff level of 1945 has been reduced by approximately one-third. Other functions that have been performed during the periodic meetings of the parties to the GATT have included: the hearing and voluntary settlement of trade disputes, the negotiation of waivers regarding the commitments of various members under the GATT, efforts to reduce trade barriers that have been erected as a consequence of balance-of-payments difficulties, the encouragement of customs simplification, and the general discussion of mutual trade problems.

Because the GATT has developed as the principal center for trade negotiations, the economic bodies of the United Nations have played a rather modest role in this field. Nonetheless, debates in the Economic and Social Council have explored certain commercial policy questions, particularly in relation to economic development, commodity problems, and East-West relations. The regional commissions have devoted considerable attention to the trade problems of their areas. The Economic Commission for Europe, for example, has taken the lead in examining the possibility of increasing East-West trade. The United States has participated in these efforts but has seldom encouraged the active intervention of the UN and its various economic commissions in this area.

Recommendations for the Future

Major premises governing this analysis. The most fundamental premise that deserves special and continuing emphasis is that the trade policies of the United States should be measured ultimately not by the yardsticks of well-worn and emotionally charged arguments for and against "free trade" but by their contribution to the principal objectives of United States policy: the promotion of the security, well-being, and democratic processes of the American people. If United States policies do not serve these ends, they should be revised in that direction even though such revision may tread on the toes of the hallowed theories of either the "reductionist" or "protectionist" variety. Every critic or defender of United States policy should be challenged to justify his views in terms of these larger objectives rather than in terms of narrow considerations of immediate profit or loss.

A second assumption underlying this analysis deals with the relation between commercial policy and the first broad objective of the American people: security. This consideration has frequently been used to justify a protectionist policy on the ground that tariffs and other trade barriers build a dike that shelters our essential enterprises from the ruinous ravages of international competition and makes us less dependent upon external suppliers and customers who may be separated from us in time of crisis. It is the position of this Committee, however, that such arguments often go to extremes in coddling industries that may not be absolutely essential or, if they are, might be stronger if they were left to fend for themselves against all reasonable competition. The more highly and complexly developed the world becomes, the more impossible it is to think in terms of anything approaching autarky in either war or peace. Rather our basic concern should be to develop the most productive and stable economy possible, which requires world-wide cooperation—not isolation. We should also assist our allies to maintain equally efficient and healthy economies.

To the extent that some protection seems feasible and necessary, it should be restricted to only those enterprises that appear to be absolutely essential in time of war and that could not be quickly strengthened during a period of crisis. The weight of expert opinion, moreover, tends to favor some form of preference other than tariffs, subsidies for example, that can be applied more selectively and the effect of which is more likely to be carefully watched and reviewed.

A third assumption is that international trade is a necessary and important means of achieving another of the basic objectives of United States foreign policy: the promotion of the economic and social well-being of the American people. Trade across national boundaries, as well as within them, is the blood stream of the world's economy whereby raw materials and finished goods may move from supplier to customer according to the principle of comparative advantage, encouraging each individual and community to supply what it is best equipped to supply and to consume what best meets its needs, regardless of origin. This world-wide commerce heightens productivity and thereby can help to increase the world's standards of living.

The contribution of international trade to the promotion of democratic processes, the third major objective mentioned above, is simply that, by providing better material conditions, it furnishes the foundation for a healthier political life. History has demonstrated that democracy does not thrive in a climate of privation. Poverty is the parent of desperation and extremism, not restraint and compromise. A better standard of living may, of course, produce short-range tensions and is, even in the long run, no absolute guarantee of successful democracy. But it seems likely that improvements in living conditions should, under most circumstances, ultimately help to alleviate discontents and provide the leisure and cultural conditioning that seem to be essential ingredients of an effective democracy.

A final assumption underlying this analysis is that there are some arguments for the protection of United States suppliers that deserve serious consideration but that these positions justify the establishment or retention of tariffs less than they justify the use of other more effective devices such as the subsidies mentioned above. There is, for example, the fact that protective measures have assisted the economic development of some industries, including those of the United States, but there are also the dangers of over-protection, the favoring of enterprises that can never be expected to survive outside the hothouse of preferential assistance, and the continuation of aid long after a reasonable developmental period has elapsed. The thesis that justifies protection to assist essential defense industries has already been discussed. There is, however, no valid basis for the thesis that United States products must be protected against lower foreign labor and other costs since lower costs, regardless of the cause, are part of the competitive process and will benefit consumers at the same time that they injure some producers. The answer should be not to erect barriers against such competition but to strive to meet it, while taking care to eliminate practices that are generally recognized as unfair, or to transfer one's resources to other endeavors in which one has a comparative advantage.

Recommendations regarding future United States policy. In the light of the above assumptions, which argue for a policy aimed at freer trade as a major means of promoting the broad objectives of United States foreign policy, *it is recommended that the United States adopt a bolder and more consistent position in favor of freer commercial relations with the rest of the world, to be pursued primarily through the GATT and other world-wide multilateral arrangements.* Although the Commission is interested mainly in problems of international organization rather than national law it must recognize as a basic fact of life that American trade legislation determines the limits and establishes the form of international trade cooperation within the free world. The central element in the American trade policy is the Reciprocal Trade Agreements Act. The Act was first adopted in 1934. Since that time, revolutionary changes have taken place in the political and economic position of the United States as a member of the world community. The Act has not been altered

to take account of these changes; on the contrary it has been subjected to periodic amendments which have moved against rather
than with the current of world events and American needs. We
need nothing less than a thorough redrafting of the Act so that it can
become an effective instrument of international economic organization.

The following are some specific proposals for reform in the Trade
Agreements Act:

1) *Purpose.* The purpose now stated in the Act is to increase
American exports by offering reciprocal market opportunities in
the United States which do not injure American producers. The
President is bound to administer the Act within the framework of
this purpose; Congressional and public debate on the merits of the
legislation is also confined to this narrow statement of objective.
The stated purpose of the Act should be redrafted to include other
purposes of United States trade policy, viz.: (a) increasing the
real income of the American consumer; (b) reducing the United
States export surplus and the foreign-aid burden on the American
taxpayer; (c) assisting the repayment by foreign countries of
their private and public obligations to the United States; (d)
promoting United States foreign policy; and (e) protecting United
States security.

2) *Powers.* The President is presently very seriously restricted
in his authority to modify tariffs and other trade barriers. For
example, the President is authorized to act only pursuant to the
conclusion of a trade agreement. This rules out any unilateral
changes in American trade policy or even the making of such
changes in exchange for non-trade commitments on the part of
other countries. Moreover, the President is permitted to vary tariff
rates only by very small percentage amounts which are utterly inadequate as a basis for trade liberalization, and is prohibited
further from transferring items from the dutiable to the free list.
Consideration should be given to abolishing or at least modifying
substantially all of these limitations on the President's power.
Finally, the duration of the President's authority, presently limited
by short-term extensions of the Act, should be made indefinite or
at least much longer than the current three-year period. The
present system of short-term renewals puts an unnecessary burden
on the proponents of trade liberalization, facilitates the incorpora-

tion of crippling amendments, and causes uncertainty abroad.

3) *The Injury Exception.* The present Act provides by means of the "peril point" and "escape clause" provisions that the President's power shall not be employed when it will cause or threaten injury to a domestic industry. Consideration should be given to eliminating this qualification entirely and making the finding of injury the occasion, instead, for government assistance to domestic industries, workers, and communities adversely affected by exercise of the President's power.

Whether or not the "no injury" rule is replaced by a program of transitional assistance to injured interests, the present administration and definition of the injury concept should be reexamined. For example, the Tariff Commission should no longer be the government agency primarily concerned with administering the injury rule, and the definition of injury should be amended to exclude certain concepts now embodied in the Act or in Tariff Commission decisions, e.g., that injury consists in a decline in the share of the market enjoyed by a domestic producer and that injury exists by virtue of declining return in one line of production even though a producer can successfully shift to other lines.

4) *The Defense Exception.* The present Act requires the President to withdraw concessions and to refrain from making them in order to protect industries considered necessary for the national defense. This exception, recently incorporated in the Act, constitutes a serious threat to economic cooperation. Consideration should be given to eliminating the exception and devising alternative methods (such as subsidies and government contracts) of maintaining essential defense industries. As an alternative, consideration should be given to devising a more adequate definition of national defense interests (which takes into account the injury to national defense as well as any gain to national defense which results from trade restrictions) and also to devising more adequate procedures for making determinations in this area.

The United States should reverse its present policy of influencing other countries to impose "voluntary" export quotas. In recent months the United States Government has devised a new formula for protecting domestic producers from foreign competition without direct domestic legislation. This is the technique of "voluntary" export quotas accepted by certain exporting nations (such as Japan). In practice, these quotas are exacted from such countries under threat of direct United States import barriers and serve to save the Administration from the embarrassment of resorting to direct protection in possible violation of international agreements to which the United States is a party. This technique should be thoroughly condemned. It obstructs trade just as effectively as direct measures of protection and has the further disadvantage of derogating from the-most-favored-nation principle, since it affects selected countries in a manner that would be illegal under the GATT if accomplished by traditional measures of protection.

As part of a more liberal trade policy, the United States should approve the Agreement on an Organization for Trade Cooperation. This Agreement was negotiated during the Ninth Session of the Contracting Parties to the GATT which convened at Geneva, Switzerland, from October 1954 to March 1955. The Agreement provides for the establishment of the Organization for Trade Cooperation (OTC) as a permanent organization to facilitate the improvement of world commercial relations on a more continuing and efficient basis than in the past. The chief benefits to be gained by creating the OTC are to make it clear to the world that the United States is prepared to commit itself to a liberal trade policy on a long-range basis and to provide a permanent organization to oversee this aspect of international economic relations. Perhaps the most significant advance will be the creation of a permanent staff that can devote itself to the largely anonymous but all-important functions of research, recommendation, negotiation, and surveillance that are important, though little understood and appreciated, forces for the building of a true sense of world community. Failure to approve the Agreement will not simply run the risk of wrecking the OTC but may wreck the entire trade liberalization movement. President Eisenhower has warned, "Failure to assume membership in the OTC . . . could lead to the imposition of new trade restrictions on the part of other countries, which would result in a contraction of world trade and constitute a sharp setback to United States exports."[1]

The United States should also continue to encourage the closest possible coordination between the trade negotiations under the GATT and the activities of related specialized agencies and United

[1] Press Release, The White House, Augusta, Georgia, April 14, 1955, p. 4.

Nations bodies. There is particular need for a more intimate linking of policies between these trade efforts and the International Monetary Fund (IMF). It was originally intended that these two programs would be geared very closely together, but at times they have operated with all too little reference to each other. Probably the creation of the OTC will help to improve this situation.

It would also be helpful if the United States would use its influence to achieve a closer coordination between the trade deliberations under the GATT and those under the Economic and Social Council and its various commissions, especially the regional commissions. The regional commissions have become popular and important forums for discussing problems common to particular geographic areas, but they could be more vigorous in pursuing the objectives of the GATT and OTC.

MONETARY POLICY

One of the major innovations in postwar economic and social organization has been the establishment of a permanent and independent International Monetary Fund to facilitate world-wide cooperation on questions of monetary policy. The basic objectives of the Fund are to promote realistic and stable exchange rates, to eliminate exchange restrictions, and to help Member States correct maladjustments in their balance of payments without competitive depreciation and other destructive measures. In comparison with the feeble prewar international activities in the monetary field, the Fund is more authoritative, more widely representative, more fully staffed, and better financed. Yet there are still obvious shortcomings in its powers, organization, and performance. The following paragraphs briefly sketch the broad pattern of its development and suggest how it might be improved.

Record of the Fund

Because of the economic and financial crisis at the end of the Second World War, the Fund, with its limited scope, authority, and resources, was in no position to be a major factor in stemming the tide. The brunt of that task fell on the European Recovery Program. Nonetheless, the Fund's consultative function has been utilized constantly to exert the agency's influence in the direction of improving domestic monetary policies as the basis for sound exchange rates, greater stability of such rates, some adjustments in rates where they seemed appropriate, and opposition to multiple-rate systems and other payments restrictions. And, as the international monetary situation has improved since the earliest postwar years, the Fund has felt able to be more active in making its resources available to assist member states in coping with short-run monetary problems.

Proposals for the Future

The most fundamental recommendation for the future is that every effort should be made to pursue the same general course regarding monetary policy that has been suggested above for commercial policy: *eventually to establish a single international system of effective coordination and cooperation that will treat the international community as a unified whole.* If the world is ultimately to be thought of and to act as a single economic unit, its monetary relations should be treated in the same unitary spirit, together with all other aspects of economic activity. Again, this is a goal that will obviously be extremely difficult to achieve, but its validity seems unassailable.

A related but more immediate goal should be to *expand the resources of the International Monetary Fund so that it may have stronger financial backing to strengthen its influence.* Between the time of its establishment in 1946 and 1956, the Fund "sold" the equivalent of approximately $1.9 billion to member governments. This represents remarkable progress compared to international monetary activities before the Second World War, but the present IMF holdings of approximately $3.2 billion in convertible currencies and gold are not very large compared to what might be required in the event of a serious monetary crisis. It has been estimated that $10 billion might need to be drawn by all countries other than the United States in case of a two-year depression in the latter comparable to that of 1937-38 in order to maintain the flow of commodity exports from the United States.

In addition, the authority of the Fund should gradually be reinforced in harmony with the basic objective expressed above. More specifically the Fund should be accorded and allowed to exercise greater power in promoting healthier national monetary policies affecting the level and stability of exchange rates. To a great extent, this objective can be achieved by means of a liberal interpretation of the present Articles of Agreement, but there are limits to this procedure beyond which it will be necessary to contemplate fundamental constitutional changes.

Another desirable objective would be to *have the Fund approach more closely the pattern of operations of the European Payments Union, particularly in the direction of increased central coordination and greater automaticity in extending credit to help governments weather short-run monetary problems.* Admittedly this is more difficult to achieve on a world-wide scale than it is within a region such as Europe. Nonetheless, such a move would be a great boon to the international monetary system and, in conjunction with other economic advances, seems not to be beyond the realm of practicability. Of course, a shift of this kind would be related to the question of the size of the Fund's resources discussed above.

A final recommendation regarding the Fund is that *the operations of the Fund should be coordinated more closely with other universal and regional arrangements concerned with investment, commercial, monetary, and other economic policies.* In the immediate future, particular efforts should be made to establish closer links between the Fund, on the one hand, and the General Agreement on Tariffs and Trade and the European Payments Union, on the other.

TRANSPORTATION AND COMMUNICATIONS

In no field have technological developments since the Second World War brought nations into closer touch with each other and seemed to require more intimate international collaboration than in the area of transportation and communications. These developments, which have shrunk the world so dramatically, have given rise to some significant strides in the utilization of international organizations to help foster collaboration on a universal basis.

Yet it is all too evident that such international arrangements lag far behind the scientific progress that they are concerned with and that the world development of transportation and communications—despite its challenging potential—is still largely a captive of nationalism. National interests, policies, and institutions still dominate the scene. There is, nonetheless, a growing body of thought and action, associated particularly with the United Nations and the specialized agencies, that operates in terms of an emerging sense of identification with, and responsibility to, a community that is broader than any single nation.

The basic question to be dealt with in this section, as in the others, is: how should the United Nations and the specialized agencies be encouraged to develop their transportation and communications responsibilities in order to take maximum advantage of the potential in these fields? First, a brief background review assesses the general pattern of development since the Second World War. Second, some specific recommendations suggest possible improvements for the future.

Reflections on the Past

The general pattern of postwar international cooperation regarding transportation and communications has been characterized by considerable unevenness, decentralization, and regional emphasis, with primary attention devoted more to technical advancement than to questions of rates, routes, and other matters of substantial economic significance. The gaps in the structure and its strong centripetal tendencies are due, in part, to the fact that there was a long history of international collaboration in these fields before the Second World War which produced several institutions, including the Universal Postal Union and the International Telecommunication Union, that had an identity and tradition of their own and tended to resist any wholesale integration under the United Nations. There were, of course, additional factors that favored a considerable degree of decentralization, including the concept of the specialized agencies, patterned largely after the International Labor Organization and the United Nations Relief and Rehabilitation Administration, and the desire to make it possible for the Soviet Union to join the United Nations without having to participate in all of its economic and social activities.

Within the United Nations, the chief forum for attempting to deal with the total transportation and communications picture and to exert some mild coordinating influence with regard to the specialized agencies concerned with these subjects is the Transport and Communications Commission of the Economic and Social Council. The Commission performs its general directing and coordinating functions chiefly by reviewing the work of the other organizations and occasionally by issuing recommendations to them. Because there are not specialized agencies to deal with all aspects of this area, it is also necessary for the Commission to cover certain specific substantive fields, including problems of passport and frontier barriers as well as minor features of international road transport and shipping relations.

On the other hand, it has been agreed that conditions of inland transport—rail, water, and road—are so different in various parts of the world that these aspects should be dealt with chiefly by the regional economic commissions of the United Nations. The most active regional program has been the European one, but even there the Inland Transport Committee of the Economic Commission for Europe has been severely restricted by strong national governments and competing regional programs, including a European Conference of Ministers of Transport sponsored by the Organization for European Economic Cooperation.

The most significant specialized agency in the transport and communications field is the International Civil Aviation Organization (ICAO). Because air travel so frequently reaches beyond national and even regional boundaries and because there was some institutionalization of world-wide cooperation in this field before the Second World War, it seemed especially appropriate to deal with this area through a specialized agency of universal membership. Here, again, it has proved easiest to win agreement on so-called "navigation" matters (development and standardization of technical equipment and procedures) and most difficult on "transport" questions (rates, routes, volume, and general financial questions). Nonetheless, ICAO negotiations have been very useful in facilitating bilateral agreements in even the latter sphere and have helped to settle at least one major aviation dispute stemming from political tension between India and Pakistan. Moreover, ICAO has been an active participant in the Expanded Program of Technical Assistance.

It has proved particularly difficult to erect a comparable organization to oversee maritime shipping. Negotiations towards this end began as early as 1946 and resulted in the adoption in 1948 of a convention providing for an Inter-Governmental Maritime Consultative Organization. This convention had not yet gone into effect as of July 1, 1957, however, chiefly because of the refusal of various governments to limit their freedom of action on a variety of issues. To the extent that there is any significant international cooperation in this field, it is channeled primarily through the non-governmental organizations of private shipowners.

There are two venerable and relatively effective specialized agencies in the communication field: the International Telecommunication Union and the Universal Postal Union. The former has been utilized to foster cooperation in connection with radio, telegraphy, and telephony and, most notably, in facilitating a more satisfactory allocation of radio frequencies, which has proved to be a most arduous task. The Postal Union continues to perform its undramatic but essential function of supervising the international movement of mail with particular attention being devoted since the Second World War to the comparatively novel problems of air mail.

Recommendations

The governing assumption that lies at the base of the following recommendations is that the modes of travel and communication can best be developed when they are planned and administered as a single network embracing the entire earth. It is obvious, of course, that this objective cannot be gained easily or quickly in view of the patchwork of national institutions and vested interests that stand in the way and inevitably resist such change. Furthermore, even if events move in the desired direction, it is unrealistic to expect that integration can take place much faster in the fields of transport and communications than in other economic and social areas. Nonetheless, if the aim is sound, it must not be foresaken but must be steadfastly pursued by whatever method seems most practicable at the moment.

One step in the right direction would be to *utilize every means possible to encourage the maximum coordination of all governmental policies regarding transport and communications so that the world may be treated as a single unit for this purpose.* This means linking the United Nations and the specialized agencies more closely with other arrangements, including both private and public activities of both a national and regional character. Naturally, this will be extremely difficult because the most traditional and parochial arrangements are the most deep-rooted and widely supported. The minimum goal should be world-wide coordination under the United Nations by means of voluntary agreement.

A related and complementary recommendation is that *governments should make steadily increasing use of existing and future international arrangements by endowing them with greater authority and funds than they now enjoy.* More specifically, the participating governments, and particularly leading nations like the United States, should recognize, in keeping with the controlling premise set forth above, the desirability of authorizing organizations such as the International Civil Aviation Organization to make binding decisions on the most important, as well as the less important, questions. This might well include sensitive issues such as rates, routes, and volume. These organizations should also be utilized to a greater extent than at present to engage in direct operations including facilities such as airports, airlines, communications transmitting installations, and international highways, rail lines, and waterways. These operations should include an even greater volume of technical assistance to underdeveloped countries—a program which has proved to be one of the most constructive achievements of entities such as the International Civil Aviation Organization as well as specialized agencies in other fields of endeavor.

Still another objective should be to *fill certain gaps in the international apparatus that now exist so that all modes of transport and communications may be given adequate attention.* In the transport field, for example, there is only one active specialized agency, the International Civil Aviation Organization. International cooperation is noticeably weaker in the other transport fields, and what there is flows largely through bilateral and a few regional arrangements. A first step should be to strengthen United Nations and specialized agency activity in all of these fields by one means or another, including the establishment of the Inter-Governmental Maritime Consultative Organization. Subsequently, in keeping with the first recommendation above, the separate regulatory entities should be amalgamated into a single international commission, preferably within the framework of the United Nations. The nature of that commission will depend, in some measure, on the future evolution of the whole economic and social structure of the United Nations which is discussed below.

ORGANIZATION OF ECONOMIC ACTIVITIES

A major theme that dominated the planning of the organization of United Nations economic activities was the desire to separate these matters more sharply from the political sphere and to encourage them to develop more vigorously and independently than had been the case under the League of Nations. In many respects this effort was successful. The Economic and Social Council has given far greater and more sympathetic attention to economic issues than the League Council gave its technical committees. And most of the economic programs, particularly those of the specialized agencies, have enjoyed substantial freedom of action. Yet, in other respects, the Organization has failed to live up to the expectations of many of its architects. The following paragraphs will briefly review the general organizational pattern as it has evolved and recommend certain possible changes for the future.

Pattern of Organization

Although the United Nations structure to deal with economic problems owes a great deal to the inspiration and experience of the League of Nations, it also embodies many significant innovations. Put as briefly as possible, the major differences between the League and the United Nations in this respect are that the economic system of the latter is a far more prominent part of the structure than under the League, it is more clearly separated from the political arena (although that has not made it immune to political pressures), its membership contains a far greater and more influential representation of underdeveloped countries, the specialized agencies are more independent than were the technical committees, and all of these activities are better financed, more adequately staffed, and more oriented towards direct field operations than before.

Although these changes have produced important advances in international cooperation, there are still serious flaws in the system. One difficulty is that the independent status of the specialized agencies has, on occasion, been carried to aggravating extremes and has made it particularly difficult to formulate and administer an integrated technical assistance program. Another problem is that, perhaps because the less developed countries do not feel that they are adequately represented on the Economic and Social Council, they have frequently tried to bypass the Council, largely by resorting to the instrumentality of the General Assembly. Many of the commissions of the Council have also proved disappointing in their performance for a number of different reasons, including the inadequate caliber of some representatives, a lack of effective authority to get anything done, and the limiting effect of national instructions.

Recommendations

In order to ensure the most effective coordination among the various international economic programs, the specialized agencies

should be brought into closer relationship with the United Nations.
The closest bond would be that of complete integration. While this
is the logical goal to provide maximum unity of planning and operations, there are obvious practical difficulties that stand in the way.
Such a shift would require amending the constitution of each agency.
It would conflict with the traditional independence of these organizations and might expose them to even greater political tensions than
now afflict them. It might result in a reduction of support for some
of their programs and injure the morale of their staffs and constituents.
There would also be the problem of reconciling different memberships
and the regulations governing admission to membership. Because of
these and other difficulties progress towards this goal must necessarily
be slow and painful. Nonetheless, steps should be taken in this direction, initially through strengthening all available coordinating devices
and particularly through increased central control of funds and
programming.

*The Economic and Social Council can best be strengthened not
through any fundamental recasting of its structure and status but by
improving its internal procedures and the quality of representation.*
Specifically the Council should strive even more diligently than in the
past to free its agenda and deliberations of non-essential functions
and issues and to concentrate its business in such a way that cabinet
ministers and other high-level officials can attend its meetings to
deal with matters of concern to them. This calls for more effective
preparatory work, greater delegation of authority to the Secretary-
General and other agencies, and, most important, increased readiness
on the part of national governments to support and expedite the
work of the Council. In order to give more adequate representation to
the major groupings of Member States, some thought might also be
given to the possibility of increasing the size of the Council slightly,
perhaps to twenty-four, although it is already the largest of the UN
Councils, with a membership of eighteen.

*To expose the United Nations to the challenge of the most com-
petent and disinterested expertise available, the Organizations
should encourage increased utilization of independent experts as
distinguished from governmental representatives.* If scientific objectivity has any validity and utility, it should be given expression in
the deliberations of the United Nations as a means of countervailing
the vested interests of particular governments. It is, of course, neces-

sary ultimately to submit expert recommendations to governmental review and approval in order to win official support. This is the function of the Economic and Social Council and its commissions. At the same time, greater support should be given to the device calling upon independent experts, within or outside the Secretariat, to prepare advisory proposals that do not simply reflect the official views of some particular government or governments.

H. FIELD HAVILAND, JR., CHAIRMAN
RICHARD N. GARDNER
GEORGE L. RIDGEWAY
STEPHEN M. SCHWEBEL
AMOS E. TAYLOR

8 ECONOMIC DEVELOPMENT OF LESS DEVELOPED COUNTRIES

INTRODUCTION

The activities of the United Nations with regard to the economic development of underdeveloped areas are based on the Charter objective of promoting "conditions of economic and social progress and development." (Article 55) This objective is only one of a number of goals for international economic and social cooperation set forth in the Charter, all of which are designed "with a view to creation of conditions of stability and well-being which are necessary for peaceful and friendly relations among nations." (Article 55)

As matters have evolved over the past decade of experience, the economic development of underdeveloped areas has emerged as the major concern of the United Nations in the economic field. In part, this emphasis reflects the fact that another major problem—the much feared postwar depression—has not developed. Also responsible is the fact that under the one-member-one-vote system, the direction of United Nations discussions has been largely determined by the economically less developed countries, to which economic development has become an outstanding goal of national policy.

In considering the United Nations achievements in this field and how they might be enlarged it is well to bear in mind that the economic development of a country depends primarily on action taken by that country itself. At best the United Nations can only lend a helping hand. Its help can be along one or more of the following lines.

1) By bringing persons with different viewpoints and experiences

into active, creative contact with one another, the United Nations stimulates both the enlargement and the dissemination of knowledge and understanding of economic development and how to achieve it.

2) Through its recommendations for national action to promote economic development the United Nations strengthens the hands of political groups sponsoring such action within the different countries. This may be effective in promoting acceptance of appropriate policies both in the less developed countries and in the economically advanced countries whose cooperation is needed to make rapid development possible.

3) By sponsoring international agreements the United Nations can assist in freeing trade, stabilizing the markets for primary products, and otherwise promoting the economic well-being of underdeveloped countries and enlarging the resources available to them for development purposes.

4) By providing an instrumentality for channeling technical knowledge and capital from economically advanced to less developed countries the United Nations can directly aid economic development.

The United Nations has to its credit some very real achievements along all of the four lines just mentioned. Few persons, however, would contend that it has done all it might have done. Criticisms of its shortcomings should be tempered by recognition of the fact that the United Nations can do only what its Member States wish it to do and are prepared to support by necessary national action. In the economic field the United Nations does not have taxing power or police power,[1] much less the economic or military force to compel compliance with its economic decisions. While at some future time national states may grant an international organization such powers, it would be unrealistic for our Committee to consider the matter at the present time. For the foreseeable future the United Nations presents, at least in the economic field, an instrument for cooperating rather than for governing. Many criticisms of the United Nations for ineffectiveness in promoting economic development should be leveled instead at the Member States which have narrowly limited their cooperation.

In view of these limitations on United Nations action in promoting

---

[1] Except for the authority conferred by Article 41 on the Security Council to call on Members to take economic measures to enforce its decisions with respect to threats to the peace, breaches of the peace, and acts of aggression.

economic development, along what lines should efforts to enlarge and improve such action be taken? One way is to improve the effectiveness and efficiency with which the United Nations implements those measures on the desirability of which the Members are generally agreed. Another way is to seek out and eliminate any aspects of organization or procedure which have made Members unwilling to use the United Nations as an instrument for promoting economic development. Either may involve in a particular case a change in the Charter, a change in structure under the Charter, or only a change in the operation of the existing structure. These kinds of changes are not of equal difficulty to secure and other things being even approximately equal, the preference would be for the change that was easiest to make.

In the following paragraphs we examine a number of criticisms that have been made of United Nations action, or inaction, with respect to economic development, and analyze several proposals that have been made to increase the scope and effectiveness of such action.

CRITICISMS OF UNITED NATIONS ECONOMIC DEVELOPMENT ACTIVITIES

Criticisms of the United Nations work in the economic development field are directed against sins of commission, sins of omission, and the sin of waste.

With regard to sins of commission—of what has been done—in the economic development field, the criticisms are relatively few. In general, the resolutions that have been passed and the operations that have been undertaken have met with widespread approval, perhaps because little has been done in the absence of a large measure of agreement. The Soviet bloc has its own theories of economic development; it has disparaged some types of international action—for example, loans of the World Bank—and opposed others—for example, Secretariat activities in the tax and fiscal fields. Economically advanced countries have criticized some resolutions—for example, the so-called nationalization resolution passed in 1953. Some of the reports and resolutions of regional economic commissions also have been criticized. In the United States Congress some members have been very hostile to all steps taken toward the stabilization of the prices of primary commodities.

For the most part, the criticisms of the United Nations regarding its work in economic development have been directed not at what has been done but rather at what has not been done. The criticisms have come, of course, from those who vainly sought action, not from those who opposed action. A major criticism that has been stressed by the less developed countries is that no final action and little discernible progress has been made regarding proposals to use the United Nations as a channel for providing capital to less developed countries through the establishment of an economic development fund. The program of United Nations technical assistance also has been criticized on the grounds that it is too small to meet the needs under present, much less under possible new programs. Criticism also has been directed against the failure to establish an international trade organization. Blame in this matter should not be directed at the United Nations since the basic reason for the failure of the projected International Trade Organization (ITO) was that the United States changed its mind with regard to it. Criticisms likewise are made of inaction or frustration in connection with certain proposed measures, notably those concerned with the elimination of restrictive business practices and with the stabilization of commodity prices. Here again the United States has a measure of responsibility for the failure of action to take place. Another cause for criticism is the continuing long delay in establishing the Inter-Governmental Maritime Consultative Organization (IMCO) due to failure of enough important maritime countries to ratify its charter. In this case the skirts of the United States are clean. Finally, there has been criticism that in recent years very few new ideas have even been considered by the United Nations, let alone adopted.

The principal object of criticisms of waste motion have been directed at the Economic and Social Council (ECOSOC) and at the administration of technical assistance. Against the ECOSOC the criticisms have been made that its sessions are too long, that the level of government representation is too low for final decisions to be reached, that the ECOSOC spends its time in political discussion which must be repeated in the General Assembly, and that it has failed in its responsibility to coordinate the work of the specialized agencies. The criticism is made that members of ECOSOC tend to overlook their responsibilities as representatives of all the United Nations, thus strengthening the tendency of countries that are not members of ECOSOC to insist on considering in the General Assembly all matters of importance to them. In short, it is urged that the ECOSOC does not operate as a professional body to discuss economic and social problems, and that as a political body it is an unnecessary extra step or "fifth wheel."

By no means all of the apparent failures of the ECOSOC are chargeable to the organization itself. In considerable part its problems have been a consequence of the struggle between the Free World and the Soviet bloc. In the course of this struggle large amounts of time and energy have been spent in acrimonious political debates. These debates, while presumably contributing to the political strategy of the two sides, retarded constructive economic action. The ECOSOC has suffered also from the fact that countries that opposed action but wished to escape criticism for their opposition sometimes have engaged in delaying tactics that tended to discredit the organization. The United States has from time to time been a party to such tactics—for example, with respect to private restrictive business practices, the stabilization of markets and terms of trade for primary products, the International Finance Corporation, and the Special United Nations Fund for Economic Development (SUNFED).

The decline in the level of governmental representation to the ECOSOC since around 1950 appears to have been partly the result of a sense of disillusionment growing out of the problems just described and partly in imitation of the reduction in the level of representation made by the United States. The declining level of representation further reduced the chance that the governments would use the ECOSOC as an instrument for important international economic action.

As will appear later, the fact that the ECOSOC is open to criticism does not necessarily mean that an easy method can be found to remedy the situation.

Criticisms of wasted motion in the Expanded Program of Technical Assistance (EPTA) stress the dual character of its administration. The Technical Assistance Board, under the supervision of the Technical Assistance Committee, carries on part of the administration, in that it helps develop programs, evaluates projects, and allocates funds for their execution to the specialized agencies and the United Nations Technical Assistance Administration (UN-TAA). These agencies also help develop the programs and engage in recruiting, compensating, and making arrangements for experts, and otherwise occupy themselves with administrative details as well as with the substantive task of rendering effective technical assistance. As a result there was for several years a good deal of criticism within as well as outside the United Nations of duplication of staff and costly overhead in the administration of the program, although the situation has been considerably improved in recent years. In part, such criticism overlooks the experience that all forms of counseling, whether private or public, require a considerable overhead burden to assure their efficiency and effectiveness. Moreover, a substantial increase in the size of the technical assistance program would not result in substantial increases in the overhead costs and accordingly would reduce their percentage of total cost. Another reason for heavy cost is the scattering of aid among many countries in many kinds of projects. This is a consequence of political pressures and should not be charged entirely, perhaps not even largely, against the administrators of the program or the structure of the organization.

Analysis of Proposals for Strengthening Economic Development Work

We now turn to consideration of certain proposals that have been made for strengthening the economic development work of the United Nations. The items with which we deal do not exhaust the subject but seem to us to be the most important. We shall consider them under four headings: (1) proposals for improving the ECOSOC, (2) proposals for improving relations between the specialized agencies and the United Nations, (3) proposals for expanding technical assistance functions, (4) proposals for an economic development agency. We recognize that structural changes designed to strengthen performance of the economic development function may fall also within the scope of the assignments of other committees of the Commission.

The Economic and Social Council

Among the alternative proposals that have come to our attention for meeting the deficiencies in the operation of the Economic and Social Council, to which reference has previously been made, are the following: To abolish the ECOSOC; to strengthen the ECOSOC and make it the head of what would be in effect an economic and social United Nations; to turn the ECOSOC into a professional rather than a policy-making organization; to merge the ECOSOC and the Security Council. We are not prepared to recommend any of these proposed modifications. Before indicating some modest suggestions we shall point out why in our opinion the rather drastic proposals just mentioned are based on erroneous assumptions or conclusions concerning the ECOSOC and its work.

One commonly held error is that the ECOSOC really is a principal organ of the United Nations. The Charter of course so states, but allocates powers and responsibilities in such a way as to leave the ECOSOC with very little independence. Unlike the Secretary-General and the Security Council it was not granted executive powers, unless calling international conferences can be so designated. Unlike the International Court of Justice it has no judicial powers. Unlike the Security Council it can only recommend; the Member States have not promised to abide by its decisions. Its power to make recommendations to Member States through the passage of resolutions is limited, as they can be overturned by the General Assembly. Perhaps for this last reason and perhaps also because of the limited membership of the ECOSOC, its recommendations are taken much less seriously than are Assembly resolutions, as is evidenced by the fact that almost all important matters are taken to the Assembly, whatever decision the ECOSOC may have made. The ECOSOC has no power to appropriate funds; any of its decisions requiring the expenditure of funds must be supported by Assembly action to be effective. In short, although the ECOSOC is a body of some importance, it is very largely a subsidiary organization of the General Assembly.

Another belief held by many observers which, in our judgment, is erroneous is that the ECOSOC serves no very useful purpose and could be abolished to good advantage. The fact that debates take place in the ECOSOC and are later repeated in the Second and Third Committees of the General Assembly is, to be sure, time consuming and often exasperating to governments and observers alike. Much the same thing would almost certainly occur, however, if these Committees were served by an interim or preparatory subcommittee. Considering the volume of work, such a subcommittee would be necessary unless Committees 2 and 3 were prepared to sit either formally or as interim bodies for extended periods in addition to the annual session of the General Assembly, a practice which would be both cumbersome and costly. With eighty-one Members and probably more to come, these Committees approach in size the United States

Senate, which of course does most of its work through smaller committees. In many respects the Economic and Social Council serves as a preparatory committee for the General Assembly. Strengthening this role, for example, by a consistent Assembly practice of referring all new matters to the ECOSOC before consideration in the Assembly, would seem a wiser approach than drastic reorganization.

Still another assumption or conclusion which seems to us erroneous is that the ECOSOC could be made into a body for the consideration of questions on a professional or "scientific" level. The idea is that the ECOSOC could work out the technical problems, leaving political discussion for the General Assembly. We do not consider this a feasible approach. The achievement of discussion at the professional level is not feasible because the questions that come before the ECOSOC are of such great variety that no one delegate or small number of delegates would be able to discuss them with professional competence. Large delegations would be expensive and the results of discussion would not necessarily present a consistent pattern. Perhaps more important is the implicit assumption that the ECOSOC could usefully consider economic and social questions without reference to their political implications. Such discussion is possible only when narrow terms of reference have been set up that exclude consideration of conflicting interests and competing value patterns. "Scientific" study does not reveal the solutions to economic and social problems, which are indeed among the most important of political questions, since "political" includes everything that calls for governmental action. It may be possible to have a specific economic or social question considered in a non-political fashion by an ad hoc group of specialists in a particular field if the terms of reference of the group are defined very narrowly. The ECOSOC can appoint such groups or ask the Secretary-General to do so. It seems highly unlikely, however, that it could itself successfully engage in discussion at a professional level.

It must be recognized that the political character of the discussions in the ECOSOC has been due in very large measure to major conflicting interests, notably between the West and the Soviet bloc, but also between the economically advanced and the less developed countries.

A final assumption which we believe to be erroneous is that the deficiencies of the ECOSOC are due to its structure and legal relationships. To be sure, the exalted view of its functions which ECOSOC sometimes takes may lead it to take its recommendations to governments too seriously and its function of preparing and screening problems for the General Assembly not seriously enough. It is our belief, however, that the basic reason for the failure of the ECOSOC to function better is the conflict between countries that have not been willing to do important things in the economic and social fields and other countries that have been pressing hard for such measures.

On the basis of this analysis it would seem unwise to abolish the ECOSOC since the necessity would then arise to set up one or more committees of comparable size to do much the same thing as the ECOSOC has been doing. It would also be unwise to try to give the ECOSOC more power and detach it from the General Assembly, giving it the last word on economic and social questions. The countries that are not members of the ECOSOC would not have respect for the organization. In a world of sovereign states the Economic and Social Council, as a representative body, cannot possibly carry the weight of the full Assembly since countries are not likely to respect recommendations which they have not helped to frame. Finally we do not think the ECOSOC should be forced to try to behave as a group of social scientists, as we believe ad hoc groups and the Secretariat are much more likely to do constructive work along these lines.

The recommendations that we would make for the ECOSOC are modest. Some increase in its size to make it more representative would be appropriate, although the advantages of small size suggest that the increase should be limited. More recognition needs to be given to the ECOSOC as a body serving the General Assembly; this means that the General Assembly should not consider matters until they have first been submitted to the ECOSOC, and that less emphasis should be placed on the ECOSOC as a body making recommendations to Member States. A much higher level of representation is needed and the same persons should also be representatives to the Second and Third Committees of the General Assembly. In other words, we think that the ECOSOC should see its major role as being in effect a committee of the General Assembly and that the Assembly should take the ECOSOC much more seriously in this capacity than it has in the past.

At the present time none of the functional commissions of the

ECOSOC has substantial responsibilities in the economic development field. We see no point in adding to the present structure a functional commission with such responsibilities. The regional economic commissions of the ECOSOC are making substantial contributions to economic development and have proved their value in the United Nations system. These commissions encourage mutual education of representatives of the countries of the region, facilitate the systematic study of its special problems, and stimulate joint action in attacking many of these problems. It is a matter for regret that various obstacles have arisen to the establishment of regional economic commissions for Africa and the Middle East. The opposition of the metropolitan powers, in the case of Africa, and the Arab-Israeli struggle in the case of the Middle East, continue to present particularly delicate and difficult problems. We look forward to the establishment of economic commissions in these regions as soon as conditions permit.

A logical effect of the activities of the regional commissions has been to stimulate the growth of regional viewpoints and of emphasis on regional interests. This is beneficial in that it encourages a cooperative attack on regional problems. It presents the danger, however, that a concentration of attention on the conflicting interests of various geographical areas might gradually lead to the break-up of the United Nations as an economic body into competing and possibly conflicting regional organizations. The General Assembly and the ECOSOC should be alert to prevent the regional economic commissions from contributing to such a development.

Relations of the Specialized Agencies and the ECOSOC

Relations of the specialized agencies to the United Nations fall within the assignment of this Committee because a number of the specialized agencies perform important roles in promoting economic development. Recommendations have come to our attention which call for the abolition of the specialized agencies and the merging of their work in the United Nations. In conflict with these are proposals to establish at least one more specialized agency to take over the economic and social functions of the Secretariat, with the ECOSOC serving only as a coordinating body. We do not favor action along either of these lines at this time. The specialized agencies are well established and doing work of importance in a manner generally satisfactory to the Member Governments; to propose their abolition or subjection to the United Nations could only lead to confusion. Moreover, the specialized agencies have the rather important advantage that they are less dominated by political considerations than is the United Nations; this leaves them relatively more free to carry on constructive programs than they could if they were subject to the political orientation that is inevitable in a body concerned with policy in all its aspects.

Setting up another specialized agency to carry on the economic work of the United Nations would leave the ECOSOC and the General Assembly no functions as far as economic and social matters are concerned, except passing hortatory resolutions. Greater powers of coordinating the specialized agencies might be granted to the United Nations, but such coordination would in the nature of the case reduce the independence of the specialized agencies. In the long run this kind of arrangement might have on balance substantial advantages, but to recommend it at the present time might boomerang by strengthening the hands of those who seek to widen the gap between the specialized agencies and the United Nations.

The only major coordination among specialized agencies now being carried on is in connection with the Expanded Program of Technical Assistance. We believe coordination has improved substantially over the past few years with respect to the administration of this program, but much remains to be done to reduce complications, to improve country programming, and to achieve more complete cooperation between the country representatives of the Technical Assistance Board (TAB) and those of the specialized agencies. It would be economical to increase the centralization of administrative details— for example, recruiting, arrangements for housing, and compensation of experts—so that the agencies could concentrate substantively on the direction and execution of technical assistance projects, which is where their particular competence lies. It would be a major mistake for governments to move in the opposite direction and to fragment the Expanded Program by making their technical assistance contributions to the specialized agencies instead of to the Special Account.

The unit overhead administrative costs of technical assistance would be decreased also if the size of the Expanded Program could be substantially enlarged. The machinery is adequate to carry a larger program without additional overhead expense. A more important reason for enlarging the size of the Expanded Program is the unsatisfied need for technical assistance.

Expanding Technical Assistance Functions

A report by the Technical Assistance Board to the Administrative Committee on Coordination in 1956 outlined a number of different areas in which technical assistance might be expanded with advantage. We would like to see the work of the technical assistance program of the United Nations expanded along those lines. There are three particular lines of expansion on which we want to comment.

1) With respect to the proposal of the Secretary-General to set up a sort of international secretariat to provide underdeveloped countries with qualified administrative personnel who would help carry on their operations and training programs, we consider this a good idea in principle. An experiment along this line in Bolivia is generally reported as having been highly successful. The success of the idea on a broader scale would seem to depend in the first instance on the willingness of the underdeveloped countries to make use of such a secretariat. Undoubtedly such persons would need to be labeled as "advisors" and kept in the background. Governments are reluctant to run the political risk of admitting that the administrative personnel of the country is so deficient that outsiders need to be brought in. Unless a considerable number of countries indicate their willingness to participate in such a plan it would not be possible to give the long-term employment contracts necessary to recruit the high caliber of persons required for this sort of service.

Some people would be concerned lest the Soviet bloc use an international advisory secretariat of this kind as a method of getting its technicians into key spots in governments of the less developed countries. Perhaps this would not be as serious as would appear at first glance, since no country would be obliged to accept an advisor it did not wish to have.

To some extent the problem of an international advisory secretariat might be solved by enlarging certain branches of the Secretariat to include some "spare parts." These persons could alternate between work in the Headquarters, the regional economic commissions, and various country administrations. This idea of a mobile secretariat, although attractive, would meet extreme difficulty in practice on account of such factors as the degree of specialization necessary for effective administration and the problem of language.

2) Another proposal of interest is to place greater emphasis on extractive industries in the technical assistance program of the United Nations. The development of the extractive industries has in the past proved to be a valuable method of financing other aspects of economic development and of enlarging the long-run opportunities for industrialization. Activities by the United Nations in providing geological surveys and otherwise promoting the extractive industries might be especially welcomed by many of the less developed countries. The extractive industries represent a sector of economic life with respect to which many countries seem to be fearful of exploitation by foreign companies. Some countries have been reluctant even to receive government aid in this sector from any single country.

3) Another proposal that has been made is that the United Nations establish an information service, listing investment opportunities in different countries and also companies seeking such opportunities. We believe that such a service is needed and would help promote economic development. There are, however, certain reasons for believing that the United Nations as such is not the organization that should provide the service. The political implications of invidious comparisons would present an obstacle to honest and objective reporting. Moreover, any advice that later proved to be incorrect might give rise to serious criticism and antagonism to the operation and to the United Nations Secretariat. It is conceivable that an international private organization could be developed to supply information of this type; this would more likely be done on a partial basis for private profit than as a public service available to all. The International Finance Corporation would be perhaps the most appropriate organization now in existence for the performance of this function. If an economic development agency were established in the United Nations or elsewhere, the function might be undertaken there if not already being undertaken elsewhere.

An Economic Development Agency

During the last half-dozen years there has been a great deal of discussion pro and con regarding the establishment of an economic development agency in the United Nations. The form in which this proposition has been before the ECOSOC and the General Assembly is the Special United Nations Fund for Economic Development (SUNFED). The establishment of SUNFED or of some similar body has become a controversial national and international issue.

In considering this issue we assume that economic development of the less developed countries is in the interest of the United States and other economically advanced countries and that some international flow of public capital will be necessary to help provide the economic and social base without which various aspects of development, notably industrialization, are not likely to proceed very fast or very far. Given these assumptions, the central question is whether all such public capital should be provided unilaterally by capital-exporting countries, particularly the United States, or alternatively, in whole or in part through the instrumentality of an international agency.

The case for using an international agency to channel public capital to less developed countries rests largely on two propositions. One is the fairly obvious but not unimportant point that the public acceptance of the whole idea of international organization is strengthened by using international agencies to do important jobs. The other proposition is that economic development of less developed countries can be more effectively undertaken through an international agency than through bilateral arrangements. Several advantages of international agencies in this connection may be noted, as follows.

1) An international agency should be better equipped than the bureaucratic or legislative machinery of any individual nation to evaluate relative world needs for aid and to decide what conditions, if any, should be attached to such aid.

2) Conditions imposed by an international agency would be more readily accepted by beneficiary governments than the same conditions imposed by any single nation. This would be especially important where conflicting local interests were involved—for example, with respect to such conditions as fiscal reform, or the creation of agricultural credit facilities to displace firmly entrenched money lenders, or the breaking up of large landed estates.

3) To the extent that all donor nations, including the Communist states, could be induced to channel their contributions to world economic development through the United Nations, economic assistance would be stripped of the overtones of competitive power politics.

4) An international agency could draw upon the skills and capital resources of a number of states; the United States contribution would have a leverage or multiplier effect.

5) An international development agency would be in a better position to promote a system of international protection of private foreign investment than would a single country, in view of the widespread fear of economic imperialism.

The objections to an international development agency are of various kinds and degrees of persuasiveness.

1) The official United States position that it cannot afford to provide funds through such an agency is not persuasive, in view of the size of its bilateral program, part of which could readily be shifted to the agency.

2) Persons opposed to international organization in general may be expected to oppose any steps that would strengthen them or enlarge their scope.

3) The advantages of an international development agency would be realized, it is urged, only if set up and operated along sound lines. The United States cannot be sure that it would meet this test.

4) The decision to join an international development agency means undertaking a commitment for a financial program of considerable duration, since anything less would be abortive and would damage our national prestige. Persons who consider international economic aid to be a highly temporary expedient would certainly oppose the making of such a commitment by the United States.

5) Finally there is the argument that bilateral arrangements are superior to an international agency in that they enable the United States to employ its aid funds in such a manner as to achieve political advantages in other countries. This seems a sound and potent argument with respect to some countries, but with respect to others the attempt to achieve such advantages seems likely to boomerang. Nationalism and the hatred of colonialism and economic imperialism are powerful forces in national and world politics. The belief that United States aid is being used to achieve political goals may lead governments to refuse to receive aid, as in the case of Burma, or to offset the internal political effects of receiving such aid, through actions and gestures to demonstrate the country's independence. Moreover, the charge that United States bilateral aid is a form of economic imperialism is a potent element in Communist propaganda.

6) Many persons think it inconceivable that the United States should provide funds for distribution by a body in which the Soviet Union or its Satellites were members. If this proved to be a very powerful obstacle it might be met, as will be discussed below, by attaching the agency to the World Bank in which, at least for the present, there are no Soviet bloc members. However, the fear of the Soviet Union and its Satellites seems to be unnecessarily great in this connection. They would constitute a small minority of members and their presence in the program would diminish the fear that the recipients of funds might have of being placed in a compromising position with regard to their international political relations.

On balance we find the case for establishing an international development agency to be strong and persuasive. We do not suggest that all United States economic aid should be channeled through such an agency. Indeed, the international character of the agency would be impaired if an overwhelming proportion of its investment were to be made by any one country.

Although we strongly favor the establishment of an international development agency we are less certain regarding what should be its structure and relationship to the United Nations and international organizations. Several possible patterns of structure and relationship have been suggested for such an agency. Each of them is open to criticism along some lines. One reason for difficulty is that if the agency had available to it the amount of funds necessary to make it a real force for promoting economic development, it would be by far the largest, strongest economic body in the United Nations family, except perhaps the International Bank. Wherever the agency was located organizationally, it would tend to attract power and functions to it. For example, the technical assistance program would almost certainly be turned over before long to the Economic Development Agency, at least with respect to the allocation of funds among the various agencies providing technical assistance. The organization of the Agency is thus a matter of considerable importance for the future of the United Nations family.

One possible arrangement would be for the Economic Development Agency to be set up as a subsidiary of the World Bank. This would avoid Soviet participation and would give the United States and other contributing countries a controlling voice in policy and administration. Coordination of international financing of economic development would be reasonably assured. Whether the Agency would be looked upon as a sufficiently "international" organization in membership and distribution of voting power to be generally acceptable throughout the world may be open to some question. The answer probably differs widely among countries, in view of their statements in the General Assembly. Aside from this possible obstacle, the results of operation would depend largely on the answer to another question, namely, whether the attitude of the Bank toward various problems of economic development would be broad and comprehensive or would consider the Agency's funds merely as a method of "sweetening" Bank loans. Still another question is whether centering virtually all international economic power in the Bank would have a substantially adverse effect on the rest of the United Nations system. Separating the Agency from the Bank would, of course, also raise problems, since the Agency would constitute a competing center of economic power and activity. This competition would present an element of confusion and might play into the hands of countries seeking to play off one organization against the other in order to get financial help on the most favorable terms. There is some doubt in our minds with respect to the answers to these various questions and accordingly as to the desirability of setting up the Agency as a subsidiary of the Bank.

Another possible arrangement is to make the United Nations itself the development agency, under the control of the ECOSOC and the General Assembly and administered by the Secretariat. This would strengthen the United Nations in general and the General Assembly in particular by adding the prestige, dignity, and bargaining power that accompany control over a large amount of money. However, activities of any organization under the control of the General Assembly could be dominated by the numerous small recipient countries making up the large majority of Member States. It may be doubted that an agency so dominated would achieve an intelligent objectivity in evaluating world needs or would impose and make effective the politically unpalatable but economically necessary conditions for making economic aid most effective. The distribution of voting power would undoubtedly constitute an insurmountable obstacle to the acceptance of this arrangement by the United States, without which any development agency would be largely an empty shell.

Another proposal has been that the Economic Development Agency be run by the Secretary-General of the United Nations and the President of the World Bank, together with another director of their choice. Aside from the problems of making such an organization work harmoniously, it may be objected that too much power would be given to the secretariat personnel to determine the operations of the Agency. The allocation of funds and the setting of conditions under which those funds will be granted, together with the determination of rates of interest and conditions of repayment, are not purely administrative tasks but are policy matters of great significance.

The Agency might also be set up as a specialized agency. This would add to the present proliferation of largely independent international organizations and would almost surely become the most powerful one of all—even more powerful in the economic development field than the United Nations itself. A relationship somewhat intermediate between the specialized agency and direct control by the General Assembly was proposed in the original SUNFED plan in which it was provided that half the members of the Board of Directors of SUNFED be chosen from the contributing countries and the other half from the receiving countries. On examination this proves to be a rather vague arrangement. The vagueness might be eliminated by another proposal to the effect that there be, say, ten directors of which five would be appointed by the five principal contributors and the other five would be elected by the General Assembly—presumably largely if not entirely from the recipient or non-contributing countries. The voting in the operation of such an agency would depend to a considerable extent on what countries were elected by the General Assembly. To reduce bizarre results the proposal has been made that the decision of the Board must be agreed to by a majority of directors in each group of five. One objection to such an arrangement is that there is no assurance that any action at all would take place. The organization might wind up deadlocked on all vital questions. Another objection is that the arrangement would result in a sort of "collective bargain" between the industrialized and the underdeveloped countries. It would tend to keep alive the conflict that may be present from time to time between the two sets of countries, instead of strengthening the cooperative aspects of international action.

While we are uncertain as to which of the previously described forms of structure and relationship offers the greatest balance of advantage, we believe that several of them are promising and that negotiations should be pressed toward the establishment of an economic development agency. It may well be that out of such negotiations will come the invention of an improved organizational relationship and voting power distribution which will command the confidence and meet the justifiable interests of the contributing and recipient countries alike.

Various ramifications of a development agency may be visualized. For example, regional development bodies closely affiliated with the agency might be established and used in administering its development loans and grants. The value of such regional organizations has been demonstrated by the experience with the Marshall Plan in Europe and with the Colombo Plan in Southeast Asia. In at least one part of the world—the Middle East—some countries in a group of countries that look upon themselves as a region have substantial resources which might be employed internationally to finance needed economic development throughout the region. In a situation of this kind the establishment of a more-or-less self-contained regional development organization seems strongly indicated.

ROY BLOUGH, CHAIRMAN
DANIEL BENEDICT
ROYDEN DANGERFIELD
FRANK P. GRAHAM
SAMUEL GUY INMAN
WALTER H. C. LAVES
LELAND REX ROBINSON
EUGENE STALEY

9 CONTROL OF OPEN TERRITORY

Introduction

One of the recommendations made by the Commission to Study the Organization of Peace a decade ago was this: "An international regime for the Antarctic continent should be established, with direct administration by the United Nations. Such a step should not be difficult if undertaken promptly, since none of the powers has yet acquired important interests on that continent, there are no native inhabitants, nor have any strategic resources been developed."[1]

The philosophy implied by this and similar recommendations can be stated quite simply. If there had been a well-developed international community at the time new land areas were "discovered" by the European colonizing nations three centuries ago, it is safe to say that much bloodshed and misery would have been avoided. Those areas might have been attached to the community instead of to any one claimant. There is only one such land area remaining: Antarctica. Parts of it have long been claimed by several nations, but so far none of those claims has been clearly recognized. But recognition appears to be imminent, in the sense that at least one nation has established the skeleton of a government on the land it claims.[2] Another virgin area is about to be invaded this year: outer space. These two areas are the prime cases, but the high seas and the sea-bed are somewhat analogous.

---

[1] Commission to Study the Organization of Peace, *Fifth Report*, Security and Disarmament Under the United Nations, June 1947, p. 22.

[2] New Zealand, with the establishment of Ross Dependency and the issuance of postage stamps in January 1957.

Certain other areas are less clearly appropriate to this philosophy, but they are certainly affected by it. When political, economic, and social interests—particularly defense interests—become vested over the years, the international community cannot be brought into the picture without lopping off large or small pieces of national sovereignty. Unclaimed territory can be the cause of bloody friction, but statesmanlike handling can turn it into a common asset. We have an opportunity to do this.

It is a debatable point whether there is an international community today sufficiently developed to perform the functions recommended. This Committee believes that the United Nations stands at this stage. We believe it should take a major step from adolescence toward maturity, but bold action will be required. One way for the United Nations to *become* a true international community is for it to *act* like one.

The recommendations which follow would not, in our opinion, require amendment of the Charter. They would in some cases require new expenditure at the outset, but they can also be expected to bring in added revenue. At least one of the recommendations is almost sure to bring large returns in the not-distant future—ownership of the resources of the Antarctic. Another may prove valuable in the more distant future—ownership of the resources of the sea-bed.

RELATIONSHIP OF THE UNITED NATIONS TO THE HIGH SEAS AND THE SEA-BED

The high seas have long been regarded as common property, free for the use of all, and subject only to rules of law necessary to safeguard this freedom in the interests of the international community as a whole. The fundamental concept of the freedom of the seas has been recognized as including not only freedom of navigation and freedom to fly over the oceans, but also the freedom to fish, to lay cables and pipe lines, and to conduct scientific research and exploration on the high seas. The "regime" of the high seas based on customary and treaty law has been largely concerned with defining and delimiting the rights of national states so as to ensure the exercise of these freedoms.

Resources

In recent years there has been an increased awareness of the value of the natural resources of the seas and a growing realization that the principle of the freedom of the seas and existing rules of law may not be fully adequate to protect and conserve these resources. The fisheries of the high seas have become an increasingly important part of the world's food supply and constitute an indispensable source of protein food for the rapidly growing population of the globe. While modern techniques and scientific knowledge have vastly enlarged the yield of fish, they have also greatly increased the danger of waste and extermination of fish and other marine fauna. Coastal States concerned with predatory exploitation of fisheries by foreign nationals have tended to take strong measures of self-protection which have not always been fully consonant with existing law and which have consequently produced friction and tension in international relations. In addition, pollution of the seas by oil and oil-producing installations, and more recently by the dumping of radio-active waste have also seriously contributed to the dangers to the living resources of the seas. It has become evident that these problems cannot be solved in terms of freedom of the seas alone, but require more positive measures of international cooperation and control.

Scientific developments and technology have also opened the possibility of making available to mankind the mineral resources of the subsoil of the oceans. Their exploitation has already been undertaken on the "continental shelves" adjacent to the coasts and beyond the area of the territorial sea, and Coastal States have asserted exclusive rights to such exploitation. While there has been a tendency to recognize exclusive rights on the continental shelf, there still remain unsettled problems regarding the submarine areas beyond the continental shelf. At the present stage of technology, such areas are not practically exploitable, but it has been anticipated that in the not-too-distant future these portions of the "res communis" may also yield valuable returns.

There are therefore three general problems—conservation of fisheries, prevention of pollution, and exploitation of the sea-bed—which warrant fresh consideration of the "regime" of the high seas in terms of the interest of the international community as a whole.

Fisheries Example

It is instructive to consider the experience of international cooperation in promoting conservation of fisheries. The need for joint action by the states concerned has brought about the establishment of a number of international bodies created by treaty and empowered to recommend specific conservation measures in particular regions of the world. At present there are eleven such international conservation organizations and a number of international conventions involving more than forty different states. These organizations and international conventions have undoubtedly achieved a certain measure of success in restoring and maintaining the productivity of the fisheries with which they have been concerned. At the same time it is evident that their efforts have fallen considerably short of achieving a substantial solution to the many problems of conservation which exist throughout the world.

The reasons that they have been handicapped in achieving a solution can be summarized briefly. In the first place, there are a number of important sea fisheries, either newly discovered or old-established fisheries, which are not at present subject to any international measures of cooperation. In the second place, the international conventions and organizations do not include a number of states that are engaged in fishing operations. So it has not been possible to prevent regulatory measures adopted by agreement among certain states from being nullified by refusal on the part of other states, including those newly participating in the fishery concerned, to observe such measures.[3] A further important difficulty is that the conventions do not contain sufficiently precise stipulations as to the procedures and conservation measures to be applied and, as a result, states are not afforded a specific indication of the action to be taken.[4] Disagreements which arise cannot as a rule be authoritatively settled by the international bodies. The fact that these organizations have been entrusted merely with recommendatory functions as distinct from authority to issue binding regulations has also been an important reason for their failure to take effective action.

Need for a New Organization

These inadequacies of the present system of international conservation strongly suggest the advisability of establishing a new worldwide international organization within the framework of the United Nations to deal with problems of the high seas and the sea-bed.

An international organization of this kind, which would be es-

[3] See report of the International Technical Conference on the Conservation of the Living Resources of the Sea (Rome, 1955), paragraphs 60 and 78.

[4] *Ibid.*, paragraph 51.

tablished by treaty on the pattern of the specialized agencies, would overcome the present disadvantages for the following reasons. It would, as indicated, be a world-wide organization including in its membership virtually all of the states of the United Nations and, therefore, all of the governments concerned with exploitation of fisheries. It would, consequently, be in a position to apply international measures of conservation to the various sea fisheries which are not at present subject to them and it would also make possible action in regard to fisheries in separated areas which depend upon the same species.[5] An international authority would also be in a position through administrative action to establish a precise and specific system of conservation measures which could be varied and interpreted to meet changing circumstances and unforeseen difficulties. Moreover, it could through action of its administrative organs or, in some cases, through quasi-judicial bodies, settle disagreements which may arise among states regarding technical questions as well as questions of a legal character. A further obvious advantage of such a comprehensive international conservation organization could be the establishment of an international research staff which could engage in scientific research and investigation, collate the results of studies made by national conservation research organizations, and reach conclusions which would have an authoritative technical standing.

These reasons would in themselves be sufficient to justify the establishment of an international organization for the high seas even if its authority were to be limited to the making of recommendations. However, the urgency and importance of the problems of fisheries warrant serious consideration of proposals to entrust such an international body with the power to make binding regulations. While this might be considered as a far-reaching step in present-day international administration, it finds ample justification in the inadequacy of merely recommendatory action and in the necessity of reducing friction and tension produced by conflicts among states regarding conservation measures.

It is not necessary, however, to endow the proposed international authority with the power to enact binding regulations in all circumstances. On the contrary, it may be desirable to enable the states directly concerned to exercise their authority in the first instance. Proposals on these lines were made several years ago in the report

[5] See, for example, *ibid.*, paragraph 69(c).

of the International Law Commission of the United Nations for 1953 as follows:

1) A state whose nationals are engaged in fishing in any area where the nationals of other states are not thus engaged may regulate and control fisheries activities in such areas for the purpose of protecting fisheries against waste or extermination.

2) If the nationals of two or more states are engaged in fishing in any area of the high seas, the states concerned shall prescribe the necessary conservation measures by agreement.

3) If, subsequent to the adoption of such measures, nationals of other states engaged in fishing in the area and those states do not accept the measures adopted, the international authority would be empowered to declare the regulations binding upon the states in question and upon their nationals.

4) In the contingency that none of the interested states is able to reach agreement, the international authority would issue regulations with binding effect.

Pollution

An organization of this kind would also be an appropriate international body to deal with the ever-increasing problem of pollution of the high seas. Such pollution occurs on a large scale through the discharge of oil from ships and through leaks in pipe lines or defects in installations for the exploitation of the sea-bed. While most maritime states have attempted by regulation to prevent such pollution in their internal waters and their territorial sea, these regulations are not adequate. Petroleum products on the high seas are washed toward the marine fauna as well as creating fire risks and pollution of beaches. It has long been obvious that an international solution of the problem is necessary, but an international convention for the prevention of pollution by oil, which was drafted in 1954, has not yet come into force.

The problem of pollution also arises through the dumping of radio-active waste in the high seas. Such dumping, which appears to be practiced in various parts of the world, is likely to be a serious source of danger to fish and fish eaters. The gravity of the problem is increasingly evident and effective measures of international action are undoubtedly required to prevent serious damage to marine life and human beings. An international body staffed by competent scientific investigators and empowered to issue binding regulations for the high seas generally would appear to be the most effective way to combat this problem.

Sea-Bed

Such an organization would also be in a position to regulate the exploitation of the floor under the high seas when exploitation becomes a practical possibility. It could operate in almost exactly the same way as the suggested organization for dealing with fisheries and pollution, or it could be of a more sweeping type, such as that suggested for handling Antarctica. The Committee recommends the latter, which means that the floor under the high seas should be recognized as "res communis" and its ownership and control be conceded to the United Nations under an arrangement parallel to the one recommended for Antarctica in the next section of this report.

RELATIONSHIP OF THE UNITED NATIONS TO ANTARCTICA

The recommendation made in 1947 by the Commission to Study the Organization of Peace has been stated in the introduction to this chapter. Developments since that time have added urgency to this recommendation.

An increasing number of weather stations are being maintained all year. In 1955 there were eighteen stations, most of them maintained on Palmer Peninsula, by Argentina, Britain, and Chile. Palmer Peninsula is claimed by all three of these countries, and the disputes about these claims have grown in intensity. Since 1948 annual trilateral agreements have been negotiated among these countries providing that none will indulge in a provocative show of naval strength in the area. However, in 1952, a British mission to reestablish a weather station was forced off the beach by machine gun fire over their heads by Argentine forces, and was only able to land after governmental negotiations in Buenos Aires.

For the next year or two, national differences may be expected to be set aside in order to make a success of the coordinated explorations and research in Antarctica planned for the International Geophysical Year. Some forty countries are cooperating in this scientific venture. Both the United States and the Soviet Union are establishing weather stations. However, as the possibilities in Antarctica become better known, the competition and claims are likely to increase. This will involve military bases, weather and scientific stations, and economic exploitation.

At present there are already conflicting claims to much of Antarctica. British Commonwealth countries claim more than half of the continent. The United States, which has a claim to discovery of the continent and has conducted a number of pioneer expeditions, has steadily refused to recognize any of the other claims, and also has made no claim to sovereignty itself on the ground that no effective occupation was possible. In 1950 the Soviet Government put the United States, Britain, France, Argentina, Chile, Australia, Norway, and New Zealand, the main Antarctic powers, on notice that it considered the disposition of Antarctic territory a matter for international agreement. Some of the other claimants are currently pressing the United States to proclaim its sovereignty over a portion of Antarctica so as to give force to their own claims. New Zealand actually established the nucleus of a colonial government in its sector in January 1957 and issued four postage stamps from the "Ross Dependency."

Should Antarctica be divided up like a pie among colonial powers? We believe not, if there is an available alternative. Antarctica is the area—because of its prevailing winds and its location—in which least harm can be done by the fall-out from any atomic and nuclear test explosions which might have to be set off. It is also the area in which some nations may wish to bury their atomic wastes. It is a strategic center from which air and naval fleets may control vital seaways around the far corners of the African, South American, and Australian continents. The world does not need another strategic area to be struggled for, and such a struggle between the United States and the Soviet Union would appear to be inevitable if the continent is to be divided up by occupying powers as Africa once was.

Even aside from the desire to keep the continent from becoming the prize in what *The New York Times* has predicted "may well develop into the world's cold war II," the difficulty of untangling the present claims (excluding the United States and the Soviet Union) in a solution satisfactory to them all is immense and almost insurmountable. And although there are no native inhabitants to lead anti-colonial revolutions, it hardly seems sensible to leave this 10 per cent of the world's land area as the subject of a new kind of national colonialism.

One alternative to such a policy of dangerous drift would be direct United Nations administration of the whole continent. The world security interest in removing Antarctica from the field of military competition alone seems to us a sufficient reason for proposing direct UN administration of the continent. In addition, there are more positive reasons why such direct UN administration seems desirable. The continent is believed to have vast quantities of minerals. Large deposits of coal have been spotted, although of a low grade; and there are verified deposits of copper, magnesium, molybdenum, and indications of oil and uranium. As the world's more accessible resources are exhausted, it is likely that there will be efforts to discover and utilize the resources under the Antarctic ice cap. Unlike the Arctic, the Antarctic ice cap covers a continent of land and not merely ocean, and the ice cap can be melted in places and full-scale exploitation of the mineral resources undertaken. Thus the power which owns, uses, and regulates Antarctic economic development may in time reap great benefits. The resources of this 10 per cent of the world's land area, we believe, should be owned, used, and regulated for the common good of the world.

In 1948 the United States suggested formally to other Antarctic powers, which did not at that time include the Soviet Union, that the solution to the problem of conflicting claims might be found through agreement upon "some form of internationalization." The form of internationalization which the United States then had in mind was not direct UN administration, but was probably some form of multilateral convention among the claimant countries. The response to this suggestion from other countries was negative, and since then the Soviet Union has become an Antarctic power. There are no indications that the United States still endorses its suggestion of "some form of internationalization."

On the other hand, both the United States and the Soviet Union might now be willing to see this strategic area removed from their field of competition through direct UN administration. Or at least they and the other half dozen or so Antarctic powers might acquiesce in such a solution if it were adopted by an overwhelming vote of the General Assembly of the United Nations. Such a decision by the United Nations does not seem impossible, and we believe it should now be pressed in all practical ways.

What form should the UN administration of Antarctica take? The form should, of course, fit the functions. The functions would be the defense and government of a largely uninhabited region and the economic development and exploitation of the region.

The task of governing this nearly uninhabited territory should not be overly difficult once the authority is granted. In the beginning it might mean chiefly the regulation of the various existing weather stations and the licensing of new weather stations. The International Geophysical Year has already produced a valuable beginning for coordination of this important meteorological observation.

Since the empty continent is a possible site for testing atomic explosions or long-range missiles, and since the United States is already reported to be alarmed about possible Soviet experiments there, a UN administration would need a small police or inspection force to patrol the continent, at least by air.

The administration would need the ability to undertake or arrange for resource development, either by licensing specific countries or private corporations, or by securing the funds to exploit the region itself. When there are any proceeds to the UN administration above administrative costs and the development needs of the region, they should go to the UN, either as part of its general income or earmarked for the work of all or some of the specialized agencies.

To carry out these tasks, the UN administration should itself be a specialized agency of the UN, established by the General Assembly, with an independent budget. Like the Tennessee Valley Authority, it should be a corporate body with the powers of an independent corporation.

This is the time to begin the experiment. National interests and investments in Antarctica are still relatively small. The possible profits still seem remote, although the contesting claims are growing more intense. Effective occupation in terms of international law has not yet taken place. Thus Antarctica is a continent in search of a sovereign. The United Nations ought to establish its sovereignty there.

RELATIONSHIP OF THE UNITED NATIONS TO OUTER SPACE

Several events in recent months have shown that the time is near when the invasion of outer space will be practical and agreement about its use and control will be a real problem. The International Geophysical Year has intensified the development of the earth satellite, and the launching of experimental models is scheduled for the current year.

In the summer of 1956 the Assembly of the International Civil Aviation Organization, meeting in Caracas, called for early consideration of the problem. The President of the United States has stated officially that the United States "is willing to enter any reliable agreement which would . . . mutually control the outer space missile and satellite development . . ."[6] In January 1957 the United States placed this problem before the United Nations, as a part of its comprehensive proposal for the control of armaments. Referring to "earth satellites, intercontinental missiles, long-range unmanned weapons, and space platforms," the United States representative said: "The first step toward the objective of assuring that developments in outer space would be devoted exclusively to peaceful and scientific purposes would be to bring the testing of such objects under international inspection and participation."[7]

Problem

The use of outer space by either satellites or ballistic missiles is almost certain to be an added threat to world peace, and hence to the security of the United States. A broader but less vital problem is the threat to the free use of that space. The purpose of international control, therefore, is primarily to assure the *peaceful* use of outer space; a secondary purpose is to assure the free use of that space by all nations. Contemporary air law does not cover flight instrumentalities such as rockets, satellites, and other spacecraft when they are in "outer space."[8]

While the scientific uses of the earth satellite are being stressed at the present time, there is no doubt whatever that it will have warlike potentialities when fully developed. These are of four kinds: (a) The surface of the earth can be observed in astonishing detail for the purpose of target identification. This is important to both the strategic offense and the strategic defense. (b) Defenses can be breached by jamming the radar signals that currently protect the major powers from surprise attack. National fences could thus be

[6] President Eisenhower's "State of the Union" message, as quoted in *The New York Times*, 11 January 1957, p. 9.

[7] Ambassador Henry Cabot Lodge, Jr., addressing the Political Committee of the UN General Assembly, as quoted in *The New York Times*, 15 January 1957, p. 4.

[8] John C. Cooper, "Legal Problems of Upper Space," address delivered before the annual meeting of the American Society of International Law, Washington, D. C., April 26, 1956, privately reproduced, p. 3.

knocked down all over the world. (c) Psychological warfare can be carried on more effectively because it will probably be impossible to jam the signals emanating from a satellite. (d) A manned space platform is theoretically possible and missiles could be launched from such a vehicle, although perhaps with no more effectiveness than from land.[9]

Alternative Policies

To achieve the purpose of international control over outer space, what are the alternative policies that might be proposed?

1) Place control in the hands of individual states. Contemporary air law applies to "activity in the gaseous air with machines requiring support from such air,"[10] and states have jurisdiction over the airspace directly above their territory. This doctrine might be extended upward to include space beyond the atmosphere indefinitely, or to include only that distance upward which the most advanced state is able to control at any given time. This alternative seems entirely impractical for obvious physical reasons.

2) Place ownership and operation of all or certain types of spacecraft in an international agency, presumably the United Nations. Only in connection with a thoroughgoing system of international control over armaments, including international inspection and a police force, would this alternative seem to be politically practical. It should not be considered separately from the crucial question of international inspection which is now under discussion.

3) Registration of all or certain spacecraft with the United Nations, plus notification and verification of each flight well in advance. This would involve inspection by the UN (or its subsidiary international agency) in order to verify the peaceful nature of any flight.[11]

Recommendations

1) That the *principle* should be accepted that outer space is not subject to ownership or control by individual states but only by the international community, represented by the United Nations.

[9] Wernher von Braun, "Missile-Carrying Satellite," in *Missiles and Rockets*, November 1956, p. 31.

[10] John C. Cooper, "Air Law—A Field for International Thinking," in *Transportation and Communications Review*, Vol. 4, No. 4 (Oct.-Dec. 1951) at p. 6.

[11] Compare the suggestion of Myres McDougal in *American Journal of International Law*, Jan. 1957, p. 77.

2) That alternative 2)—international ownership and operation of all or certain types of spacecraft—be adopted as the long-run goal of United States policy.

3) That alternative 3)—international registration of spacecraft and verification of flights—be adopted as the short-run policy of the United States regarding *earth satellites*, but only after more than one nation has launched such a satellite.

4) That the *missile* which is designed to travel in outer space, but not in an orbit, be treated as any other piece of armament. It would therefore be handled by any program of arms control that may result from current and future international discussions.

5) That the international agency administering the registration, inspection, and verification function recommended here should be a branch of whatever international body may be agreed upon to carry out arms control as a whole, and should share in the powers of enforcement granted to that body.

Reasoning Behind Recommendations

1) Missiles that do not travel in an orbit—such as the Intercontinental Ballistic Missile when it is perfected—can be considered simply as extensions of the long-range gun, different in degree but not in kind. The fact that they pass through outer space at one stage in their flight is not a governing consideration. Therefore they fall within the scope of present and future discussions of the UN Disarmament Commission, and are not essentially a problem in outer-space control.

2) Earth satellites would spend almost all their lives traveling an orbit in outer space, which is about to be occupied for the first time this year (1957). According to the philosophy mentioned in the introduction to this chapter, it is more practical to establish "governmental" controls over an area before it is occupied than after.

3) The earth satellite seems to provide the best point at which to break into the classic vicious circle surrounding arms control. Public knowledge of these satellites is widespread even before their launching, and the international cooperation brought about by the I. G. Y. presents an opportunity that may never be duplicated.

4) Earth satellites will not be vital to national defense until after a period that is probably long enough for a system of international control to take hold. Satellites many times the size and power of

those being launched by any nation this year would be needed for important defensive or offensive purposes, and even then there is some question that they would be fully reliable. Furthermore, by the time such satellites are perfected for non-peaceful purposes they may be quite superfluous against an enemy's defenses because the Intercontinental Ballistic Missile (I. C. B. M.) will have rendered national radar defenses ineffective anyhow.

5) Since the earth satellites will not for a few years yet be important to national defense or capable of national offense, the only chance for effective international control seems to depend upon vigorous effort in the near future.

6) Once the earth satellite has been enlarged and perfected to the point where it is a dangerous military weapon, the only true security for any nation will lie in airtight international control.

7) If international registration of the relatively harmless satellites of the present stage is accomplished, and the machinery for notification and verification of the peaceful nature of flights is set up soon, the system of control might be able to keep up with the progress of satellite development. As the satellite grows gradually into a dangerous weapon, there is some chance that attitudes necessary to make international control feasible would also grow at the same rate.

8) It may seem paradoxical to seek international ownership of a dangerous instrumentality only after it has been overshadowed by a far more dangerous and uncontrolled one. Yet the Committee believes that the principle of establishing full international control—even extending to ownership—over the realm of outer space is highly important as a precedent. Control of spacecraft of other types—including perhaps the I. C. B. M.—might be less difficult after the vicious circle is broken in this way.

DIRECT ADMINISTRATION OF OTHER TERRITORY BY THE UNITED NATIONS

In the case of territory, whether land, sea, or air, that is not yet substantially occupied, United Nations policy regarding direct administration can be guided by abstract principle to a high degree. In the case of inhabited territory, policy can usually be made only on the basis of a crisis which already shows signs of dangerous tension between nations. Once in a while, however, the crisis can be resolved in such a way as to promote the abstract principle. The United Nations has such an opportunity at present.

If the principle were the only thing to be considered, in 1957 the United Nations might speculate about temporarily administering such disputed territories as Kashmir, the Gaza Strip, or Cyprus. And it might consider permanent administration of such international waterways or control points as the Suez Canal, the Turkish Straits, or Gibraltar.

In practice, however, there are only two areas which seem to be within the realm of possibility in 1957. One of these is the Suez Canal, because of the following passages in the resolution adopted in October 1956 by the Security Council, which agreed "that any settlement of the Suez question should meet the following requirements: . . . (3) the operation of the canal should be insulated from the politics of any country; . . ." Yet the tone of that resolution does not indicate agreement on UN administration, but rather on international arrangements of some other sort. The other possibility is the Gaza Strip, and perhaps some other parts of the Sinai Peninsula not yet evacuated by the Israeli Army at the time of writing.

The Committee has no recommendation at this time with regard to the Suez Canal except that it should remain *actively* before the United Nations until a generally acceptable permanent arrangement is reached.

The Committee recommends that the UN seriously consider occupation of the Gaza Strip for an indefinite period if it can possibly arrange to enter and remain there. For several reasons, this presents a unique opportunity to test the efficacy of direct administration by the UN in the interests of peaceful settlement. (1) If Israel occupied the Gaza Strip, the armistice agreements painfully negotiated in 1948 and 1949, and just as painfully maintained in general up until October 1956, would be grossly breached because the territory would have been taken by force. On the other hand, if Egypt resumed its position there and the UN Emergency Force left the area and disbanded, the legal status quo would have been restored but there would be no better assurance than there was in 1956 that either country would refrain from attacking the other. (2) A military force under direct control of the UN did actually enter the Gaza Strip. It may be presumed on the basis of UN experience, there and elsewhere, that this force—made up of troops from ten Member Nations located in four different continents—would not be fired upon by either side except through unauthorized accident. (3) The troops could be augmented, as they would have to be, by civil administrators operating under military authority but supervising the establishment of native government. This would not be condominium, but a military government by the UN. (4) While there is no specific provision in the Charter permitting such an occupation, there is also no specific prohibition apart from the "domestic jurisdiction" clause. That clause is powerful in a situation where the "domestic" territory is clear-cut, but this is not quite the case with the Gaza Strip. The border is a temporary one pending a peace treaty, and it has been under observation for years by the UN Mixed Armistice Commission. While it is a very long step from border conciliation to military occupation, it may not be an impossible step.

In making this recommendation, the Committee realizes the difficult political and legal issues which the experiment would have to face, both in obtaining UN approval and in maintaining the flow of supporting funds. The actual presence of an organized UN force, however, solves what would otherwise be a difficult issue—the physical one of raising a force and placing it in the disputed area. On balance, the Committee feels that this is an opportunity without precedent, and one which should not be allowed to pass.

SUMMARY OF RECOMMENDATIONS

1) That Antarctica be owned and administered directly by the United Nations, through a Specialized Agency to be set up for that purpose.

2) That a new organization be set up, having a relationship to the United Nations similar to that of a Specialized Agency, to deal with problems of the high seas.

3) That the floor under the high seas be recognized as "res communis" and its ownership and control be conceded to the United Nations.

4) That the principle be accepted that outer space is owned and controlled by the international community represented by the United Nations, and that international ownership and control of all spacecraft be adopted as a *long-run* policy.

5) That as an immediate policy, international registration and

verification of earth satellite flights be adopted after more than one nation has successfully launched such a satellite.

6) That the Suez Canal issue remain actively before the United Nations until a generally acceptable permanent arrangement is reached.

7) That the United Nations occupy and administer the Gaza Strip for an indefinite period.

RICHARD W. VAN WAGENEN, CHAIRMAN
CLARENCE A. BERDAHL
OSCAR A. DE LIMA
HARRIS WOFFORD, JR.

IV
Center for International Organization

10   THE GENERAL ASSEMBLY*

The history of the development of the United Nations during the
first decade of its existence is marked by a continuing growth in
the powers and responsibilities of the General Assembly, partially at
the expense of the Security Council, and, to a lesser extent, of the
Economic and Social Council.

The abuse of the veto in the Security Council, the failure to implement such provisions as Article 43 of the Charter contains for
an international police force, and the impotence of the Military Staff
Committee have combined with other factors to produce a substantial
shift of the peace-preserving functions of the Security Council to
the General Assembly. The Economic and Social Council also has
not developed the executive potential some quarters hoped it might.
The significant, if essentially limited, executive and political powers
of the Secretary-General, which, by the terms of Article 99, are tied
in with those of the Security Council, have tended to develop in a
fashion that has complemented, rather than competed with, the
General Assembly's powers. For its part, the General Assembly has
adopted procedures which have accelerated and institutionalized its
accrual of power. The Interim Committee was a first, if unproductive,
step; the Uniting for Peace Resolution has proved more significant.
The General Assembly, moreover, has resorted to special, and suspended, as well as emergency, sessions, and its regular annual meetings on occasion have extended over half a year. The Assembly has
thus tended to become a permanent as well as the primary United
Nations organ.

* Footnotes A-G in this chapter refer to comments by William R. Frye and
Hans Kohn.

At the same time, the character of the General Assembly has been considerably altered, in fact if not in form, by the admission of new Members. While in itself a desirable development, which has endowed the Organization with something approaching universality, the admission of new Members has had an undoubted impact upon the balance of voting power.

Broadly speaking, the balance of power in the Assembly as originally constituted lay in the hands of the relatively developed and wealthy nations of Western Europe and the Americas (who could usually count upon the votes of the less developed Latin American States as well). It has lately tended to shift towards the economically less developed, poorer nations of Asia, Africa, and the Middle East, with whom the Latin American delegations sometimes ally.

The Atlantic community initially dominated the Assembly's political decisions. Its influence upon the voting in the economic, social, non-self-governing and trust territories fields was greater in the earlier years of the Organization's life than it is today. But the Atlantic powers, and the Scandinavian and Commonwealth States that often share their views, in any case did not and do not habitually vote as a bloc, unlike the representatives of the Asian-Arab, Latin-American, and Soviet blocs. And the Soviet group, while often the object of critical United Nations resolutions, has increasingly managed to align itself with or to align with itself many of the economically underdeveloped States. The gap in living standards between the underdeveloped countries and the Atlantic community has widened at the same time that the voting power of the underdeveloped Members has increased in an Assembly whose effective powers have also increased.

One profound problem which thus promises to arise even more acutely in the future than in the past is that of an imbalance between those nations who will have to supply the greater part of the funds with which the United Nations must be endowed if it is to realize its maximum potential, and the Assembly majority consisting of nations which, broadly speaking, would be the chief economic beneficiaries of a fully functioning world organization. Unless effective measures are taken to solve this problem, critics of the United Nations are likely to attract a widening audience for such crude and inaccurate epigrams as, "We pay and you decide what is to be done with our money." It is precisely this sort of inelegant oversimplification[A] that is likely to arouse a negative attitude towards the United Nations in the Congress of the United States and in the parliaments of the other more prosperous democracies.

A second problem which expansion of the General Assembly's functions and membership has aggravated is political decision or recommendation by an "irresponsible majority." The disabilities of a voting procedure that accords an equal voice to El Salvador and the United States, to Yemen and Pakistan, or to Cambodia and India— of a system that could permit States representing less than a fiftieth of the world's population to adopt resolutions purportedly expressing the will of the world—are evident. The dangers[B] of decision-making by a majority which may be disproportionately composed of small States, and disturbingly impelled by motivations of nationalism, or communism, or racism—by some or all of these and other doctrines that may or must conflict with the principles of the United Nations Charter—are urged by some to be real and perhaps imminent. It is "nonsense," Lord Cherwell recently declared, for nations to submit their "vital interests to a body so absurdly constituted" as the General Assembly,[1] and his is a view not without advocates. The possibility of the United Nations Emergency Force, or a more powerful United Nations armed instrument, operating not in accord with a clearly defined and just international law, but rather under the direction of a wilful majority of minor and misguided States, abetted by one or more Great Powers, may be one to be reckoned with. International organization, after all, evidently is not an end in itself, but a means for the achievement of the ends of peace and human well-being. International organization can be positively and profoundly destructive insofar as it is turned away from those ends—insofar as it is led to act in an arbitrary fashion which does not accord with justice. The growth of a powerful international law has been slow, or, at least, too slow to meet the need; the processes of international legislation,

A. This is not an oversimplification. It is a distortion. Nothing of the sort has happened or is likely to happen; the potential recipient states have shown great restraint and responsibility, if only because they know very well that the United States and other donor countries will not in fact pay if others are to decide what is done with the money. W. R. F. & H. K.

B. There are no such dangers in practice. This view reflects a misunderstanding of how the General Assembly operates. W. R. F. & H. K.

[1] *The New York Times*, January 15, 1957.

of universal law-making, remain desperately primitive; the substance of a more powerful international law is unresolved. Enactment of international law by treaty, and accretion of international law by custom, are, or at any rate have been, inadequate for the demands of our time. The General Assembly is charged by the Charter with "encouraging the progressive development of international law and its codification". (Article 13) But its fitness to perform that high function is open to question. The Assembly's resolutions do not, generally speaking, carry the force of law. In view of the Assembly's voting system, that is perhaps desirable and probably inevitable. The importance of devising an international legislative process within the United Nations that will genuinely and significantly advance the achievement of the purposes which Article 1 of the Charter sets forth, and that will merit the confidence of those States which, in the nature of things, will bear the primary responsibility for implementing the Organization's decisions, is transcendent. But it may well be asked whether the General Assembly can—or should—gain greater political or legislative strength as long as it adheres to the system of equal votes for unequal Members.[c]

Yet the case for weighted voting, or the case against the existing system, can be and often is overstated. While in form the United States has a General Assembly vote no weightier than Guatemala's, in fact its influence within and without the Assembly is immeasurably greater. Not only does the particular vote of the United States, representing as it does that of the most powerful Member, carry more influence in itself than the votes of others, but the United States vote tends to carry those of many other States with it. The votes of the Latin American nations, and of some other Members as well, usually may be counted as coinciding with that of the United States, at least on the graver political issues. The Soviet Union, for its part, in fact may count not only on the three votes of the Soviet republics which are represented in the Organization, but on those of its Satellites. The influence of the other larger powers, while not so far-reach-

C. This passage is full of fallacies and false assumptions. The General Assembly is not a legislature. Its members do not have equal influence on the outcome of votes; it is ludicrous to speak of "a voting procedure that accords an equal voice to El Salvador and the United States . . ." The United States can almost always command at least 30 to 35 votes from friends and supporters. W. R. F. & H. K.

ing as that of the United States or the USSR, unquestionably in actuality extends beyond that represented by their formal voting power. Moreover, the possibility of the small Powers banding together in large numbers to run the General Assembly would appear to be more theoretical than immediate.

A more serious danger may be the inability of the General Assembly to reach any meaningful decisions on "important questions." The Asian-African bloc, which consists of 28 of the Organization's 81 Members, is in a position to prevent the adoption of any resolution demanding a two-thirds majority, as "important questions" do, even without the support of the 10 Communist votes; the United States, if it stands together with its Latin American and some other friends, is in a similar position. The possibility of stalemate, and the probability of resolutions which at best represent healthy compromise, and at worst reflect essential inaction or less healthy compromise, has grown with the growth of "neutralism" and the notable expansion in membership of the Asian-African bloc.

Let us assume that the United Nations should be endowed with greater powers, and essentially the power to take certain limited legislative decisions, of politics and of the purse, which would be binding upon its Members without their individual consent.[D] What voting system, if any, might be expected to permit such an extended endowment? And, even assuming no fundamental increase in the Organization's powers (indeed, it today possesses, at least in theory, significant political and economic powers and still greater potential), what voting system, if any, would enable the Organization as otherwise presently constituted to develop more fully its political, economic, and other potentialities? The discussion which follows will survey possible responses to these questions (especially the second).

Many of those who advance what might be termed a "constitutional response" primarily envisage the introduction of some sort of system of weighted voting (probably, but not necessarily, through amendment of the Charter).

Various formulas have been advocated. Perhaps all of them may

D. This is an assumption we would not wish to make. The remainder of the paragraph appears to prejudge the necessity or desirability of a different voting system. W. R. F. & H. K.

be said to seek in one way or another to give greater representation to the more populous countries without creating an Afro-Asian, chiefly non-white, dominance. Some of these proposals provide for weighting population figures with other factors, such as productivity or literacy or both. Essentially, they would combine the criteria of population with economic strength to determine the number of votes to be allotted to each Member. Others, notably the carefully worked out Clark-Sohn proposal, seek to achieve a fair balance not by the addition of factors other than population, but by a plan of weighting in accordance to population which would place a top limit upon the representation of any nation, thus according the most populous countries equal voting power despite their differences in population, while classifying the smaller States in population groups which would be represented in a roughly proportionate manner.[E]

Another school suggests a bicameral United Nations legislature, analogous to the two-house system of the United States. One chamber would be chosen from States in numbers proportionate to their population. A second chamber would give equal representation to each Member, irrespective of its population or other elements of power. Resolutions might require adoption by simple majorities of both houses. Or perhaps the functions of the houses might in some manner be divided, one acting as an "upper" and the other as a "lower" house. A more promising plan, which would avoid difficulties inherent in a two-house structure, would be that of preserving a single Assembly, but providing that each vote in the General Assembly be tallied twice. The first tally would correspond to the present Assembly system of each Member casting one vote; in the second count, votes would be awarded to States in accordance with some formula of weighting population, or population together with economic strength,

E. Such schemes are completely impracticable, since they require a Charter amendment which would have no chance whatsoever of ratification by the large number of states which were being asked to sacrifice relative voting power. Even if practicable, however, such schemes would not be desirable. To the extent that they were based on population, they would increase the present voting power of the Soviet Union, India, and China more than that of the United States. Were China to be represented one day by the mainland regime, such "reformers" might find they had created the hostile majority they now profess to see on the horizon. Other criteria, such as productivity, may not always be "safe." W. R. F. & H. K.

military power, and so forth. A simple majority under each of the tallies would be necessary for the General Assembly to take a decision. John Foster Dulles has advanced a plan of this kind.[2]

The possibilities of a regional approach appeal to still others. It has been suggested that United Nations membership be divided into a small number of regions, each of which would have a voting power weighted in accordance with population and other pertinent factors. It is anticipated that the disparity among the regions would be significantly less than would be the national disparities which would flow from directly weighting the votes of each State. Arrangements within each region for allocation of voting rights among its members would be a matter of regional discretion. The regional organizations would have limited powers for the advancement of regional interests, particularly those of an economic character;[F] the nations composing the regions otherwise would retain their autonomy and internal independence. Some proponents of such a regional approach would entrust the Assembly in which the regional units would vote with legislative powers in matters materially affecting the safety and vital interests of the world community, while reconstituting the Security Council as the Assembly's executive arm.

The prospect of acceptance by the necessary majority of any of the plans for weighted voting seems far from bright. The smaller States, which are of course the more numerous, may be expected to resist weighting. Plans that are designed to institutionalize the situation of power and privilege of the more developed and largely white-populated minority of nations would promise to encounter still stronger resistance. Yet, weighting proposals, if perfected and adopted, would more accurately reflect power realities[G] than does the present voting system of the General Assembly, which is qualified only in its requirement of a two-thirds majority for "important questions." These very power realities possibly could be applied to realize such proposals, for evidently the influence of the Great and Middle Powers, and of

F. Would the advocates of such a scheme wish to "freeze" the Eastern European bloc under Soviet control? W. R. F. & H. K.

[2] U. S. Senate Committee on Foreign Relations, Subcommittee on the United Nations Charter, "Representation and Voting in the United Nations General Assembly," Staff Study No. 4, p. 9, 83rd Cong., 2nd Sess. (U. S. Government Printing Office, Washington, 1954).

the economically advanced countries, vastly exceeds their voting strength in the Assembly. Were the Great Powers to stand together constitutionally as they did at San Francisco, the prospects for reform might be substantial. But of course the prerequisite of Great Power unity on constitutional questions is a towering one; it has been pointed out that if East-West relations were such as to enable Great Power agreement on fundamental Charter amendment, there would be far less need for such amendment. The difficulties of achieving Great Power agreement on weighted voting can hardly be minimized. No system of weighted voting with even a remote chance of general acceptance can be expected to give the United States and its allies a two-thirds majority; whether because of the rectitude of their policies or the reach of their power, they have, for most purposes, a simple majority today. Any relatively practicable system of weighted voting may be expected to enhance the voting strength of the Soviet bloc, especially if China is added to it. Asian voting power would likewise benefit, while Latin-American and Arab voting power would decline, with mixed effects for the influence of the democracies. Only a severely modified plan of population weighting, or a plan which weighed in economic power, would promise to favor the influence of those Western nations which are the heart of the free world.

This is not to say that voting reform is altogether dependent upon Charter amendment. Professor Sohn has noted that:

The solution finally adopted for the voting arrangements need not be embodied in a Charter amendment, but may be included instead in a separate agreement binding the ratifying countries to certain courses of action, if the General Assembly should adopt a decision not only by the majority provided for in the Charter but also by a majority calculated in accordance with a formula embodied in that special agreement. Alternatively, the parties to the special agreement may establish a second Assembly, in which seats would be allocated in accordance with a particular formula. In that case, they may further agree to accept certain specified recommendations of the General Assembly of the United Nations as

G. Perhaps. But "power realities" ten years from now may be based on entirely different criteria—the possession of uranium or thorium, for example, might be one. The whole "power reality" which is centered presently in Moscow might have been altered fundamentally. Would it be wise to base a system of weighted voting on today's "realities," even if they could be defined and agreed upon? W. R. F. & H. K.

binding upon them if they have been properly endorsed by the second Assembly.[3]

A measure of effective weighting might more easily be achieved within the Organization, with respect to the peace preservation problems within the Security Council's purview, if that organ could be revived and reformed. If the membership of the Security Council were enlarged to assure permanent or semi-permanent membership to other of the primary Powers, and to the Middle Powers (perhaps rotating among themselves), and if the voting procedures of the Council were amended or applied so as to confine the veto to questions of breaches of the peace and acts of aggression, then the arguments for refashioning the present voting system of the General Assembly would lose much of their force. For, in the Organization as a whole, a measure of weighting would in this way be achieved. Such a development would be the more attractive were the proposals respecting voting on economic questions, which are discussed in the following section, to prove feasible.

It may perhaps be that no fundamental expansion in the Organization's political powers may be expected as long as the present voting system prevails. But, unsatisfactory as that system may be in principle, the General Assembly in practice has not been predominantly irresponsible thus far in the exercise of its powers. A not unpersuasive argument may be made for leaving well enough alone for the moment; of postponing fundamental constitutional reform while exploring the possibilities of special voting procedures for the less explosive areas of the General Assembly's concern.

Advocates of what might be termed a "functional response" are inclined to ask, first of all: "What do we want the United Nations to do, or to do more effectively? What hampers its operations at present? Which of the existing obstacles can we most readily remove?"

It lies beyond the frame of reference of this Committee to discuss the political tensions which at present inhibit the full functioning of a world organization. We are concerned here solely with the means by which the United Nations may be enabled to do more effectively

[3] Louis B. Sohn, "The Role of the General Assembly and the Problem of Weighted Voting," Commission to Study the Organization of Peace, *Charter Review Conference*, 1955, p. 94.

that which it can do in spite of the existing tensions.

These presently practicable functions consist primarily in the prevention and suppression of aggression—prevention being by far the more important.

Prevention of aggression embraces the whole area of action to ameliorate those conditions of real or fancied injustice that move men to violence. It includes the work of the specialized agencies which are working to eliminate hunger, disease, and ignorance. It includes every aspect of the war on poverty, backwardness, and oppression of the weak by the strong. It includes technical assistance and capital assistance to the nations that have been left behind by the industrial and technological revolutions and are now trying to catch up with the twentieth century. The prevention of aggression includes the timely mobilization of the moral forces of the world against any putative aggressor; it equally includes the invocation of processes of peaceful settlement of international disputes (by the Security Council, the General Assembly, the International Court of Justice, and the Secretary-General), the development of public sentiment throughout the world in support of arms reduction and control, and, pending that achievement, preparedness and willingness to combat aggression should it occur.

The *suppression* of aggression, if necessary by force, is a function which clearly can be reliably fulfilled by the United Nations only in conditions of world law and world law enforcement that do not as yet exist. Nevertheless, United Nations action in Korea and, in some measure, in the Middle East, illustrates how, to a limited extent, the United Nations can act even in the prevailing circumstances.

Both prevention and suppression require more authority and more physical resources than are at present at the disposal of the Organization. Increased authority in part depends upon Charter revision but, even within the present Charter, experience has shown that the United Nations authority can be expanded when world opinion supports the expansion.

With regard to physical resources, the case is different. The effectiveness of the United Nations in eliminating the social, economic, and psychological causes of war is limited by the physical means at its disposal. The specialized agencies could all profitably use larger funds. United Nations technical, and especially, capital assistance programs (which to date consist primarily of cautiously advanced loans) are severely hampered by lack of money.

This is where the functional approach comes to grips with the problem of voting rights in the General Assembly.

It is perfectly understandable that the United States and other developed nations will hesitate to place their resources at the disposal of an Assembly in which the have-not nations may exercise a disproportionate influence in reaching the decision as to how the funds are to be spent.

The functional approach to this problem would suggest the creation of a United Nations Development Authority, so constituted as to give appropriate representation both to the nations supplying it with funds and to those seeking assistance. This could be done without Charter revision by resolution of the Assembly.

A United Nations Development Authority might be constituted along the lines of the Board of Governors of the International Atomic Energy Agency; that is to say, with the major contributors of funds occupying permanent seats and with rotating regional representation of the beneficiary countries. There would be no veto, but it might well be provided that all programs must be approved by a majority of the permanent (net contributing) members, or by a majority of the votes they might be entitled to cast. The voting power of the contributors could be weighted in accordance with their net contributions, in a fashion analogous to the procedures of the International Bank and the International Monetary Fund.

The creation of such a Development Authority might be accompanied by the creation of regional subsidiaries, similar to the regional bodies created by the Economic and Social Council. Each regional Development Authority would sift the problems and opportunities existing in its area and would assign priorities to projects within the region. It would then, through its annually rotating spokesman on the parent Authority, present its case for consideration. The fixing of priorities among regions, as well as the actual allocation of funds, would then be determined by the parent body, in which the majority of the votes of the contributing nations would exercise the decisive influence.

Were such a device to be adopted, the ground would have been cut from under a major (though admittedly not the sole) rational objection to channeling development funds through the United Nations. That is not to say that irrational or selfishly nationalistic objections would also thereby be eliminated. However, with one of the chief rational objections met, the already cogent case for multilateral aid channeled through the United Nations, in place of bilateral aid, would be the more compelling.

It is the belief of this committee that, while Charter revision of voting procedures should be explored, Charter revision does not offer great promise of meeting the immediate problems presented by the changed nature of the General Assembly. It is felt that one principle immediate problem—that of reversing the growing gap between the living standards of the world's privileged and underprivileged peoples—may best be handled by the establishment of a United Nations Development Authority duly insulated against the vagaries of majority rule in the General Assembly.

Admittedly, the proposal advanced does not deal with the problems inherent in the present voting procedures of the General Assembly in matters other than the disbursement of funds. The committee does not minimize these problems, but it is not hopeful that they can, at this juncture, be overcome by constitutional change. On the other hand, the committee believes that, if the United Nations is enabled to act more effectively in promoting world-wide economic and social development, political problems may perhaps be solved more readily. In due course, the achievement of weighted voting in the sphere of economic development might be extended to other areas of United Nations endeavor—even, eventually, to the arena of political combat.

NORMAN COUSINS, CHAIRMAN
EDWARD A. CONWAY, S.J.
WILLIAM R. FRYE*
HANS KOHN*
STEPHEN M. SCHWEBEL
JAMES P. WARBURG

* Minority Report

This study gives a disproportionate amount of attention to a supposed necessity to "reform" the voting procedures of the General Assembly, which necessity is frequently assumed but never convincingly established. The net effect is to implant doubts and give substance to prejudices which it should be the purpose of this Committee and the Commission to combat, not to encourage.

The United States does have greater difficulty in leading and influencing the present General Assembly of 81 nations than the 1946-55 Assembly of 60 nations. The 30-35 votes which the United States can almost always count upon mobilizing cannot be expanded into a two-thirds majority of 54 as easily as they could a two-thirds majority of forty. Some twelve of the 21 new Members belong to the neutralist Afro-Asian bloc. But the realistic and practical answer to this problem is to win the cooperation and support of a sufficient number of these Afro-Asian countries—a task by no means so difficult as it sometimes is portrayed. A shift of from two to six votes would be all that would be required in many instances; and such countries as Ethiopia, Tunisia, Nepal, Ghana, and (at this writing) Jordan are by no means as rigidly aloof from the United States as India and Indonesia. At least six of the Afro-Asian nations are often fully cooperating friends of the United States: Turkey, Iran, Pakistan, Thailand, the Philippines, and Japan. On the Hungarian issue, even Burma and Ceylon eventually supported the United States position.

Imaginative diplomacy and far-sighted leadership would regain for the United States its full influence in the General Assembly. The Afro-Asian nations see three issues as paramount: economic development, colonialism, and prestige. If the United States were to channel more of its foreign aid through the United Nations in the form of economic assistance, give more consistent political support to peoples seeking self-government, and learn to accord persons whose skins are tinted full recognition of their dignity and equality, great strides would be made, if indeed the problem would not be wholly solved. Brotherhood is good international politics. Instead of thrashing about in search of some "gimmick" such as weighted voting, and seeking to impose it upon unwilling smaller countries—an impossible task, in any event—we could make of the present General Assembly an even greater influence for good by being a sympathetic and understanding friend of the emerging nations on issues they consider important, and thus winning their support on issues which we consider vital.

The implicit assumption in many schemes for "constitutional reform" is that the United States, because of its population, productivity, military might, etc., possesses a near-monopoly of wisdom, virtue, and enlightened policy. We should not have the arrogance to propose that our vote be weighted any more heavily than, in practice, it already is. Insofar as it is desirable, such weighting can be achieved naturally in proportion as we lead, not seek to drive, nations smaller than we in size and physical resources but often rich in history, culture, wisdom, and other non-material assets.

WILLIAM R. FRYE
HANS KOHN

11 THE SECURITY COUNCIL

The question of the composition and role of the Security Council holds a prominent place among the problems to be faced in considering the future of the United Nations. Originally designated as the organ with the "primary responsibility for the maintenance of international peace and security" (Article 24 of the Charter), the Security Council has not been in a position to play this role under the conditions existing during the past decade. Severe international tensions between the Soviet Union and the Western Powers prevented the consensus which was essential to the functioning of the Security Council as contemplated by the UN Charter. In 1950, the aggression in Korea found the Soviet Union and the Western Powers backing opposite sides of the conflict, and the Security Council was able to take action initially only because of the fortuitous absence of the Soviet Union from meetings to the end of July.

It became apparent that, for the duration of the cold war, if anything was to be done in the absence of effective action by the Security Council, action would have to be taken by the General Assembly in the exercise of a residual responsibility for the maintenance of international peace and security and that Members would have to rely increasingly on collective arrangements established under Article 51 of the Charter. The Security Council became relatively less important and the central role in the United Nations peace and security system shifted to the General Assembly.

Although the implications of present and prospective world political conditions are of basic importance, there are other reasons for reviewing the place of the Security Council in the United Nations. It was agreed at San Francisco in 1945 that provision should be made both for individual amendments to the Charter and for a general review conference if desired by a sufficient majority of UN members. Furthermore, it was stipulated that if a general review conference had not been called during the first ten years, the question would be placed on the agenda of the General Assembly and a decision to hold such a conference could be made by a majority of the General Assembly members and any seven members of the Security Council (Article 109, para. 3, of the Charter). Under this provision, it was decided in 1955 that a Charter Review Conference would be held when world conditions were propitious, and that preparatory work would be undertaken. This gives fresh incentive for the study of issues and problems related to the objective of strengthening the United Nations, including the important question of the future of the Security Council.

Still another reason for considering this problem is the substantial increase in the membership of the United Nations—from the original 51 to a total of 81 early in 1957. With the increase in UN membership the question has been raised of whether the Security Council as at present constituted can be adequately representative. Arguments have been made that a total of six elective members on the Security Council is not sufficient to do justice to all the major geographical, political, and security interests of the present UN membership, and that an increase in size of the Security Council would give new UN members, especially, a chance to play a more effective part. Whether or not this line of reasoning can be accepted as conclusive, it deserves serious consideration.

The problem of a revised Security Council involves five key questions: functions, relations to other UN organs, size, composition, and voting procedure. The recommendations of this Committee on these points are as follows:

1) The question of *functions and powers* represents the basic issue in considering proposals for a revised Security Council, since the assumption made on this point will determine to a large extent the conclusions reached on the other questions listed above.

The distinctive function assigned to the Security Council by the UN Charter was that of exercising the "primary responsibility for the maintenance of international peace and security." This included a major responsibility for the pacific settlement of international disputes and of situations likely to disrupt the peace; the taking of enforcement measures in case of a threat to the peace, a breach of the peace, or an act of aggression; control of military forces made available to the United Nations under the agreements contemplated by Article 43 of the Charter; and the formulation of plans for the regulation of armaments. Other functions of the Security Council include recommendation of new Members for admission to the United Nations, recommendation of a candidate for Secretary-General, and participation in the election of judges to the International Court of Justice.

In considering possible revision of these functions as assigned by the Charter, two questions arise. First, should the Security Council retain its primary responsibility in the area of peace and security? Second, should the role of the Security Council in other matters be increased, diminished, or left *in statu quo?*

Relatively little attention has been given to the problem of Security Council functions. Proposals for revising the Security Council have centered instead on the problems of the veto and, after that, on questions of size and composition. There has been, it is true, some discussion of removing the Council's authority to make binding decisions on enforcement matters and substituting an authority to make recommendations. Suggestions of this type, however, are directed toward a solution of the veto problem by removing the compulsory powers of the Security Council, and not at the question of functions. Even if such a proposal were adopted, it would merely limit the Council's formal authority but it would not affect its basic function with respect to international peace and security.

While the Charter provisions placing primary responsibility for the maintenance of international peace and security on the Security Council and prescribing the manner of its exercise have been largely inoperative because of relations between the Soviet Union and the Western Democracies, there was undoubted justification for the view that the maximum effectiveness of the Organization in this area required cooperation among the Great Powers. The Committee therefore believes that these provisions should be largely retained to provide the basis for future cooperation if it should become possible. Other provisions of the Charter, notably Articles 10 and 11, have provided adequate legal basis for the development of the role of the General Assembly to the extent necessary to fill the gap left by the Council's ineffectiveness under present political conditions.

The Council has other functions that need to be considered. The provision for the Council's recommendation on the admission of new Members to the United Nations has been the focus of acrimonious controversy, has intensified the veto problem, and in the past has delayed the admission of some twenty applicants. It seems desirable for the Security Council to retain some role in the important function of admitting new Members. We believe, however, that the veto privilege should not apply to this question. We suggest, therefore, that new Members be admitted to the United Nations by a recommendation of two-thirds of the members of the Security Council and a two-thirds vote of the General Assembly. Admittedly, this problem is not so serious as it was prior to the Tenth General Assembly. Nevertheless, Germany and several other states remain to be admitted at some time in the future, and the question retains a considerable degree of importance.

It is important to the effectiveness of the United Nations that the Secretary-General have the confidence and support, to the greatest possible extent, of all the Great Powers, as well as that of the other UN members. Therefore, we suggest no change in the requirement that the General Assembly, upon the recommendation of the Security Council, appoint the Secretary-General. However, the competence of the General Assembly to designate an Acting Secretary-General in the event of a prolonged deadlock in the Security Council must be recognized. Participation of the Security Council in the election of judges to the International Court of Justice is well established and we see no reason to suggest a change in this practice. It might be possible to argue that the Security Council should share in other functions now vested entirely in the General Assembly, such as budgetary and financial questions. However, we do not believe that any gain in effectiveness would be accomplished in this manner, and the result might be further confusion in an already complicated procedure.

In short, the Committee recommends that the basic function of "primary responsibility for the maintenance of international peace and security" should remain as originally established. We do not propose any changes in the Charter relating to the functions of the Security Council, as distinguished from its size, composition, and voting procedure.

2) *Relations to other UN organs.* The Security Council and the General Assembly were originally designed as coordinate principal

organs of the United Nations, with distinct but interrelated functions. The Security Council was to operate primarily in the area of peace and security, while the General Assembly was given broad powers of deliberation and recommendation in all areas of concern to the United Nations, as well as an important supervisory, elective, and fiscal role. The Security Council incorporated a special, but not exclusive, position for the Great Powers, while the General Assembly provided equality of voting and talking for all states, large and small. The decline of the Security Council and reliance on the General Assembly to perform functions originally contemplated for its companion organ brought about an imbalance in the United Nations system. This question suggests itself: What implications ensue for the future relations between the Security Council and the General Assembly?

It has already been suggested that the provisions of the Charter defining the responsibilities of the Security Council in the maintenance of international peace and security should be retained. The extent to which the Security Council will be able to exercise these responsibilities in fact and the degree to which the General Assembly will continue to perform the role which it has assumed in the course of the past decade will be determined by political conditions. No doubt under more favorable conditions the Security Council will be able to regain part at least of its earlier position but it is doubtful if the relationship between the Council and Assembly which was initially envisaged in the Charter or which existed at the beginning of the Organization's functioning will ever be restored. This Committee is of the opinion that the relationship should be left for definition as needs and circumstances arise within the broad and flexible framework of the Charter as at present written, except for the specific matters covered elsewhere in this report.

As regards the problem of relations with other UN organs, the suggestion of consolidation has been made, more particularly of the Security Council and the Economic and Social Council. This would bring together, organizationally speaking, the responsibility for dealing with immediate breaches of the peace and the responsibility for ameliorating the social and economic conditions which produce international tensions. Such a combination of short-term and long-term functions might lead to a more effective integration, de-emphasize military aspects of international relations, increase the prestige of the revised Council and attract a high caliber of representation in its deliberations. On the other hand, if the responsibilities of the present Councils are functionally distinct, it is not necessarily a constructive move to merge them into one organizational entity. The result in practice might be a split into sub councils (a sort of two-platoon system), introducing a new problem of coordination with no gain in effectiveness or prestige.

3) *Size*. The number of Security Council members was determined at the San Francisco Conference largely on the assumptions (a) that it should be as small as possible in order to operate expeditiously, and (b) that it should include the Great Powers, possessing most of the industrial and military resources of the world, plus a group of other states chosen from the entire United Nations membership. These assumptions were consistent with the fact that the functions assigned to the Security Council would require quick action in an emergency. A large number of members was not necessary in order to include the states on which the chief responsibility for maintaining the peace would fall, and the General Assembly would provide broad and inclusive representation in the work of the United Nations.

Thus, the size of the Security Council was deliberately made small and it was rigidly specified in the Charter at the figure of eleven, five permanent and six non-permanent members. These provisions were in contrast to those of the League of Nations Covenant, which allowed the Council and the Assembly to increase the number of Council members. That arrangement had the advantage of flexibility, but it also led to political difficulties arising from pressures to increase the size of the Council from time to time. The United Nations Charter obviated this difficulty by requiring a formal amendment to change the size of the Security Council. It is widely agreed now, however, that the UN Charter goes too far in this direction and that a greater degree of flexibility would be desirable.

Most of the discussion since 1945 concerning the size of the Security Council has retained the assumption that it should continue as a small body. There has developed, however, a widely shared opinion to the effect that some increase should be made in the number of Security Council members. Discussion along this line usually has been based on the argument that, with only six elected members, it is not possible to satisfy the legitimate demands of all geographic areas, groups of states, and important "middle powers." An increase in

United Nations membership from sixty to eighty-one between December 1955 and March 1957 has given impetus to the belief that a Security Council of eleven members is not adequately representative, and discussion of this matter in various official and non-official circles has been intensified. In December 1956, the General Assembly debated a resolution introduced by nineteen Latin American countries and Spain, proposing to increase the number of non-permanent members from six to eight. Another resolution, introduced by a group of Asian-African countries, provided for establishment of a committee to make a further study of the problem. Although these resolutions were concerned primarily with geographic allocation of Security Council membership, they necessarily involved the question of size.

Assuming that some increase in the size of the Security Council is appropriate, three alternatives present themselves.

First, one might argue for a minimum increase, to reach a total of thirteen or fifteen members. There are several advantages in this approach. It retains the assumptions that a small Security Council can operate more effectively in an emergency, and that a larger number is not necessary in order to include the leading industrial and military states together with a sufficient representation of other countries. From a practical point of view, it would probably be easier to obtain a moderate increase in the size of the Security Council than to secure approval of a more drastic proposal. Certainly this approach is in line with the resolutions recently debated in the General Assembly.

The second alternative is that of enlarging the Security Council substantially, to a membership of twenty or so, on the assumption that this would allow adequate representation of the broad range of geographic and other interests. It is also possible to suggest a variation of this approach, for example, that the maximum size of the Security Council be fixed at a fraction (one-fifth or one-fourth) of the total number of UN members. Proposals of this type make the implicit assumption that the Security Council should be representative of the entire United Nations membership, rather than that it should be a small body including those states having the resources and power to implement decisions with respect to the maintenance of international peace and security.

The third alternative follows a different approach by introducing the concept of flexibility. If the Charter is merely amended to allow a moderate increase in the size of the Security Council, serious difficulties will continue to exist for any further adjustments which may become desirable. Why not, then, provide that the Council itself with the approval of the General Assembly may establish the number of members of the Security Council? It is the consensus of this Committee that this approach is preferable to any attempt to specify the precise size of the Security Council. This recommendation is made with full realization of the difficulties which the League of Nations encountered with a rather flexible arrangement. Nevertheless, we believe that the UN Charter went too far in the other direction, and that discretion in this matter should be placed with a qualified majority of United Nations members. We believe that this is the appropriate location for this responsibility and that we are entitled to assume that it will be prudently exercised. In order that a group of small states will not be able to increase the size of the Security Council when all or most of the Great Powers might be opposed, a decision on this matter should reflect the support of a majority of the permanent members. This Committee proposes, therefore, that the Charter be amended to provide that the size of the Security Council be determined by a two-thirds vote of the members of the Security Council, including a majority of the permanent members, with the approval of two-thirds of the members of the General Assembly.

4) *Composition.* The basic problem involves the number and identity of permanent members, the number of non-permanent elected members, and the balance between them.

The Charter provisions relating to permanent members should be changed in two ways. First, the five "Great Powers" of 1945 named in Article 23 do not accurately reflect the present distribution of world power, and the arrangement is almost certain to become progressively unrealistic. India, for example, might well become a permanent member of the Security Council, and the claims of Germany and Japan are an obvious future problem. Certainly, the list of permanent members is likely to be enlarged rather than reduced. One suggestion has been that the distinction between permanent and non-permanent members be abolished and that the General Assembly elect all members, expecting that the major powers would always be chosen (just as they are in the Economic and Social Council). This proposal, although it may be desirable theoretically, does not seem to be practical in the near future.

Second, revision is needed in the method of designating additional permanent members, since it is generally agreed that the naming of particular states in the text of the Charter is undesirably rigid. One method, that used by the League of Nations, is to declare certain members eligible for immediate re-election. Another suggestion is that it might be possible to devise some objective criteria, related to actual and potential capacity to contribute to the suppression of aggression on the analogy of appointing certain states of "chief industrial importance" to the Governing Body of the International Labor Organization. No one has devised, however, a satisfactory formula that could be automatically applied. Designations might be made by the General Assembly, thus leaving to future sessions of that organ the competence to make additions or modifications. This possibility has some merit, but it is open to the criticism that the small countries might have too much influence in the matter. A better arrangement, and the one recommended by this Committee, is to utilize the same procedure as for determining the size of the Security Council, namely, by a two-thirds vote of the Security Council, including a majority of the permanent members, with the approval of two-thirds of the General Assembly.

Another important question concerning the composition of the Security Council is that of the criteria for selecting the non-permanent members. The Charter (Article 23) provides for "due regard being specially paid, in the first instance to the contribution of Members of the United Nations to the maintenance of international peace and security and to the other purposes of the Organization, and also to equitable geographical distribution." In actual practice the latter criterion has been the dominant one, and the six non-permanent members of the Security Council usually have been distributed with two seats for Latin America, one for Western Europe, one for Eastern Europe, one for the British Commonwealth, and one for the Middle East. The resolution debated by the General Assembly, in December 1956, proposed an increase to eight non-permanent seats distributed as follows: two for Latin America, two for Western and Southern Europe, one for Eastern Europe, two for Asia and Africa, and one for the Commonwealth. Representatives of Asia and Africa objected to this proposal on the ground that it discriminated against those continents, whether considered on the basis of geographic distribution, population, or total number of states involved. It was claimed, for example, that 130,000,000 Europeans would get preference over 386,000,000 Asians, and this was completely unacceptable to the latter. The Asian-African countries offered a resolution of their own providing for a committee to study the problem, in the hope of obtaining a more favorable arrangement by delay and further consideration.

The General Assembly debate on these two resolutions was almost entirely concerned with the criterion of geographical distribution. On the other hand, there is indisputable merit to the suggestion that eligibility for membership in the Security Council should be based on contributions to world peace. Admittedly, there is a serious question as to whether this criterion can be applied accurately and objectively, and it must be recognized that a similar provision already in the Charter had very little significance in the first decade of the United Nations. The selection of non-permanent members in practice can be expected to result in some type of "balanced representation" of geographic regions and groups of states. Nevertheless, this Committee strongly recommends that the criterion of contributions to peace and security be retained in the Charter. This is an eminently sound principle, and it should not be eliminated simply because it is not easy to apply. If this principle does not make much difference in the geographical distribution of Security Council seats, it may still find application when choices are made between candidates within a given region or group of states. This would give a better chance of selection to the "middle powers," a fact which in itself should increase the effectiveness of the Security Council.

No change is proposed in the present method of electing non-permanent members of the Security Council by a two-thirds vote of the General Assembly.

5) The *voting procedure* of the Security Council must be changed if the size and composition of the Security Council are altered, since the Charter provisions for decision-making in that organ are in the form of absolute numbers rather than in proportions. Various suggestions have been considered, and this Committee agrees on the recommendation that procedural matters be subject to a majority vote and that substantive decisions be made by a two-thirds vote of the total Security Council membership. The two-thirds vote required for a decision on matters under Chapter VII of the Charter or for recommending the appointment of a Secretary-General should in-

clude the concurrence of the permanent members, and a vote to alter the size or composition of the Security Council should include the concurrence of a majority of the permanent members.

The rule of unanimity among the permanent members, or veto privilege, has been one of the most controversial provisions of the Charter. At the San Francisco Conference, the smaller states objected to the voting procedure as proposed for the Security Council but the Great Powers insisted on it. Subsequent abuse of the veto privilege by the Soviet Union seriously weakened the Security Council and made its voting procedure the object of more discussion and proposals for revision than any other provision of the Charter. The United States has been on record since 1948 as supporting an elimination of the veto privilege on questions of admission to membership in the United Nations and of recommendations for the pacific settlement of international disputes. The Committee supports this position. Certainly, the veto should not apply to recommendations for pacific settlement and the privilege should not be invoked except on issues of vital importance. The Committee agrees that the rule of unanimity among the Great Powers should continue in force with respect to questions of enforcement (or other action under Chapter VII of the Charter). In saying this, we recognize that it is possible to think of arrangements with varying degrees of flexibility. For example, a distinction might be made between a recommendation which would authorize enforcement action and a decision which would impose an obligation to take enforcement action. Or, there might be merit in a provision that a resolution receiving two-thirds vote in the Security Council, but lacking unanimous support of the permanent members, be formally transmitted to the General Assembly for its information and guidance.

In the event that the composition of the Security Council is changed to provide for one or more additional permanent members, a special problem arises on the question of requiring unanimity of the "permanent members" for substantive decisions. The Committee agrees that the veto privilege should *not* be extended to new permanent members. This would result in two different categories of permanent members, those with and those without the veto privilege. It is to be hoped that this would not be a serious political problem, especially if questions subject to veto are restricted as suggested. In any case, we do not believe that the veto should be extended to any additional Security Council members. If this were done, it would probably make decisions even more difficult since the prospects of unanimity are diminished as the number of participants in a decision increases.

Summary. This Committee recommends that:

1) The functions of the Security Council should remain as stated in the Charter.

2) No change should be made in the Charter provisions establishing the Security Council as a principal organ coordinate with the General Assembly. The relationship in practice should be left for definition in accordance with needs and events, within the broad and flexible framework of the Charter.

3) Article 23 of the Charter should be amended to provide that the size and composition of the Security Council be determined by a vote of two-thirds of the members of the Security Council, including a majority of the permanent members, with the approval of two-thirds of the members of the General Assembly.

4) The voting procedure of the Security Council should be changed so as to restrict, but not remove, the veto privilege.

WILLARD N. HOGAN, CHAIRMAN
HARDING F. BANCROFT
BENJAMIN V. COHEN
LELAND M. GOODRICH
BOYD A. MARTIN
PAUL E. SMITH

12 BUDGET AND REVENUES

THE MULTIPLICITY OF BUDGETS IN THE UNITED NATIONS SYSTEM

The promotion of peace and international cooperation through the United Nations system gives incalculable rewards to the nations of the world. Facilities for the adjustment of international frictions and conventions which advance economic standards, health, communications, and human dignity literally cost the peoples of the world but pennies. If the entire United Nations budget, the budgets of all the specialized agencies, and every existing program of the United Nations had been charged against the United States alone in 1955, it would still have cost each American less than $1.25. Only during the three years of the Korean war was the cost to United States citizens for United Nations actions high enough to constitute a real burden—estimated to have been about $38.00 per capita.

Before examining the adequacy of revenues for the future development of the United Nations system, it is important to understand the multiplicity of the budget arrangements that now exist. The United Nations *Organization* has at least five separate budgets; the United Nations *system* has at least fifteen, as indicated in the table at the end of this chapter. The complicated financial relationships which result constitute a major problem that requires careful consideration before judging whether the United Nations should have more or less money to spend on the functions which governments have assigned to it.

The regular budget of the United Nations amounts to about one quarter of the costs of the United Nations system; the budgets of the specialized agencies to about 17 per cent, and the voluntary programs to about 58 per cent. The regular budgets of the United Nations and the agencies are based upon assessments which all Members have to pay if they wish to remain in the various organizations. The voluntary programs depend entirely upon the voluntary contributions of states and non-governmental organizations.

The five budgets of the United Nations are coordinated by the General Assembly, as is the budget for the Expanded Program of Technical Assistance, although to a somewhat lesser degree. The regular budgets of the specialized agencies are not coordinated or integrated in any way, as each agency is a completely independent entity. Article 17 of the United Nations Charter provides a means for some coordination of the budgets of the specialized agencies by the General Assembly—an authority that has not been used effectively to date.

The Regular Budget of the United Nations

The regular budget of the United Nations for the past six years has hovered between $48,000,000 and $50,000,000 while that of the entire United Nations system has fluctuated between $155,000,000 and $211,000,000.

The regular United Nations budget is based upon decisions by the General Assembly and other organs, which are then translated into proposals by the Secretary-General and scrutinized by the Advisory Committee on Administrative and Budgetary Questions; recommendations by the Fifth Committee; and final approval in the General Assembly. Although many discussions in recent years have revolved about the question of putting a ceiling on the regular budget, or at least stabilizing it, there is still need for a better understanding of how the money is now spent on the main functions of the Organization. For the purposes of the report,[1] these functions are considered to be (1) political, (2) economic and social, (3) trusteeship, (4) legal, and (5) public information. What seems to be needed is a form for the regular budget that would, for example, show whether the United Nations,

economic and social function   costs nearly 44 per cent of the total regular budget, as suggested in column III of table 1 below, or 26 per cent, as suggested in the official documentation; whether the

[1] This section of the report is based upon a book by Clyde Eagleton and Waldo Chamberlin, entitled *The United Nations Organization Functions and Procedure*, which will be published in 1957 by the Brookings Institution as a volume in its United Nations series.

political function	costs 30 per cent or 6 per cent; whether the
public information function	costs 12 per cent or 10 per cent; whether the
trusteeship function	costs 7 per cent or 2 per cent; whether the
legal function	costs 2 per cent or 1 per cent; and whether the
undistributed, or undistributable costs	are more nearly 3 per cent or 52 per cent.

The annual *Budget Estimates* contain five different forms of summaries of expenditures, which appear in Table 1 below as "Form" A to E. The problem is to find a means for determining how, in terms of functions, the "undistributed" is spent. Columns II and III in Form E represent an attempt to "distribute the undistributed" by using as a base the documentation produced for each function. Table 2 shows the actual production in 1951, the latest year for which data was available.

TABLE 1: Five Forms of the 1954 Budget Estimate of $48,123,000[2]
(In thousands of dollars)

Form A.   *The main presentation*—in eleven parts

I. Sessions of the General Assembly, Councils, Commissions and Committees	$ 866– 1.8%
II. Investigations and Inquiries	2,566– 5.3%
III. Headquarters, New York	30,282–62.9%
IV. European Office, etc.	5,441–11.3%
V. Information Centers	899– 1.9%
VI. Regional Economic Commissions	2,077– 4.3%
VII. Hospitality	20– – (0.04)
VIII. Contractual Printing	1,649– 3.4%
IX. Technical Programs	1,392– 2.9%
X. Special Expenses	2,149– 4.4%
XI. International Court of Justice	778– 1.6%

[2] The figures in Forms "A" and "D" are from the UN General Assembly, Eighth Session, *Official Records*, Supplement No. 5, *Budget Estimates . . .* 1954, pp. vii and 167; those for Forms "B" and "C" and in Column 1 of Form "E" below are from Supplement No. 5A. *Information Annex II to Budget Estimates . . .* pp. 4-7 and 13-17. The same summaries for 1957 appear on pages vii and 105 of the *Estimates* and pages 4-7 and 14-16 of Annex II.

TABLE 1 (*Contd.*)

Form B. By "*Standard Objects of Expenditure*"—in three groups

I.	Personal Services	31,513–65.5%
II.	General Services	11,930–24.8%
III.	Special Projects and Activities	3,901– 8.1%
IIIA.	International Court of Justice	778– 1.6%

Form C. By "*Main Activities*"—in five subdivisions

I.	General Policy	1,033– 2.2%
II.	General Administration and Services	22,772–47.3%
III.	Program Operations	17,772–36.0%
IV.	Undistributed Common Costs	6,061–12.6%
V.	Other Budgetary Provisions	908– 1.8%

Form D. By "*Main Objects of Expenditure*"—in seven subdivisions

I.	Salaries and Wages	27,854–57.9%
II.	Common Staff Costs	4,531– 9.4%
III.	Travel and Transportation	2,368– 4.9%
IV.	Contractual Services and Supplies	6,951–14.4%
V.	Property and Equipment	2,520– 5.2%
VI.	Grants and Subsidies	1,797– 3.7%
VII.	Undistributed	2,100– 4.4%

Form E. By "*Main Fields of Activity*"—in six schedules

Functions	Column I Secretariat estimates	Column II "Distribu- tion of the Undistrib- uted" $25,- 521,000 in Column I	Column III Total of dollars in Columns I and II
Economic and Social	$12,629–26.2%	$ 8,932–35%	$21,561–44.8%
Policy and Political	3,124– 6.5%	11,229–44%	14,353–29.8%
Public Information	4,810–10.0%	1,021– 4%	5,831–12.1%
Trusteeship and Non- Self-Governing Territories	1,303– 2.7%	2,297– 9%	3,601– 7.5%
Legal	736– 1.5%	510– 2%	1,246– 2.6%
SUBTOTAL	$22,602–46.9%	$23,989–94%	$46,591–96.8%
Undistributed	25,521–53.1%	1,532– 6%	1,532– 3.2%
TOTAL	$48,123–100%	$25,521–100%	$48,123–100%

TABLE 2. WORKLOAD IN TERMS OF DOCUMENTATION (1951)

	Translations: pages	Meeting records: pages	Typing for Reproduction: pages	Mimeographing and offset printing: pages	Contract Printing: pages	Average of other columns
General Assembly	51%	36%	45%	20%	42%	39%
Security Council & AEC	4%	5%	6%	5%	5%	5%
ECOSOC	19%	32%	20%	36%	6%	22%
ICEF	1%	5%	1%	1%	–	2%
Trusteeship Council	3%	21%	5%	8%	6%	9%
Administrative Tribunal	–	1%	–	–	–	–
Sub-total	**78%**	**100%**	**77%**	**70%**	**59%**	**77%**
% for each department of the Secretariat						
Office of Secretary-General	2%	–	2%	3%	–	1%
Security Council Affairs	–	–	–	–	–	–
Economic Affairs	4%	–	4%	3%	15%	5%
Social Affairs	6%	–	5%	2%	5%	4%
Trusteeship & NSGTs	2%	–	1%	–	3%	2%
Legal Department	2%	–	1%	1%	9%	2%
Public Information	1%	–	2%	10%	5%	4%
Administrative & Financial Services	–	–	1%	2%	–	1%
Conferences & General Services	2%	–	3%	6%	2%	3%
Technical Assistance Administration & Board	1%	1%	3%	3%	2%	2%
Others				1%		
Sub-total	**20%**	**1%**	**22%**	**31%**	**41%**	**23%**
TOTAL	**98%**	**101%**	**99%**	**101%**	**100%**	**100%**
Pages	153,308	55,415	228,666	178,948,800	71,772	

Note: Totals of the percentages will not balance at 100 because of fractions used and because items under one per cent are not entered. Averages are not weighed and a page in one column may well represent considerably more work than a page in other columns. The figure of 178,948,800 mimeographed pages does not include 70,000,000 produced in Geneva, nor other millions done at the various regional offices.

The data in Table 2, arranged according to function, provides the following totals, which are those in Column II in Table 1:

Political
General Assembly	39 per cent	
Security Council	5 per cent	44 per cent

Economic and social
ECOSOC	22 per cent	
UNICEF	2 per cent	
TAB	2 per cent	
Secretariat		
Economic Affairs	5 per cent	
Social Affairs	4 per cent	35 per cent

Trusteeship
Council	9 per cent	
Secretariat	1 per cent	9 per cent[3]

Legal	2 per cent
Public Information	4 per cent
	94 per cent
Undistributed	6 per cent
	100 per cent

The political function is heavily overweighted because all General Assembly documentation is listed thereunder. Similarly, the other functions are underweighted, particularly economic and social. There may well be some better base than documentation to provide the key to a performance budget which would "distribute the undistributed," and the material set forth herein is but a suggestion of the type of analysis of United Nations expenditures that is needed. Advocacy of more, or less, money for the United Nations would at least require a better understanding of how the money is now spent than can presently be obtained from any official publications.

The Secretariat has made some effort to move in the direction of a performance budget but the process has been complicated by the fact that different governments want different information, and by the very great difficulty of determining how certain expenditures should be distributed among functions.

[3] The Total of 9 per cent results from the fact that the components which make it up include fractions which make the total closer to 9 than 10.

FINANCING THE REGULAR BUDGET OF THE UNITED NATIONS

The United Nations Charter provides, in Article 17, paragraph 2, that "the expenses of the Organization shall be borne by the Members as apportioned by the General Assembly." The task of assessment is actually delegated to a ten-member Committee on Contributions which is guided by several resolutions of the General Assembly, notably that the expenses of the Organization be apportioned broadly according to capacity to pay. To help the Committee's evaluation of "capacity" the Secretary-General prepared a list of states according to their gross national products, which, in turn, is based upon available information submitted by the national governments.

It is now the rule, moreover, that no state shall be assessed more than 33⅓ or less than .04 per cent of the entire budget and Member States may pay a part of their obligations in foreign currencies other than United States dollars. Since the spring of 1956, which saw the inclusion of sixteen new members in the assessment tables, the wish that no state would be assessed more on a *per capita* basis than the state making the largest contribution (the United States) to the Organization has become a fact.[4]

Although there have often been individual objections to the rate of assessments by the Committee on Contributions when they are received by the Fifth Committee of the General Assembly, the schedule is invariably recommended intact to the plenary session where it is adopted by a two-thirds majority of those present and voting. The rates of assessment are being fixed for the three-year period 1956-1957-1958 to be comprehensively reviewed again in 1958.

In addition to the annual contributions of Member States, certain other revenues from direct sources have been flowing into the United Nations general fund as miscellaneous income. The sale of United Nations stamps by the UN Postal Administration, the sale of gifts in the UN Gift Shop, the sale of publications in the UN Headquarters and through distributing agencies, and the guided tours purchased by thousands of visitors to the United Nations have all produced direct revenues for the Organization. Although these sums are relatively modest, perhaps amounting to half a million dollars net in 1957, the first year for which proper figures are available, the principle of estab-

---

[4] Canada, Iceland, New Zealand, and Sweden had been assessed more *per capita* than the United States of America.

lishing activities that can produce revenues without the intercession of national governments is an important one. The development of this principle could make the Organization less rigidly dependent upon the annual contributions of Member States with various implications for the future development of the United Nations as a corporate entity. One immediate use for these funds, however, would be the new and imaginative programs which require some assurance of a dependable yearly income and that now stand apart from the regular budget of the United Nations. This would clearly assume that all direct revenues would be added to the contributions of the Member States and not merely used to offset the present assessments.

THE VOLUNTARY PROGRAMS

The finances of the voluntary programs are more volatile than those of the regular budget of the United Nations. Since such activities often have an emergency nature, as the International Refugee Organization or the Children's Fund, or are of limited regional interest, as the Relief and Works Agency for Palestine, the contributions and the expenditures of the voluntary programs tend to fluctuate widely. More disturbing is the practice of voting a program, but not contributing to it. Authorized $266,000,000 in 1953, the Korean Relief Agency had collected only $112,000,000 one year later—and 93 per cent of that came from four governments. Only 37 nations have thus far made contributions to the Palestine Refugees Relief. In its Final Report (1956) on Review of the United Nations Charter, the United States Senate Foreign Relations Committee pointed out that of the total membership of the United Nations, only 22 had pledged contributions to all the voluntary programs, yet the General Assembly had approved all of them by a majority vote. So serious had the practice become of establishing programs which failed to receive adequate financial support, that the General Assembly, at its Tenth Session in 1955, requested all Members to take account of the probabilities of collecting contributions before approving such voluntary programs and appealed to those Members who had been laggard in their contributions to make every effort to support such activities.

Arrears in the payments of assessments against Members of the Organization have thus far not constituted a serious problem. Article 19 of the Charter which provides that a Member in arrears, equal to the two preceding years of contributions due from it, shall have no vote in the General Assembly is a sound admonition. Nevertheless, Member States have frequently sought to reduce or limit their assessments while, as indicated previously, failing to meet their responsibilities to the voluntary programs by adequate voluntary contributions. In view of the increasing responsibilities of international organizations, the need for better budgeting and increased revenues must be courageously faced by the Members of the United Nations.

ADMINISTRATIVE AND PROGRAMMATIC BUDGET

The campaign in recent years on the part of many states to stabilize or put a ceiling upon the United Nations budget represents an effort to reach some kind of equilibrium for the expenses of the Headquarters, its branches, its personnel, printing, and other administrative expenses. Although there is a strong argument for a clearer understanding of how the money of the United Nations is being spent in the interests of efficiency, an international organization which is dedicated to the score of laudatory purposes set forth in the Preamble and Article 1 of the Charter must be responsive to ever-changing international needs, not hamstrung by rigid ceiling or stabilization figures. Indeed, the administrative expenses of the Organization have already found their levels after ten years of experience and it may be anticipated that over the years these costs will have a gentle, rising curve.

While administrative expenses can be handled through an *administrative* budget, the United Nations must now be ready to respond to unexpected international conflicts that produce material and moral devastation, calling for quick succor; the United Nations must also be receptive to imaginative plans for friendly international cooperation which may catch the enthusiasm of millions of people everywhere and demand financial support. The creation of the first United Nations Emergency Force in Egypt late in 1956 illustrates the dynamic development of the United Nations and the imperative need of finding additional sources of revenue which will be immediately and independently available to the international organization. Such activities, whose magnitude may be expected to increase rather than diminish, cannot forever depend upon sporadic voluntary contributions. If such programs are to succeed they need not only the wholehearted support of all the Members of the United Nations by financial contributions after the political vote, but also regular, dependable allocations of money from direct revenues which might flow into a *programmatic* budget.

In brief, it is recommended that the normal, administrative expenses of the Organization should continue to be borne by apportionment among the Member States under an administrative budget which clearly reveals what the money is being spent for. If the United Nations Emergency Force becomes a regular organ of the United Nations, like the Security Council, the General Assembly, and so forth, its expenses should be borne by assessment as a part of the administrative budget. Second, it is recommended that the voluntary programs which would continue to be dependent upon the voluntary contributions of states, should be drawn together in a programmatic budget; third, that all direct revenues of the United Nations which now exist or may be developed, should be allocated to the programmatic budget. To illustrate the advantages of this approach, it is notable that the Expanded Technical Assistance Program has become virtually a regular program of the United Nations to which practically every Member State makes some contribution. In the future other programs may become long-range operations of the United Nations. It is partly to sustain these meritous programs with dependable revenues and partly to cushion emergency or regional programs against the uncertainties of voluntary contributions that the allocation of direct revenues to a programmatic budget is advocated.

SOURCES OF DIRECT REVENUES FOR THE UNITED NATIONS

1) *Private contributions.* It has been suggested that the United Nations embark upon a more vigorous campaign to attract donations from individuals, corporations, and philanthropic foundations. While gifts and donations[5] have served special purposes and have been highly appreciated, nevertheless it should be recalled that the United Nations is a public international organization. Not only are individual donations undependable, but special attention to this source of revenue would be a misconstruction of the principles and purposes of a general international organization. Ultimately support for the United Nations must depend upon the governments of the world or the

---

[5] Outstanding were the gifts of the site of the Organization's Headquarters by John D. Rockefeller, Jr., the grant of the Ford Foundation to the UN High Commissioner for Refugees, and the millions of dollars collected by the Children's Fund from individuals.

peoples of the world under international government with public responsibilities.

2) *Usufruct of the Ocean Beds and Acquisition of Antarctica*. An interesting source for direct revenues for the United Nations might derive from the right to use the resources and products of the sea-bed for its own profit. Another intriguing possibility is the cession of the continent of Antarctica to the United Nations by the states that now lay claims to it. Nevertheless, it must be observed that (granted the willingness of nations to concede property rights to the United Nations) to exploit the sea-beds beyond the continental shelf or in the frozen wastes of Antarctica would probably require considerable capital investment, risk, and perhaps marginal returns. It is unlikely that the Organization could or would enter such operations directly, but once possessing the right to exploit such areas, the United Nations might contract for their development. This is a subject for further study.

3) *Defense Expenditures and Disarmament*. Since the first purpose of the United Nations is to maintain international peace and security, its organization may be properly regarded as an adjunct to national defense and its cost, therefore, a part of a national defense budget. A small percentage of a state's expenditures for armies, navies, air forces, and defense support could be assessed against the state and deposited directly in the revenues of the United Nations. Such funds would be especially appropriate in view of the creation of the United Nations Emergency Force which, in the main, would perform services otherwise required of contingents acting under purely national auspices.

4) *Taxes and Excises*. A fundamental difficulty which must be faced in any consideration of direct revenues by taxes or excises is the necessity for avoiding any direct competition with private enterprise. Thus, a tax on international carriers or on private companies engaged in world-wide commercial activities would be vigorously resisted. Even further removed from practicability at this time would be proposals which involve the imposition of a tax upon incomes, imports, or exports, many other items of taxation which are prerogatives of sovereign authority. On the other hand, there are a number of public services now provided by national governments which have an international character. It might be feasible to allow the United Nations to share a small part of the fees or excises for international mail or passports or visas—on the rationale that the United Nations helps to

maintain a world of peaceful communication, trade, and travel. A fraction of the tolls levied upon an international waterway would be another possible source of revenue for the United Nations in this category.

Even more useful would be the development of public services by the United Nations and its specialized agencies themselves which might be sources of direct revenues: consultant services to governments or private organizations by the United Nations in special matters of economic, political, or social development; fees for international radio licensing through the International Telecommunication Union; fees for international health certificates through the World Health Organization; fractions of the returns of interest on loans from the International Bank for Reconstruction and Development, the International Finance Corporation, or any other international development agency—all present challenging approaches to increasing the direct revenues of the United Nations for an imaginative programmatic budget. The services offered by international organizations can bring great savings to the nations of the world in many ways and the sharing of fees from services vested with an international character offers a reasonable way to improving the financial situation of the United Nations.

RECOMMENDATIONS

In the years to come responsible statesmen look forward to an increase of international cooperation for the maintenance of world peace. Under such conditions the United Nations may be expected gradually to expand those functions which contribute to higher standards of living, increased social dignity, and understanding between peoples, as well as improving its role as a forum of opinion and tribunal of justice. Better budgeting and increased revenues are necessary concomitants for the future. It is, therefore, recommended that:

1) The budgets of the United Nations Organization and the specialized agencies have been extraordinarily complicated due to (a) the rapid growth of the Organization with the sporadic introduction of different voluntary programs and (b) the presence or initiation of specialized agencies with differing memberships, some with constitutions predating the UN itself, and whose budgets are not effectively coordinated by the General Assembly of the UN. All international organizations should work toward *clarification, through a performance*

analysis, of how the revenues now received are spent by function. The General Assembly, with its membership of 81 nations, should now take *positive steps to review and coordinate the budgets of the specialized agencies.*

2) The United Nations Organization budget should be divided into *administrative* and *programmatic* budgets. It is recommended that the normal, administrative expenses of the Organization, including a permanent United Nations Force, should continue to be borne by apportionment among the Member States; that the voluntary programs, which would continue to be dependent upon the voluntary contributions of states, be drawn together in a single programmatic budget.

3) All *direct revenues* of the United Nations Organization which now exist or which may be developed by either the United Nations or the specialized agencies *should be allocated to the programmatic budget.*

4) Gifts and donations of individuals have greatly assisted the progress of international organization and should not be discouraged. On the other hand, the United Nations is a public international organization and its ultimate effectiveness depends upon the long-range support of governments of the world. While the administrative budget may continue to be supported by the assessment of states based upon their national income, new sources of direct revenues for the United Nations for its programmatic budget should be boldly explored.

(a) The *usufruct of the ocean beds and the acquisition of Antarctica* by the United Nations represents a bold experiment in international organization and the feasibility of this approach toward obtaining direct revenues should be explored.

(b) Taxes and excises when these are imposed *upon public services vested with an international character,* particularly when provided by an international organization itself. For illustration, a fraction of the postage fee for a passport, a fraction of the toll on an international waterway or an international carrier, a fraction of the fee for an international radio license or international health certificate, a fraction of the interest on an international loan, and so forth.

GERARD J. MANGONE, CHAIRMAN
DANA CONVERSE BACKUS
WALDO CHAMBERLIN
PAUL C. SHEELINE

EXPENDITURES OF THE UNITED NATIONS AND THE SPECIALIZED AGENCIES, 1946-56

Figures for 1946-1954 are actual expenditures; those for 1955-1956 are appropriations
(in millions of dollars)

Organization	1946	1947	1948	1949	1950	1951	1952	1953	1954	1955	1956
A. The United Nations Regular Budget	$19.3	$27.3	$38.4	$42.5	$43.7	$48.6	$50.3	$49.3	$48.5	$50.2	$48.6
B. The United Nations Voluntary Budgets											
UNRWA	—	—	—	39.1	19.2	42.1	26.8	29.2	29.2	32.2	23.4
UNICEF	—	.8	31.5	46.7	35.9	22.6	13.5	12.5	14.5	14.2	15.8
UNKRA	—	—	—	—	.5	4.1	53.0	28.7	58.1	21.4	24.5
UNREF	—	—	—	—	—	—	—	.8	.4	2.7	3.8
IRO	—	75.7	132.2	119.4	85.4	—	—	—	—	—	—
C. Specialized Agencies Regular Budgets											
ILO	2.7	3.7	4.1	5.0	5.3	5.8	6.4	6.5	6.8	7.0	7.5
FAO	.4	5.2	4.2	4.7	4.5	4.6	4.8	5.1	5.5	6.0	6.6
UNESCO	1.1	6.2	6.7	7.8	7.2	8.0	8.7	8.0	9.0	9.2	10.8
ICAO	.7	1.7	2.3	2.3	2.9	3.0	3.2	3.1	3.1	3.2	3.3
UPU	.1	.2	.9	.3	.3	.4	.4	.4	.4	.4	.5
WHO	.1	1.7	4.4	4.8	6.1	6.3	7.9	8.1	8.1	9.2	10.2
ITU	—	—	.9	3.0	1.6	1.4	1.6	1.5	1.3	1.3	1.7
WMO	—	—	—	—	—	.2	.2	.3	.3	.4	.4
D. Specialized Agencies Voluntary Budget ICAO, joint support	—	—	—	2.0	.9	1.4	1.5	1.6	1.6	2.2	?
E. The United Nations & Specialized Agencies Voluntary Budget UNTA	—	—	—	—	—	6.6	22.3	22.7	24.7	28.0*	?
TOTALS	$24.4	122.5	225.6	277.7	213.5	155.0	200.6	177.6	211.5	180.0	?

* Amount pledged by 70 governments

APPENDIX

Members of the United Nations

The members of the United Nations are classified according to their financial contributions to the Organization and also according to their geographical distribution. Their contributions are measured by the scale of assessments adopted by the General Assembly for raising revenues. Their geographical distribution is shown in accordance with the scheme usually followed by the General Assembly in the election of the non-permanent members of the Security Council. At the beginning there were fifty-one members and the subsequent admission of thirty additional members has, of course, altered the relative importance of the different geographical regions. The third column gives the number of years for which members have been elected to serve on the Security Council. The first column gives the estimates of population for 1956.

	Population in Millions	Scale of Assessment for 1957	Years Service on Security Council
A. *Permanent Members*			
United States	168.1	33.33%	12
U. S. S. R.	152.1 *	13.96%	12
United Kingdom	51.2	7.81%	12
France	43.3	5.70%	12
China	601.9	5.14%	12
	1016.6	65.94%	

* Omitting populations of Ukraine and Byelorussia.

265

B. *Elective Members*

  I. British Commonwealth
    (one seat)

Canada	15.9	3.15%	2
India	377.0	2.97%	2
Australia	9.2	1.65%	4
Union of South Africa	13.9	.71%	.
Pakistan	75.8	.55%	2
New Zealand	2.2	.43%	2
Ceylon	8.4	.11%	.
Ghana	4.1	*	.
	506.5	9.57%	

  II. Western Europe
    (one seat)

Italy	48.0	2.08%	.
Sweden	7.3	1.46%	2
Belgium	8.9	1.27%	4
Netherlands	10.8	1.15%	3
Spain	29.0	1.14%	.
Denmark	4.4	.66%	2
Norway	3.5	.49%	2
Austria	7.0	.36%	.
Portugal	8.8	.25%	.
Ireland	2.9	.19%	.
Luxembourg	.3	.06%	.
Iceland	.15	.04%	.
	131.05	9.15%	

  III. Eastern Europe
    (one seat)

Ukraine	40.1	1.85%	2
Poland	27.5	1.56%	2
Czechoslovakia	13.1	.84%	.
Romania	17.3	.50%	.
Byelorussia	8.0	.48%	.
Hungary	9.8	.46%	.
Finland	4.2	.37%	.
Yugoslavia	17.5	.36%	3
Greece	8.1	.20%	2
Bulgaria	7.2	.14%	.
Albania	1.3	.04%	.
	154.1	6.80%	

* To be determined by 12th Session of the General Assembly.

IV. Latin American
(two seats)

Argentina	19.1	1.17%	2
Brazil	58.4	1.09%	6
Mexico	29.1	.70%	1
Venezuela	5.8	.43%	.
Colombia	12.7	.37%	6
Chile	6.8	.30%	2
Cuba	5.8	.27%	4
Uruguay	2.5	.16%	.
Peru	9.4	.15%	2
Guatemala	3.3	.07%	.
El Salvador	2.2	.06%	.
Bolivia	3.2	.05%	.
Dominican Republic	2.4	.05%	.
Ecuador	3.6	.05%	2
Panama	.9	.05%	.
Costa Rica	1.0	.04%	.
Haiti	3.3	.04%	.
Honduras	1.7	.04%	.
Nicaragua	1.2	.04%	.
Paraguay	1.6	.04%	.
	174.0	5.17%	

V. Southwest Asia and North
Africa (one seat)

Turkey	24.1	.63%	4
Egypt	23.2	.36%	3
Iran	21.1	.27%	2
Israel	1.9	.16%	.
Iraq	5.2	.12%	2
Syria	3.9	.08%	2
Saudi Arabia	6.5	.07%	.
Afghanistan	12.0	.06%	.
Lebanon	1.4	.05%	2
Jordan	1.5	.04%	.
Libya	1.3	.04%	.
Yemen	4.5	.04%	.
Morocco	8.0	*	.
Sudan	9.0	*	.
Tunisia	3.7	*	.
	127.3	1.92%	

* To be determined by 12th Session of the General Assembly.

VI. Other States   *

Japan	89.3		
Indonesia	82.4	.51%	
Philippines	21.8	.41%	1
Thailand	20.3	.16%	
Ethiopia	19.5	.11%	
Burma	19.4	.10%	
Cambodia	4.1	.04%	
Laos	1.3	.04%	
Liberia	2.8	.04%	
Nepal	8.4	.04%	
	269.3	1.45%	

	Total number of States	Number of States which have served in Security Council
Permanent Members of Security Council	5	5
Other states with rate of assessment over 1%	13	10
States with rate of assessment between 1% and .1%	34	16
States with rate of assessment less than .1%	29	3
	81	34

Former Members of the League of Nations, not yet admitted to the United Nations:

Germany
Switzerland

States, not yet admitted, which have applied for membership.

Republic of Korea
Democratic People's Republic of Korea
Mongolian People's Republic
Vietnam
Democratic Republic of Vietnam

* To be determined by 12th Session of the General Assembly.

Other Reports of the
COMMISSION TO STUDY THE
ORGANIZATION OF PEACE

Preliminary Report and Monographs, International Conciliation, April 1941.

Second Report—The Transitional Period and Papers Presented to the Commission, International Conciliation, April 1942.

Third Report—The United Nations and the Organization of Peace and Papers Presented to the Commission, International Conciliation, April 1943.

Fourth Report
    Fundamentals of the International Organization, General Statement, Commission to Study the Organization of Peace, November 1943.
    Part I. *Security and World Organization,* November 1943
    Part II. *The Economic Organization of Welfare,* November 1943
            (Also published in International Conciliation, January 1944)
    Part III. *International Safeguard of Human Rights,* May 1944.

Fifth Report—Security and Disarmament Under the United Nations, June 1947.

Sixth Report—Collective Self-Defense Under the United Nations, Memorandum and Draft Treaty for Implementation of Article 51, May 1948.

Seventh Report—Collective Security Under the United Nations, July 1951.

Eighth Report—Regional Arrangements for Security and the United Nations and Papers Presented to the Commission, June 1953.

Ninth Report—Charter Review Conference, and Papers Presented to the Commission, August 1955.

NOTE: Copies of the Seventh, Eighth and Ninth Reports available from Commission to Study the Organization of Peace, 345 East 46th Street, New York 17, New York.

INDEX